EARL WARREN, ERNESTO MIRANDA, AND TERRORISM

Marjie,
To our truly
wonderful and
unique friendship.
Amos xox
Sept 6, 2018

Visit Author Website for links to images, song references
in the book, and other documents:
http://twelvetablespressauthorsite.com/amos-n-guiora

EARL WARREN, ERNESTO MIRANDA, AND TERRORISM

by
Amos N. Guiora

TWELVE TABLES PRESS
XII

www.twelvetablespress.com

P.O. Box 568
Northport, New York 11768

Library of Congress Cataloging-in-Publication Data

Name: Amos N. Guiora
Title: Earl Warren, Ernesto Miranda, and Terrorism
Description: Northport, New York: Twelve Tables Press, 2018
ISBN 978-1-946074-08-9
Subjects: Law—United States/Criminal Law
LC record available at https://lccn.loc.gov/

Twelve Tables Press, LLC
P.O. Box 568

Earl Warren, Ernesto Miranda, and Terrorism

To the memory of my brother-in-law, Yossi Beinart (1956–2017), whose extraordinary intellect was only matched by his basic decency, goodness, and humanity.

Table of Contents

Preface

You have the right to remain silent. Anything you say can and will be used against you in a court of law. You have the right to an attorney. If you cannot afford an attorney, one will be provided for you. Do you understand the rights I have just read to you? With these rights in mind, do you wish to speak to me?

This book asks one question.

Were Earl Warren alive, would he apply the Miranda warning established in *Miranda v. Arizona* to suspected terrorists? The answer is "yes."

I believe, based on interviews I conducted with those close to Warren, it would be a resounding yes. The Miranda decision was *his* decision. I am convinced that the essence of the holding—protecting the rights of the interrogated suspect—was of crucial importance to Warren. While other Supreme Court decisions in the years Warren was Chief Justice (1953–1969) dramatically shaped America, there is something fundamentally profound in the Miranda holding that sets it apart.

The weight Warren attached to the Miranda was not "by chance"; it reflected, I believe, his understanding of the

consequences of police misconduct and governmental overreach. Both caused egregious harm to innocent individuals. Warren knew this firsthand: after all, he had served as
District Attorney, Attorney General, and Governor. Perhaps
no Chief Justice has come to this exalted position better
steeped in, and more deeply versed, in how fragile individual liberties are in the face of government power.

Warren knew this firsthand because he had exercised
power during the course of an extraordinary political
career. The levers of power had been in his hands; his decisions impacted the lives of many. Sometimes, as we shall
come to see, those decisions were unfair, unjustified, and
wrong. Those decisions are, I believe, essential to understanding the importance he attached to *Miranda*.

The question we are posing addresses one of the most
urgent matters America faces today: terrorism. This issue
takes on greater meaning when terms, often ill-defined, are
casually bandied about by politicians, thought leaders, and
pundits. Terms and words have meaning, whether intended
or not. Phrases, coming from the political right and left,
serve to undermine, castigate, and possibly endanger individuals and groups.

The importance of the Miranda decision, and the rights
it guaranteed, cannot be sufficiently emphasized. Its relevance is particularly acute when individual rights are at
their most vulnerable. As these words are written in February 2017, there is justified concern regarding the rights of
the vulnerable members of society: the very class Warren

sought to protect when the Court announced the *Miranda* decision on June 13, 1966.

When Warren was appointed to the Supreme Court by President Dwight Eisenhower in 1953, he was sixty-two years old. His world was dominated by white men. Warren's wife, Nina, was a traditional homemaker; Warren expected Nina to focus on their six children.[1] Earl Warren was ambitious, tough, self-effacing and modest, fully aware of his strengths and weaknesses. When appointed to the Supreme Court, he quickly realized that unlike some of his new colleagues, he was not a brilliant jurist. He was, however, a master politician who was able to sway, convince, and cajole. That quickly became apparent when shortly after becoming Chief Justice, Warren crafted a unanimous decision in *Brown v. Board of Education*.[2] Those skills came naturally to Warren; they enabled him to achieve unparalleled success as a politician in California before his appointment to the Supreme Court.

A chief justice is "first among equals"; while he cast only one vote, there is little doubt Earl Warren was, truly, the Chief Justice of the Warren Court. His impact, imprint, and influence are undeniable; the critical decisions discussed in this book reflect his influence. That is not to diminish or disrespect the abilities and contribution of some of his fellow Justices. It is, however, intended to convey that Warren

---

1. In his memoir, Warren refers to his wife in the formal, Mrs. Warren.
2. 347 U.S. 483, 74 S. Ct. 686 (1954).

powerfully used the position of Chief Justice. By all accounts, he was respectful, perhaps deferential, in the early years of his term, oftentimes relying on the counsel of Justice Hugo Black. However, over the course of time, once confident in and of his abilities, the Court truly became the Warren Court.

As explained in the pages ahead, I served for twenty years in the Israel Defense Forces, Judge Advocate General's Corps. Different postings provided me the opportunity to gain a deep appreciation for dilemmas inherent to interrogations and the complicated relationship between suspects and interrogators. Those experiences, primarily in the West Bank and Gaza Strip, are important to my understanding of the challenges and complexities when interrogators and suspects share the same space.

Physicality, tangible and intangible alike, is an essential component of the interrogation setting. For the uninitiated, a visit to a detention interrogation facility is invariably uncomfortable. The discomfort is physical: it is hot, loud, and unnerving. However, the discomfort extends beyond the physical. The reality of the setting is stark: the state, in accordance with relevant laws, is denying basic freedoms to those it suspects committed a crime.

There can be no mistaking the reality of the circumstances: the detained individual has been, or will be, interrogated by a professional interrogator. How the interrogation will be conducted is dependent on the interrogator. The detainee knows this. The interrogator knows that the detainee knows this. In democracies, there are limits on the interrogator. How the interrogator interprets and implements these limits is a matter of professional judgment and discretion. Warren sought to establish clear limits and boundaries. That is the core of the *Miranda* decision.

A visitor to an interrogation facility instantly understands the anxiety permeating throughout. It is hard to miss. Protection of the vulnerable was uppermost in Warren's mind when he wrote *Miranda*. That is clear from both how the opinion is drafted and from Warren's subsequent comments. The question we will seek to answer is whether his concern for protecting the criminal suspect would apply to protecting the terrorist suspect. The pressure on an interrogator can be very intense. The public wants "justice," rights be damned.

Terrorism evokes visceral responses. It is somehow different from the traditional criminal law paradigm. Terrorists are not criminals. They are different. Their motivations are different. The randomness of their actions is profoundly distressing. Terrorists challenge society; they are perceived as undermining core values. Terrorists seek to destabilize our daily routine, norms, and mores.

However, given the Supreme Court's demonstrated reservation in overturning precedent—less than 250 such instances since 1789—it would seemingly require extraordinary circumstances to reverse *Miranda*. That is distinct from creating exceptions; in 1984, Chief Justice Rehnquist carved out a "public safety" exception to *Miranda* in *Quarles*

v. New York.[3] While the facts did not readily lend themselves to the holding, Rehniquist's discomfort with *Miranda*
was clear. However, the hesitation to reverse was evident
when Rehnquist, in *Dickerson v. US,*[4] balked at overturning *Miranda.* However, Rehniquist's upholding of *Miranda*
should not be interpreted as an embrace of Warren's decision; rather, it reflects additional consideration extending
beyond the jurisprudence of Warren's holding.

Exploring whether Warren would apply the *Miranda*
warning to a suspect very different from Ernesto Miranda
presupposes—at least theoretically—the following: all suspects are to be guaranteed rights, regardless of the crime
suspected of committing. That is, suspect A, suspected of
crime A is to be guaranteed the same rights as suspect B,
suspected of committing crime B.

That basic assumption is applicable in the traditional
criminal law paradigm; whether or not it applies to "other"
acts, particularly those defined or understood to be terrorism, is a matter of public discussion. Spikes in terrorist
attacks accentuate the controversy and sharpen the debate's
tone. It fosters politicians seeking to score easy points with
a scared electorate. Responsible and measured voices are
quickly drowned out.

Nevertheless, what must not be underestimated, regardless of what brought the interrogator and interrogatee

---

3. 467 U.S. 649, 104 S. Ct. 2626 (1984).
4. 530 U.S. 428, 120 S. Ct. 2326 (2000).

together are realities of the interaction. Warren doubtlessly understood those realities. Of that, there is no doubt. That is, the call to protect society in the aftermath of a terrorist attack is not cost free. After all, the individual suspected of involvement in an act of terrorism is just that: an individual suspected of involvement. A suspect is innocent until found guilty in a court of law. The consequences of minimizing, mitigating, or denying Miranda rights to a suspected terrorism are profound. Perhaps that is an understatement. The consequences extend far beyond the suspected individual; there are societal ramifications whose significance cuts to the relationship between the individual and the state.

Where this plays out, where the tension is most acute, powerful, and compelling is in the interrogation setting.

First and foremost, the interrogator is in full control. That, more than anything else, defines the relationship. That fact is essential to understanding the *Miranda* decision. Warren knew this firsthand: he had been there and recognized the inherent complexity of the circumstances. More than anything else, Earl Warren knew—not instinctively, but actually knew—that the environment was inherently coercive.

Warren knew what I knew: the imbalance between the two actors is visceral. The relationship is profoundly asymmetrical. I know this because I have seen it. For that reason, then, *Miranda* and the rights it guarantees suspects are the majestic apex of American jurisprudence. As Warren made clear, protecting the suspect is vital for a democracy.

In exploring the relationship between terrorism and interrogations, I ask if rights guaranteed by the US Supreme Court to an individual suspected of committing a rape, as Ernesto Miranda did in 1963, extend to individuals suspected of committing an act of terrorism. The question is posed regarding acts of terrorism *committed in the United States only.* The actor need not be an American citizen, resident, or alien provided the attack was conducted in the United States.

The sole exception is if an American commits an act of terrorism outside the United States and is extradited to the United States and prosecuted in Federal District Court. Detainees held in Guantanamo Bay and other installations are not guaranteed Miranda protections and therefore fall beyond our scope.

Warren was not an intellectual but a Chief Justice who dramatically changed America. A casual review of the sixteen years he served in that position leaves no doubt of that. What is also clear was, and is, the hostility felt toward Warren and the Court by politicians and the public alike.

Case in point: one of the individuals I interviewed while writing this book has a highly negative view of the Miranda holding. In response to my question what would he say to Warren were the Chief Justice to join us in our conversation, the response was quick in coming: "I'd punch him in the nose." When I expressed my surprise at the intensity of the response, my interlocutor, a highly respected member of a major city's senior law enforcement team, was succinct: "Warren caused great damage to America."

While I appreciate and respect clarity, I was initially taken aback. However, upon further reflection I came both to understand and appreciate the frankness: the former, because the decision was clearly intended to limit law enforcement's ability to interrogate; the latter, because it clearly "put on the table" the passion *Miranda* elicits. We will discuss this in the pages ahead.

To fully understand the significance and endless controversy of *Miranda,* it is necessary to engage in a historical review of that era. No Supreme Court decision can be studied in a historical vacuum; *Miranda*, perhaps more than any other decision, exemplifies that. The turbulence of the 1960s changed America. The sense of disquiet was exacerbated by a Supreme Court determined to expand individual liberties precisely at a time when traditional values and beliefs were loudly, and sometimes violently, challenged. The dissonance was obvious.

There is a certain irony that a mainstream conservative, who had his eye on the Republican presidential nomination in 1952, propelled America to a new era precisely at a time when white college students and urban African Americans said "enough" to the existing "order." As a former, leading member of the Students for a Democratic Society (SDS) told me over breakfast in New York City, the radical student movements of the 1960s must be understood in a twofold manner: their perception of racial inequality and a resulting commitment to combat that.

As we shall come to see, combating took various forms and shapes ranging from the polemic to the violent. That is an important theme in examining Miranda because of the seeming incongruity of a Supreme Court minimizing state power at the very moment "burn baby burn" was on the lips of looters and rioters.

Warren wrote the Miranda decision at the height of domestic disorder and unrest. The halcyon days of the 1950s gave way to a very different America in the 1960s.

Todd Gitlin's book, "The Sixties: Years of Hope, Days of Rage"[5] brilliantly brings this to light. Gitlin who was SDS President captures the era's intensity, in particular an overwhelming desire to directly address society's ills. The "movement" was committed to changing the status quo, challenging the establishment and attacking institutionalized racism. While SDS was opposed to American involvement in the Vietnam War, Gitlin's book suggests that US foreign policy was not the group's primary focus. That is not to gainsay the War's importance; rather, it is to reinforce the primacy of domestic issues.

SDS was largely nonviolent; however, subsequent groups, black and white alike, committed acts of violence. At the very moment, the Supreme Court was extending the rights

---

5. Todd Gitlin, *The Sixties: Years of Hope, Days of Rage* (Bantam Books, 1987).

of suspects. Viewed in that context, the anger Warren evoked and passion Miranda elicited "make sense."

There are a number of different ways to bring the turbulence of the 1960s to light. However, before describing "how" it is necessary to explain "why." For a wide-range of circumstances, the 1960s were an extraordinary decade. As discussed in the pages ahead, the events came "fast and furious," sometimes literally spinning out of control, confounding participants and observers alike. National leaders were, more often than not, scrambling in their responses that were largely ineffective, reflecting uncertainty in the face of demonstrations, anger, and violence.

How to bring this to the reader presents important challenges to the writer: after much consideration, I chose to incorporate music from that era as a means to bring it alive.[6] I made this decision before reading Gitlin's book, which explores the importance of music in general and particular songs in specific.

I was struck that we both highlighted P.F. Sloan's "Eve of Destruction," sung by Barry McGwire.

Of that song, Gitlin writes:

There had been no song remotely like this one in the decade-long history of rock music, although the

---

6. I am neither a musician nor a student of music. However, I love music. I run to music. I write to music. My music tastes are very limited: American rock, particularly of the 1960s-1980s, and Israeli musicians, particularly the iconic group Kaveret; the late Arik Einstein and Yehuda Poliker.

objections of the Christian Anti-Communist Cru-
sade suggest, that here, at long last, was the song fun-
damentalists had been anticipating through all their
years of panic, the one that would confirm their dire
prophecies about the dark, inexorable logic of "nigger
music." Nothing could have been in starker contrast
to the previous year, 1964, when the Number 1 hits
had included the Shangri Las' "Leader of the Pack, the
Beach Boys" "Deuce Coup" and "California Girls",
the Supremes' "Baby Love," and the Beattles' "A Hard
Day's Night—all bouncy." "Eve" was strident and bit-
ter, its references bluntly topical—no precedent for
that not even in Bob Dylan's allegorical "Blowin' in
the Wind."[7]

Including music gives portions of this book a sense that
it reads like a popular social and cultural history. That was
not my intention when undertaking this project; however,
during the course of research, it became clear that explaining the years Warren was Chief Justice required careful
examination of the America of his times. Doing so made
incorporating music essential; it is well-nigh impossible to
discuss the 1960s without delving into the protest music of
that tumultuous decade. Music played a unique role in
expressing the mood of the 1960s. Instinct suggests that

---

7. Gitlin, *The Sixties: Years of Hope, Days of Rage*, 196.

Warren did not listen to the music of those confronting traditional society. However, it cannot be denied that Warren's decisions *also* challenged, and confronted, basic norms of American society. The *Miranda* holding is but one example.

The protest music of the 1960s was in sharp contrast to the silence that greeted the internment of innocent Japanese Americans in the aftermath of Pearl Harbor. Protest by victims or observers was nonexistent. Neighbors did not turn on neighbors. This was very different from the Holocaust when Gentile neighbors turned on their Jewish neighbors. Rather, the primary response was one of acquiescence. That characterized neighbors, media, and artists alike. This was decidedly not the case when America was literally in flames. The music of the 1960s brings this to life: it captured the pain and anger of individuals suffering injustice at the hands of government or concerned about the nature, values, and quality of society.

There is, then, a profound lack of symmetry between the public silence, including that of song writers and musicians, that largely met the decision to violate the rights of American citizens in 1943 and the loud and cacophonous noise of the 1960s.

Warren's Miranda was written during a time of social upheaval where editors commented daily, politicians argued openly, angry Americans took to the streets, and musicians expressed their concerns publicly. For that reason, I decided to include lyrics from relevant songs in the text. The book's website includes YouTube links to the actual songs. I hope this brings the era alive.

The music I incorporated was the "protest music" of the era. Readers may disagree with how I defined that particular genre and what musicians I chose to include. That is legitimate. It is not intended to minimize the importance of groups not included in the pages ahead. However, I decided to differentiate between protest songs such as "Fortunate Son"[8] and iconic songs such as "White Rabbit."[9] That is not to suggest Credence Clearwater Revival[10] was more important or popular than Jefferson Airplane,[11] but rather to highlight how I perceive particular songs and their relevance to this book.

Examining distinct aspects of Warren's remarkable career, as politician and Supreme Court Chief Justice, is both a journey through American history and a look at contemporary America and the compelling challenges it faces. It is, I believe, essential to understanding the *Miranda* decision and its possible application—from Warren's perspective—to those endangering contemporary society through acts of terrorism.

---

8. https://www.youtube.com/watch?v=LyzUIEW-Q5E.

9. https://www.youtube.com/watch?v=WANNqr-vcx0.

10. http://www.rollingstone.com/music/artists/creedence-clearwater-revival/biography.

11. http://www.rollingstone.com/music/artists/jefferson-airplane/biography.

Acknowledgments

I have known Steve Errick, publisher of Twelve Tables Press, since I joined the ranks of American academia in 2004.

We were introduced by our mutual good friend, Professor Craig Nard. At the time, I was a Visiting Professor of Law at Case Western Reserve University School of Law. Craig, who is the Galen J. Roush Professor of Law, Case Western Reserve University School of Law suggested to Steve, then Vice President and General Manager of Aspen, that he review materials I had put together for a course I was teaching on Counterterrorism. I am forever in Craig's debt for that warm recommendation.

One phone call later, Steve and I agreed on a book deal, which was the beginning of a wonderful collaboration and terrific friendship. The book you are holding is a continuation of that relationship.

In addition, this book owes many thanks to many people; in particular, I would like to acknowledge the following: Amanda Roosendaal (Juris Doctorate Candidate 2018), S.J. Quinney College of Law, University of Utah; Anabel Alvaredo (Juris Doctorate Candidate 2018), S.J. Quinney College of Law, University of Utah; Paul Cassell, the Ronald N. Boyce Presidential Professor of Criminal Law and University

Distinguished Professor of Law, S.J. Quinney College of Law, University of Utah; John Devins; Hannah Estreicher; the Rev. Dr. John C. Lentz, JR., Pastor, Forest Hill Church, Presbyterian; Louisa M.A. Heiny, Professor of Law, S.J. Quinney College of Law, University of Utah; Kerry Lohmeier, Assistant Librarian, James E Faust Law Library, S.J. Quinney College of Law, University of Utah; and Gary Mailman.

I would be remiss were I not to add a few, additional, words regarding Ms. Roosendaal: for the 2016 to 2017 academic year, she was "assigned" to me as a recipient of the College of Law's prestigious Quinney Fellowship (Ms. Alvaredo was similarly recognized); her commitment and dedication to this project compelled her to continue editing and tweaking into the fall of 2017.

I am humbled and grateful to Amanda for her unstinting efforts that significantly contributed to the final product.

Student engagement is one of the true pleasures of academia; Ms. Roosendaal represents its very finest tradition.

I was very fortunate—and am deeply grateful—that a number of former Supreme Court clerks from different era's took the time to patiently answer my many questions about the Court, Chief Justice Warren, the *Miranda* decision, and the relationship among the Justices. Those conversations were enlightening on many levels; more than anything, however, they provided me truly unique insight into the workings of the Court.

That same warm thanks is extended to the many academics and prosecutors who generously gave their time enhancing my understanding of their scholarship and insights. I am greatly enriched by those many interactions and conversations.

Chapter One

An Overview: Earl Warren in a Nutshell

In an interview with *60 Minutes*, President Obama discussed the handling of captured terrorists and challenged those who claimed the "American system of justice was not up to the task of dealing with these terrorists."[1]

Obama said, "I fundamentally disagree with that. Now do these folks deserve Miranda rights? Do they deserve to be treated like a shoplifter down the block? Of course not."

President Obama ought to call former Attorney General Eric Holder.

In a five-page letter to Senator Mitch McConnell (R-KY), Holder laid out in exhaustive detail exactly why, in his view, "these folks" deserve Miranda rights and why his Justice Department will treat them like a shoplifter down the block.

Holder's letter responds to criticism of the Obama administration's handling of Umar Farouk Abdulmutallab, the

---

1. Steve Kroft, *Interview of Barack Obama on 60 Minutes*, CBS News, March 20, 2009, www.cbsnews.com/stories/2009/03/24/60minutes/main4890684.shtml.

Christmas Day "underwear" bomber, from McConnell and other Republicans. Holder wrote:

> The decision to charge Mr. Abdulmutallab in federal court, and the methods used to interrogate him, are fully consistent with the long-established and publicly known policies and practices of the Department of Justice, the FBI, and the United States Government as a whole, as implemented for many years by Administrations of both parties. Those policies and practices, which were not criticized when employed by previous Administrations, have been and remain extremely effective in protecting national security. They are among the many powerful weapons this country can and should use to win the war against al-Qaeda.
>
> I am confident that, as a result of the hard work of the FBI and our career federal prosecutors, we will be able to successfully prosecute Mr. Abdulmutallab under the federal criminal law. I am equally confident that the decision to address Mr. Abdulmutallab's actions through our criminal justice system has not, and will not, compromise our ability to obtain information needed to detect and prevent future attacks.[2]

---

2. Letter from Eric Holder, Attorney General, United States of America, to Mitch McConnell, Senator, US Senate (February 3, 2010), https://www.justice.gov /sites/default/files/doj/legacy/2014/09/15/ag-letter-2-3-10.pdf.

President Obama and Attorney General Holder could not agree whether or not to extend Miranda protections to suspected terrorists. This disagreement highlights the complexity and controversy of the issue. The question is brought to the forefront after every act of terrorism committed on American soil.

These acts are committed today, will be committed tomorrow, the day after, and in the coming years. Terrorism is here to stay; we will neither defeat terrorists nor win the misnamed "War on Terror." It is for that reason that we must resolve the quandary of what rights should be extended to suspected terrorists.

It is as much a legal question as a values-based inquiry; do we protect suspected terrorists in the interrogation room?

If yes, to what extent?

Careful examination of the *Miranda* holding and of Earl Warren will shed light on that question. It is to Earl Warren that we turn our initial attention.

Earl Warren

Warren: The Person

Warren served in three executive-level positions in the State of California: District Attorney of Alameda County, Attorney General of California, and Governor. To what extent those experiences impacted his position in *Miranda* will be explored in the pages ahead. The metamorphosis in his outlook, and its impact on American jurisprudence, is nothing short of remarkable.

After all, the same Supreme Court Chief Justice who wrote Miranda played a critical role in the unjustified and tragic internment of 120,000 Japanese Americans in the aftermath of Pearl Harbor. Both—*Miranda* and internment—are issues of historic proportions; perhaps the former was influenced by the latter. While Warren's memoirs do not shed convincing light on this theory, the connection between the two is, at the very least, interesting to ponder.

In the books written about him, Warren comes across as a forceful and powerful man of action. His rise in California politics was impressive; his electoral success from District Attorney to Governor suggests an enormously popular politician who enjoyed extraordinary support from right and left alike. The Warren that others portray is, frankly, a more interesting and compelling Warren than the one in his bland memoir. That is not insignificant in an effort to understand what influenced him regarding the *Miranda* decision, particularly his role in the internment decision.

Perhaps the memoir is a correct reflection of Warren: a solid, yet not particularly insightful or reflective individual, with a strong sense of self who comes across as a man with a powerful presence. That perception was reinforced in conversations I had with those who worked with Warren. They depict a reserved individual, fully aware of who he was and very comfortable in his own skin.

While some described a "warm" person, the consensus opinion was that of a person accustomed to leadership positions, not an intellectual but very much someone who knew what results he wanted. While philosophical and doctrinal underpinnings of particular Supreme Court decisions were not his focus, there must be no mistaking his enormous influence on American jurisprudence.

Warren's life and career are free of rumors or claims of financial indiscretion, embarrassing personal affairs or outrageous public conduct. Warren was a family man, preferring the intimacy and privacy of his home to socializing and mingling beyond what the call of politics demanded. From his father, whose murder was never solved, he learned the values of hard work, financial frugality, and seriousness in approaching the challenges life posed. The suggestion that Warren was almost too perfect is not unreasonable.

Warren, the consummate family man, carried himself with a strong sense of self, mission, and purpose untainted by scandal or rumor. Pictures of Warren suggest a man of formality, perhaps some stiffness, comfortable with himself, attractive in a masculine manner, and imbued with confidence that does not morph into arrogance or disdain for the other. Warren conveyed a strong sense that he knew exactly who he was.

The composite picture of Warren is of someone who had great respect both for the position he held and for the public. In that sense, the image is of a public servant in the finest sense of the word. Warren was not, according to his biographers, an internationalist nor a person engaged in deep study and analysis of foreign affairs and policy. Warren's focus was on California's affairs and politics. This was reflected in the organizations to which he belonged including the Native Sons of the Golden West, the Freemasons, the American Legion, the Loyal Order of the Moose, and the Independent Order of Odd Fellows.

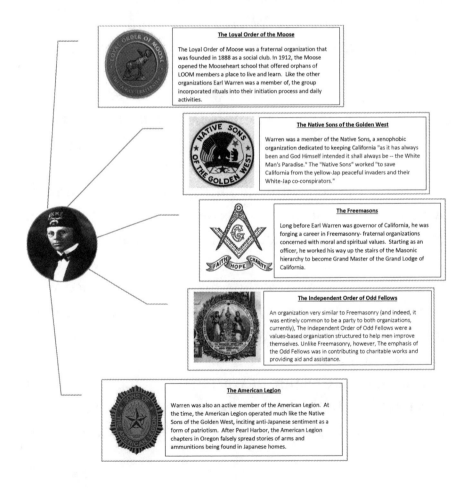

The Loyal Order of the Moose

The Loyal Order of Moose was a fraternal organization that was founded in 1888 as a social club. In 1912, the Moose opened the Mooseheart school that offered orphans of LOOM members a place to live and learn. Like the other organizations Earl Warren was a member of, the group incorporated rituals into their initiation process and daily activities.

The Native Sons of the Golden West

Warren was a member of the Native Sons, a xenophobic organization dedicated to keeping California "as it has always been and God Himself intended it shall always be -- the White Man's Paradise." The "Native Sons" worked "to save California from the yellow-Jap peaceful invaders and their White-Jap co-conspirators."

The Freemasons

Long before Earl Warren was governor of California, he was forging a career in Freemasonry- fraternal organizations concerned with moral and spiritual values. Starting as an officer, he worked his way up the stairs of the Masonic hierarchy to become Grand Master of the Grand Lodge of California.

The Independent Order of Odd Fellows

An organization very similar to Freemasonry (and indeed, it was entirely common to be a party to both organizations, currently), The Independent Order of Odd Fellows were a values-based organization structured to help men improve themselves. Unlike Freemasonry, however, The emphasis of the Odd Fellows was in contributing to charitable works and providing aid and assistance.

The American Legion

Warren was also an active member of the American Legion. At the time, the American Legion operated much like the Native Sons of the Golden West, inciting anti-Japanese sentiment as a form of patriotism. After Pearl Harbor, the American Legion chapters in Oregon falsely spread stories of arms and ammunitions being found in Japanese homes.

Warren the Lawyer Politician

Warren was a Republican, who both in the California politics of the 1930s and today would be described as a moderate. There is unanimity among Warren scholars that he was a temperate person, commanded respect among peers and subordinates, and was respectful of others. However, he was also known not to forgive and to hold a grudge for years. His complicated and contentious relationship with President Richard M. Nixon is a commonly cited example.

Reading the outstanding works of Professor George (Ted) White,[3] Professor Paul Moke,[4] and Mr. Jim Newton[5] has given me great insight into Earl Warren. To their credit, White, Moke, and Newtown neither engage in hero-worshipping nor gloss over troubling points in Warren's remarkable career. Warren reached the pinnacle of public life both in electoral politics and appointed office. An objective analysis of his decades-long career leaves one with the impression of a life truly well lived.

His popularity as a politician was extraordinary; he is the only Governor in California history to be elected three times. In 1946, he was nominated by both the Democrat and Republican parties and received more than 90% of the vote. In 1948, Warren was Thomas Dewey's vice presidential candidate; in one of the greatest upsets in American

---

3. George Edward White, *Earl Warren: A Public Life* (1987).
4. Paul Moke, *Earl Warren and the Struggle for Justice*, (2015).
5. Jim Newton, *Justice for All: Earl Warren and the Nation He Made* (2007).

presidential elections, Dewey lost to President Harry S. Truman.

There is evidence suggesting that Warren was ambivalent regarding the nomination and quickly moved on from the defeat. Perhaps he was able to rationalize the defeat as Dewey's and that he, as vice presidential candidate, bore no responsibility. However, there is no evidence suggesting that his efforts in the campaign reflected anything less than full commitment to Dewey's unsuccessful candidacy. In the long run, given the position to which he was ultimately appointed, the loss was inconsequential to Warren's career.

While Warren entertained conflicted presidential ambitions in 1952, Dwight Eisenhower received the Republican nomination and named Nixon as Vice President. The historical record does not shed absolute clarity regarding the extent to which Warren was genuinely interested in seeking the presidency. While Warren was a "favorite son" at the Republican Convention, I do not sense that he possessed the burning desire to be President that characterized others from that era including Nixon, Lyndon B. Johnson, Hubert H. Humphrey, and John F. Kennedy.

What is clear is that his relationship with Nixon was greatly impacted by Warren's perception of Nixon as manipulative, disingenuous, and devious. Warren never forgave Nixon for what he perceived as undercutting his presidential ambitions; the extent to which those ambitions were absolute is a matter of interpretation and uncertainty. What is not uncertain is that Warren's sentiments and observations regarding Nixon were widely shared and expressed.

Chief Justice Earl Warren

After the election, President Eisenhower promised Warren he would be appointed to the first vacancy in the Supreme Court. In the interim, Eisenhower named Warren as Solicitor General; it was a position to which Warren was not particularly suited or prepared for. Because of unexpected circumstances, he never served in the position. Upon the sudden death of Chief Justice Fred Vinson in 1953, Eisenhower—perhaps reluctantly, albeit with the support of Nixon who viewed Warren as a political rival—named Warren Chief Justice.[6]

Eisenhower had promised and, in all likelihood, intended to honor the commitment to appoint Warren to the Supreme Court. He had, however, not intended to appoint Warren as Chief Justice. Nevertheless, Warren was able to indirectly exert pressure on Eisenhower to honor the commitment; the evidence is clear that Warren very much desired the position and fully intended to ensure Eisenhower honor the commitment.

---

6. From Nixon's perspective the appointment was a "win-win": a conservative is appointed to the Court and a rival "moved aside."

Earl Warren's tenure as Chief Justice was highlighted by a number of cases that shaped America. Perhaps *"changed America"* is a more accurate description.[7]

Earl Warren's career as a District Attorney clearly gave him great insight regarding the reality of interrogations. A careful reading of *Miranda* makes that clear. He knew of what he wrote regarding the essence of the interrogation setting. Warren came to the Supreme Court deeply experienced in prosecutorial decision making, law enforcement, interrogations, and the confluence of the three.

Scholars argue about Warren's place in the pantheon of Chief Justices. Many place him at the height of the top tier, one notch below John Marshall. Others criticize Warren for not being a brilliant legal scholar and for failing to address constitutional issues with the depth, sophistication, and intellectual capability of Felix Frankfurter.

Justice Frankfurter was not, by all accounts, an easy and accommodating colleague. He was thought to be overbearing, oftentimes treating his Brethren as if they were his Harvard Law School students. Justice William O. Douglass was resentful of Frankfurter's lecturing tone, particularly in Conference. However, there is no doubt Frankfurter was a justice of great intellectual depth, sophistication, and capability.

---

7. *Brown v. Board of Education (Brown I)*, 347 U.S. 483 (1954); *Baker v. Carr*, 369 U.S. 186 (1962); *Mapp v. Ohio*, 367 U.S. 643 (1961); *Gideon v. Wainwright*, 372 U.S. 355 (1963).

The comparison between Warren and Frankfurter is relevant for one particular purpose: while there are some who doubt Warren's intellectual prowess, none cast doubt as to his leadership skills. There is, on that note, unanimity among biographers, scholars, and longtime Court observers. In addition to his undisputed leadership skills, Warren forcefully advocated guaranteeing individual rights in accordance with the US Constitution.

Miranda must be understood against the backdrop of Warren's commitment to protecting the vulnerable: those who would otherwise be denied opportunities and protections. That is a remarkable legacy. That is not to gainsay dark chapters in his decades-long career. There were two in particular. How they impacted the *Miranda* opinion is relevant to our examination.

Warren's holdings were clear, decisive, and left little doubt as to their meaning. Warren's career as a District Attorney, Attorney General, and Governor significantly shaped his writing style. The language is neither flowery nor highbrow. I use the word *manual* in describing Warren's writing style to my students. The word is intended as a compliment. Obfuscation benefits neither litigants nor the broader public seeking to understand ramifications of a judicial opinion. Given the extraordinary issues the Warren Court addressed, clarity was essential.

Otherwise, implementation of *Miranda* would be difficult. Absent of clarity, it would be of little relevance for those who most needed protection: the suspect. Vagueness would enable interrogators to blur the lines and, perhaps, result in interpretation to the suspect's disadvantage.

America after Warren Wrote *Miranda*

In the 50 years since Warren wrote *Miranda*, American society has faced a number of crisis points. Inevitably, there will be disagreement regarding any "top ten" or "top five" list. In the context of the question this book poses, the following are suggested:

1. **1960s radical movements, urban riots, and civil rights**
2. **Opposition to Vietnam War**
3. **9/11 and its aftermath**

All three sharply, and sometimes painfully, brought to focus the relationship between the individual and the state; the extent to which individual rights are guaranteed; the extent to which protest is acceptable and the extent to which the state can protect individual safety and security. In all three, the state came in direct contact with an individual suspected of involvement in activity that warranted interrogation, whether criminal or terrorist based.

However, the fact an individual has been arrested and identified as a suspect warranting interrogation must not mean that the state may run roughshod. Interrogate, yes; guarantee protections similarly, yes. That is the essence of the *Miranda* opinion.

In the immediate aftermath of 9/11, the reaction was one of public shock and dismay, governmental overreach, arbitrary measures, and ill-considered responses. US counterterrorism policy can best be described as a mixed bag: use of force with questionable criteria and review; an unwillingness to engage in semantic nuance; and a lack of clarity regarding the rights of suspected terrorists.

The status and rights of detained terrorists subject to interrogation have become a matter of great controversy and, unfortunately, highly politicized. Nowhere is the dilemma of individual rights more powerful, visceral, and dramatic than in the interrogation room. It is the heart of criminal procedure and of operational counterterrorism.

Benjamin Franklin's famous quote: "Those who would give up essential Liberty, to purchase a little temporary Safety, deserve neither Liberty nor Safety"[8] captures the tension between limited and unlimited interrogations.

My colleague, Professor Paul Cassell has written extensively on the impact and ramifications of the *Miranda* decision. Professor Cassell and I have debated whether Miranda warnings should be applied to suspected terrorists. We very much disagree. Paul argues there is no need to do so; I am convinced of the need to do so. Regarding *Miranda*, Paul—who argued *Dickerson v. U.S.*[9] before the Supreme Court—has written:

---

8. http://www.bartleby.com/73/1056.html.
9. 530 U.S. 428 (2000).

Miranda substantially harms the ability of law enforcement to protect society. Its technical rules prevent the conviction of countless guilty criminals, condemning victims of these crimes to see justice denied and fear crimes reprised. Its barriers to solving crimes also create substantial risks for innocent persons wrongfully caught up in the criminal justice system, who desperately need a confession from the true offender to extricate themselves.[10]

The questions, as we shall see in the pages ahead, are the extent to which rights are protected and ascertaining the costs arising from those protections. Protecting individual rights is not cost free; inquiring whether society and/or the victim pays a tolerable price is a fair question. Similarly, failure to protect the rights of the suspect imposes costs on suspect and interrogator alike. That is true regardless of the nature of the crime committed. The burden to protect suspect rights is heightened when the public is particularly engaged, if not agitated. That is very much the case regarding terrorism.

My interactions with Cassell have sharpened my understanding of the complexity of the tension. The points of disagreement are clear. I make no secret of the fact that the writings of Professor Yale Kamisar—the so-called "father of Miranda"—have been critical to my understanding of

---

10. Paul G. Cassell, *The Statute That Time Forgot: 18 U.S.C. 3501 and the Overhauling of Miranda*, 85 Iowa L. Rev. 255 (1999).

Miranda. In many ways, Kamisar's scholarship shapes how I view the interrogation paradigm, both practically (my Israel Defense Forces [IDF] career) and academically. In answering whether Warren would apply *Miranda* to terrorism, I hope to do justice both to the letter and spirit of the holding and to its writer.

Earl Warren's remarkable career spans across a number of decades bridging disparate periods in American history. He made a lasting mark on American jurisprudence and society; his opinions changed the relationship between the individual and the state. His growth as a person, his deepened understanding of the need to protect individual rights, and his recognition of the consequences of excessive state power are the basis for the *Miranda* decision. In his time period, at that very moment in American history, only Earl Warren could have penned *Miranda*. That recalls the adages that only Nixon could have gone to China; only Menachem Begin could have made peace with Egypt; only Yitzhak Rabin could have shook Yassar Arafat's hand.

Timing is, as the saying goes, everything. Earl Warren was perfectly positioned to write *Miranda*. In many ways, the opinion which I believe had to be written could only have been written by him. In the vernacular, Warren had the "chops" to do so. He personified law enforcement; he was tough, he had been an incredibly successful politician, he was a Republican. He could not be accused, best efforts aside, of being "soft on crime" or unduly sympathetic to criminals. He was not. This was a tough former district attorney, who prosecuted criminals, who had pushed the envelope regarding suspect rights. This was the same Warren who, without true reason or justified cause, aggressively pushed to deny without the modicum of due process the rights of American citizens.

Understanding *Miranda* requires exploring Warren's past.

To that we turn.

Chapter Two

Warren in California: Internment of Japanese Americans and *Point Lobos*

The Japanese race is an enemy race and while many second and third generation Japanese born on United States soil possessed of U.S. citizenship have become "Americanized" the racial strains are undiluted. It then follows that along the vital Pacific Coast over 112,000 potential enemies, of Japanese extraction, are at large today. There are indications that these were organized and ready for concerted action at a favorable opportunity. The very fact that no sabotage has taken place to date is a disturbing and confirming indication that such action will be taken. . . .[1]

---

1. General DeWitt's Final Report: Japanese Evacuation from the West Coast, 1942, and the government's brief to the Supreme Court defending Ex. Order 9066.

No Jap should come back to this coast except on a permit from my office. . . . We must worry about the Japanese all the time until he is wiped off the map.[2]

—Lt. General John DeWitt, Commanding General,
Western Defense Command (1942)

I firmly believe there is positive danger attached to the presence of so many of these admittedly American-hating Japanese in an area where sabotage or any other civil disorders would be so detrimental to the war effort. I have always felt that the concentration of these Japs (in California camps)—the reason for their concentration is based on military necessity and the Army, which is charged with the external security of our country is the only agency thoroughly familiar with the Jap and his machinations. . . . The Army should control the whole situation.[3]

—Governor Earl Warren

The immediate aftermath of the attack on Pearl Harbor on December 7, 1941, left many Americans in a state of panic and confusion. Building on these fears, and fueling the nation's sense of self-preservation, Lieutenant General

---

2. Richard Reeves, *Infamy: The Shocking Story of the Japanese American Internment in World War II*, 160 (2015).

3. Reeves, *supra* note 72, at 168.

http://renatef.xlx.pl/days-leading-up-to-pearl-harbor.php. Also can be found at HYPERLINK "http://www.radass.com/wp-content/uploads/2015/12/Pearl -Harbor-Attack-Newspaper-Headlines01.jpg" Pearl-Harbor-Attack-Newspaper -Headlines01.jpg from http://www.radass.com/author/radassbill/

John DeWitt, wartime commanding general of the Western Defense Command, made a series of announcements and proposals advocating for the removal of Japanese Americans from the West Coast. These pronouncements, enforced with similar ones from then-California Governor Culbert Olsen, and Attorney General Earl Warren, would eventually lead to the mass relocation and internment of 120,000 Japanese Americans. While DeWitt would never waiver in his conviction that Japanese Americans were best dealt with through permanent relocation,[4] editorials published at the time reflect that not all Americans were no longer advocating for permanent relocation:

> The General should be told that American democracy and the Constitution of the United States are too vital to be ignored and flouted by any military zealot. The panic of Pearl Harbor is now past. There has been ample time for the investigation of these people and the determination of their loyalty to this country on an individual basis. Whatever excuse there once was for evacuating and holding them indiscriminately no longer exists.[5]
>
> —Washington Post Op-ed, April 15, 1943

---

4. Commission on Wartime Relocation and Internment of Civilians, *Personal Justice Denied: Report of the Commission on Wartime Relocation and Internment of Civilians* (Washington, DC: Government Printing Office, 1982), 121. (In front of a House Committee on April 15, 1943, he [DeWitt] stated: "There is a feeling developing, I think, in certain sections of the country, that the Japanese should be allowed to return. I am opposing it with every proper means at my disposal.")

5. *Id.*

https://www.trofire.com/

Japanese American Internment: Background

They've sunk the posts deep into the ground
They've strung out wires all the way around.
With machine gun nests just over there,
And sentries and soldiers everywhere.
We're trapped like rats in a wired cage,
To fret and fume with impotent rage;
Yonder whispers the lure of the night,
But that DAMNED FENCE assails our sight.

We seek the softness of the midnight air,
But that DAMNED FENCE in the floodlight glare
Awakens unrest in our nocturnal quest,
And mockingly laughs with vicious jest.

With nowhere to go and nothing to do,
We feel terrible, lonesome, and blue:

That DAMNED FENCE is driving us crazy,
Destroying our youth and making us lazy.

Imprisoned in here for a long, long time,
We know we're punished–though we've committed no
    crime,
Our thoughts are gloomy and enthusiasm damp,
To be locked up in a concentration camp.

Loyalty we know, and patriotism we feel,
To sacrifice our utmost was our ideal,
To fight for our country, and die, perhaps;
But we're here because we happen to be Japs.

We all love life, and our country best,
Our misfortune to be here in the west,
To keep us penned behind that DAMNED FENCE,
Is someone's notion of NATIONAL DEFENCE![6]

Down in our hearts we cried and cursed this govern-
ment every time when we showered with sand. We slept
in the dust; we breathed the dust; we ate the dust.[7]

> —Joseph Kurihara, an internee at the Manzanar
> internment camp in California

6. Anonymous poem circulated at the Poston internment camp.

7. Amber Li & Catherine Tang, *Camp Conditions*, Fight to Freedom: Japanese American Internment (2007), http://51773304.weebly.com/camps.html.

Introduction and Warren

The link between internment of Japanese Americans as a response to Pearl Harbor and reactions to acts of terrorism is compelling. The two raise important questions about protection of individual rights; ethnic and racial profiling; public reaction media reporting (including social media in the contemporary age); and reactive, operational measures.

Public reaction often focuses on a government's failure to protect; in response, the government reacts with strong measures. Decision makers seek to ensure the public that aggressive steps are in place to both apprehend those responsible and to ensure subsequent attacks will not occur. The former is likely; the latter is a fallacy and disingenuous.

Earl Warren, in the aftermath of Pearl Harbor, succumbed to the malady of "doing something." Warren's actions included testimony before a congressional committee; providing misinformation to Walter Lippmann, the nation's most revered and feared newspaper columnist; claiming the mantle of California's "go to" person for civil defense; and engaging in a media campaign intended to draw attention both to himself and the presumed dangers posed by California's Japanese American population.

Based on a conversation with Warren and Lieutenant General DeWitt, Lippmann wrote the column (below) on February 13, 1942; Roosevelt signed the Executive Order on February 19, 1942. The impact of the article, given Lippmann's unique status and standing, was enormous. It is not by chance that Warren chose to meet with Lippmann; his purpose was to provide information, which tragically turned out to be disinformation, to the nation's most important columnist for the purpose of influencing decision makers. It is a time-tested tool used by politicians; Warren was not unique in this vein.

However, there was no factual basis for "information" Warren shared, which he undoubtedly knew Lippmann would publish. In other words, Warren and Lippmann had a convenient meeting of mutual interests: Warren wanted to push the internment decision and Lippmann was uniquely positioned to influence Roosevelt and his team. The only problem? There was no truth in what Warren shared and what Lippmann wrote:

> The enemy alien problem on the Pacific Coast, or much more accurately the Fifth Column problem, is very serious and it is very special. What makes it so serious and so special is that the Pacific Coast is in imminent danger of a combined attack from within and from without. The danger is not, as it would be in the inland centers or perhaps even for the present on the Atlantic Coast, from sabotage alone. The peculiar danger of the Pacific Coast is in a Japanese raid accompanied by enemy action inside American territory. This combination can be very formidable indeed. For while the striking power of Japan from the sea and air might not in itself be overwhelming at any one point

just now, Japan could strike a blow which might do irreparable damage if it were accompanied by the kind of organized sabotage to which this part of the country is specially vulnerable. This is a sober statement of the situation, in fact a report, based not on speculation but on what is known to have taken place and to be taking place in this area of the war. It is a fact that the Japanese navy has been reconnoitering the Pacific Coast more or less continually and for a considerable length of time, testing and feeling out the American defenses. It is a fact that communication takes place between the enemy at sea and enemy agents on land. These are facts which we shall ignore or minimize at our peril. It is also a fact that since the outbreak of the Japanese war there has been no important sabotage on the Pacific Coast. From what we know about Hawaii and about the Fifth Column in Europe this is not, as some have liked to think, a sign that there is nothing to be feared. It is a sign that the blow is well-organized and that it is held back until it can be struck with maximum effect.[8]

Whether Warren's role can be defined as "a" role as compared to "the" role" is, ultimately, not important. What is relevant is that Warren played a seminal role. Of that, there is no doubt. The historical record is clear, open neither to

---

8. Walter Lippmann, *The Fifth Column* (Feb. 13, 1942), http://www.digitalhistory.uh.edu/active_learning/explorations/japanese_internment/lippmann.cfm.

"spin" nor a claim of "fake news." Analyzing the exact extent of his influence is, perhaps, interesting. It is, however, not essential given the undeniably important role he played. For our purposes, that is sufficient as it will shed light on the larger question we are asking: would Warren extend *Miranda* to suspected terrorists. We can learn a great deal by examining Warren's actions as Attorney General.

In the immediate aftermath of Pearl Harbor, Warren was active, engaged, and determined to act. Whether the motivation was political opportunism or genuine concern regarding national security and public order, the consequences of his activity were deeply harmful to an entire ethnic group upon whom were cast unwarranted and unjustified aspersions. The harm must not be minimized. About 120,000 individuals—men, women, and children—were forced to leave their homes, lose their property and possessions, and were humiliated in front of their neighbors, friends, and colleagues. While there was no intention to kill the 120,000—in direct contrast to Nazi Germany's "Final Solution"—a profound wrong occurred.

In reviewing available literature, it is clear California and federal officials overreacted. Reading oral histories, first-person accounts, public records, and biographies of individuals involved paints a disturbing picture of "group think," profiling, and racism. The voices who opposed can be counted on one hand. However, they did not have the political, personal, or professional wherewithal to push back against an action they knew to be unwarranted. Complicit in an action they knew to be wrong, the naysayers chose to remain silent. That is distinct from Warren who was aggressively pursuing a terrible and tragic agenda. Regardless of motivation—whether predicated purely on national security considerations, personal aggrandizement, or a combination of the two—Warren's role in the internment decision is a profound blight on his otherwise lauded record as California Attorney General.

Among those who opposed the voices calling for interment was US Attorney General Francis Biddle, who argued against the growing consensus among his peers. Ultimately, Biddle acquiesced, particularly when the support of Secretary of War Henry Stimson was apparent. Biddle was of the opinion that as wrong as the decision was, priority on such matters must rest with those responsible for the nation's defense.

Japanese Americans, Pearl Harbor, and Its Aftermath

Sunday December 7, 1941 caught America unprepared for the Japanese attack on Pearl Harbor. Whether the White House had early warning and measures could have been taken to prevent the attack, or minimize its consequences, is beyond our purview.[9]

---

9. To read more on this issue, see Greg Robinson, *A Tragedy of Democracy: Japanese Confinement in North America* (2009); Jere Takahashi, *Nisei Sansei: Asian American History & Cultu* (1998); Eric K. Yamamoto et al., *Race, Rights and Reparation: Law and the Japanese American Internment* (2nd. ed. 2013); Richard

http://viaconsultationgroup.com/index.php/real/21942/

We are only interested in the internment decision forc-
ing 120,000 Japanese Americans—70% US citizens (Nisei),
30% Japanese immigrants (Issei)—to be forced into camps
within days of President Roosevelt signing Executive Order
9066. The decision is one of the most controversial, unjustified, and troubling in American history. It is a permanent
stain on America. It also offers invaluable, albeit discon-
certing, insight into how decision makers respond in times

Reeves, *Infamy: The Shocking Story of the Japanese Internment in World War II*
(2016); Roger Daniels, *Prisoners without Trial: Japanese Americans in World War II*
(Revised ed. 2004).

of crisis. The victims of the Executive Order committed no crime, gave no indication of anti-American activities, and provided no justification for the decision that would forever scar their lives.

Earl Warren did not have particular affinity, appreciation of, or respect for Californian's Japanese American population. His interaction with Nisei and Issei alike was extremely limited, if not nonexistent. Their world and culture was, largely, alien to him in spite of his years in public service. Warren's world was a traditional world for that era, dominated by white Protestant males whose social milieu and clubs did not include "others" whether African Americans, Jews, or Japanese Americans.

Japanese Americans worked small plots of land; while some owned their land, others were restricted by law from owning the land they worked. They were industrious, frugal, living a self-contained existence devoid of contact with outsiders; the only outsiders they interacted with was California's white agriculture community. Relations between the two communities were complicated; Japanese Americans were unwelcome competition and viewed with suspicion. Evidence is overwhelming that the white agriculture community benefited from the Executive Order, as valuable farm land was freed up when Japanese Americans were forced to relocate.

To give the subsequent discussion sufficient context, the Executive Order that authorized the Secretary of War to prescribe military areas must be read in full:

Whereas the successful prosecution of the war requires every possible protection against espionage and against sabotage to national-defense material, national-defense premises, and national-defense utilities. . . .

Now, therefore, by virtue of the authority vested in me as President of the United States, and Commander in Chief of the Army and Navy, I hereby authorize and direct the Secretary of War, and the Military Commanders whom he may from time to time designate, whenever he or any designated Commander deems such action necessary or desirable, to prescribe military areas in such places and of such extent as he or the appropriate Military Commander may determine, from which any or all persons may be excluded, and with respect to which, the right of any person to enter, remain in, or leave shall be subject to whatever restrictions the Secretary of War or the appropriate Military Commander may impose in his discretion.

The Secretary of War is hereby authorized to provide for residents of any such area who are excluded therefrom, such transportation, food, shelter, and other accommodations as may be necessary, in the judgment of the Secretary of War or the said Military Commander, and until other arrangements are made, to accomplish the purpose of this order. The designation of military areas in any region or locality shall supersede designations of prohibited and restricted areas by the Attorney General under the Proclamations of December 7 and 8, 1941, and shall supersede the responsibility and authority of the Attorney General under the said Proclamations in respect of such prohibited and restricted areas.

I hereby further authorize and direct the Secretary of War and the said Military Commanders to take such other steps as he or the appropriate Military Commander may deem advisable to enforce compliance with the restrictions applicable to each Military area hereinabove authorized to be designated, including the use of Federal troops and other Federal Agencies, with authority to accept assistance of state and local agencies.

I hereby further authorize and direct all Executive Departments, independent establishments and other Federal Agencies, to assist the Secretary of War or the said Military Commanders in carrying out this Executive Order, including the furnishing of medical aid, hospitalization, food, clothing, transportation, use of land, shelter, and other supplies, equipment, utilities, facilities, and services.

This order shall not be construed as modifying or limiting in any way the authority heretofore granted under Executive Order No. 8972, dated December 12, 1941, nor shall it be construed as limiting or modifying the duty and responsibility of the Federal Bureau of Investigation,

> *with respect to the investigation of alleged acts of sabotage or the duty and responsibility of the Attorney General and the Department of Justice under the Proclamations of December 7 and 8, 1941, prescribing regulations for the conduct and control of alien enemies, except as such duty and responsibility is superseded by the designation of military areas hereunder.*[10]

The only "crime" committed by those ordered to leave their homes and relocate to camps in the western US was their ethnicity. While Japan attacked Pearl Harbor, Japanese Americans living in the United States were just that— Japanese Americans living in the United States. A significant percentage of them were American citizens: in 1940, 63% of the Japanese American population in California was Nisei (second-generation immigrants who became naturalized citizens); between 1930 and 1940, the Nisei population increased from 68,357 to 79,642, while the Issei (first-generation immigrants) population declined from 70,477 to 47,305.[11]

There was no evidence they were *in any way* involved in the planning or execution of the attack. They gave no

---

10. Executive Order No. 9066, 7 Fed. Reg. 1407 (Feb. 25, 1942), https://www.ourdocuments.gov/doc.php?flash=false&doc=74&page=transcript.

11. Jere Takahashi, *Nisei Sansei: Shifting Japanese American Identities and Politics* (1997).

indication of being disloyal to America. There is no proof Japanese Americans took to the streets to celebrate the attack. The reactions of Japanese Americans mirrored that of their fellow countrymen. America was under attack and Japanese Americans were no less or more vulnerable and susceptible to foreign threats than anyone else living in America. Like any American living within reach of the Japanese Army, Japanese Americans were at risk.

Although Germany and Italy were at war with America, unlike German Americans and Italian Americans, Japanese Americans were deemed a threat to American national security. There was no basis for this assumption. Subsequent to World War II, no proof has been offered validating this assertion. The United States fought Germany, Italy, and Japan in the Second World War. However, no concerted or organized policies were considered or implemented against those who came to the shores of America from Europe.

While the Executive Order did not specifically mention Japanese Americans, it was implemented exclusively against them. That was the intent of those who recommended to Roosevelt that he sign the Order; no other ethnic or racial group was considered. Evidence suggests President Roosevelt did not meet with senior government officials to discuss the internment decision before signing the Executive Order. Perhaps the decision was not deemed sufficiently important. Undoubtedly, Roosevelt had an unfathomably complex set of responsibilities and decisions demanding his full-time attention: after Pearl Harbor, the United States was fighting a global war.

Nevertheless, his advisors did not discuss with the President the ramifications of relocating 120,000 innocent individuals whose sole "crime" was their ethnicity. Similarly, the President did not request such a meeting.

The judiciary would prove complicit in the internment process. Internment was held constitutional in three cases: *United States v. Minoru Yasui,*[12] *Kiyoshi Hirabayashi v. United States,*[13] and *Toyosaburo Korematsu v. United States.*[14]

UNITED STATES V. MINORU YASUI (1943)
&
KIYOSHI HIRABAYASHI V. UNITED STATES (1943)

These two cases were companion cases. In *Yasui,* The Supreme Court determined that curfews applied against citizens of the United States were Constitutional. In implementing Executive Order 9066, the US Military created "zones of exclusion" along the West Coast of the United States, subjecting Japanese Americans to curfews and eventual relocation.

Decided on the same day as *Yasui,* the Court in *Hirabayashi* held that application of curfews against members

---

12. 320 U.S. 115 (1943).
13. 320 U.S. 81 (1943).
14. 323 U.S. 214 (1944).

of a minority group was constitutional when the nation was at war with the country from which that group originated.

The Justice Department had expected a legal challenge to substantial portions of Executive Order 9066, including curfew, exclusion, and internment.

Yasui and *Hirabayashi* established favorable precedent for larger challenges to the entire internment process.

TOYOSABURO KOREMATSU V. UNITED STATES (1944)

In *Korematsu*, the Supreme Court ruled that Executive Order 9066's exclusion provisions, including internment, was constitutional. Fred Korematsu was a Japanese American citizen who decided to stay in California after the Executive Order, knowingly violating the Civilian Exclusion Order 34 (the internment provision). He argued that the Order was unconstitutional under the Fifth Amendment. Using the *Hirabayashi* ruling as precedent, the Court reasoned that deference was to be given to Congress and military authorities in times of heightened security. The Court explicitly rejected claims of racial prejudice.

The decision-making process was deeply troubling. It reflects unmitigated racism, unmoored to facts; it was fear-mongering resulting in the casting of unwarranted aspersions. Those involved acted for the sake of "doing something";

their actions marred by their assumptions and prejudices. It was made over the course of two short months; decision makers seemingly never stopped to ask themselves whether or not the decision was warranted. The impetus for internment came from government, politicians, military officials, and the media; the general public's reaction to the attack on Pearl Harbor largely focused on its consequences and harms. This is not to say that public outbursts did not occur; after all, 2,403 Americans were killed.[15] That, however, did not translate to public demands that Japanese Americans be removed from their homes and communities. There is no evidence of such demands; history does not record public demonstrations against Japanese Americans.

The list is long of government officials, military officers, politicians, and journalists who had a hand in Roosevelt's decision to sign the Order on February 19, 1942. While Roosevelt bears ultimate responsibility, others are culpable. These include some of America's most distinguished and recognized politicians and public officials. Among the most culpable is Earl Warren.

Earl Warren and Internment

We must carefully examine Earl Warren's actions between December 7, 1941 and February, 1942. However, as we shall

---

15. The National WWII Museum, *Remembering Pearl Harbor: A Pearl Harbor Fact Sheet* (1941), http://www.nationalww2museum.org/assets/pdfs/pearl-harbor-fact-sheet-1.pdf.

come to see, Warren's interest in questions of civil defense predated the attack on Pearl Harbor. Warren, the Republican Attorney General and Olson, the Democratic Governor, were not on speaking terms. They viewed each other with great suspicion and were at cross-hairs during the years they served together in office (1939–1943). Ultimately, their rivalry focused on the ballot box where Warren defeated Olson in November 1942.

Warren's efforts to establish himself as a civil defense expert must be viewed in the context of his political rivalry with Governor Olson. In an effort to establish his own circle of power, Warren focused on civil defense. He enjoyed the support and loyalty of District Attorney's and other law enforcement officials whose respect he earned during the years he served as the Alameda County District Attorney. Warren, neither as District Attorney nor as Attorney General, had an inherent linkage to or understanding of issues relevant to California civil defense. Nevertheless, for political purposes, the claim to expertise was important and understandable.

There is an unresolvable dissonance between different aspects of Warren's career. Warren was a man of impeccable character, strong moral fiber, moderate political views, and, for the most part, imbued with a clear sense of distinguishing right from wrong. However, at a critical moment in American history, Warren chose to allow base instincts, reflecting an unhealthy combination of parochialism and political opportunism, to guide him. It would be easy to say he got caught up in the moment. There is some justification for this suggestion. As an elected official, there was an understandable need to act on behalf of a public under attack. That is within the range of acceptable. What is not acceptable is what Warren did.

His decision to aggressively lobby for internment of innocent American citizens is the unpleasant—and disturbing—reality of his career. It reflects his world view at the time; his testimony before the Tolan Committee, when he pointed an unjustified accusatory finger at Japanese Americans, makes that abundantly clear. Warren the cautious lawyer, who I believe respected individuals and the rule of law, had no basis for any of the arguments he presented before the members of Congress. However, I do think he genuinely believed what he was saying, even though his words were devoid of factual basis.

The available literature suggests Warren was not a racist, but rather a man who, like many of his peers and social milieu, possessed a parochial and limited world view. In a sense, he was a "man of his times" who did not understand "the other." Nevertheless, that limited world view must not be understood as justifying his conduct, statements, and viewpoints. The argument "that was the times" has been used to explain—justify is another word—the actions of anti-Semitic, anti-black, and antiwomen behavior by white males through the ages. The term *genteel racist* has been used over the years to define—perhaps excuse—someone who is a "good person" but lacks empathy regarding the other.

The 2016 presidential election highlights the danger of conflated and heated terminology. However, to truly understand Warren's actions in the internment decision, we need to ask uncomfortable questions regarding Warren. The risk in doing so is that we judge Warren through the lens of 2017, not 1941. That is, admittedly, a danger. Nevertheless, as discussed below, Warren's words and actions directly contributed to a terrible injustice.

Warren, as Attorney General, could not claim, "I was only following orders"; the phrase "I was but a cog in the machine" would not apply to Warren. That is obvious given his position, influence, and dominant role in the internment question. Warren did not directly speak with Roosevelt; there is no documented evidence suggesting Roosevelt inquired as to Warren's position on the issue. Nevertheless, there is no doubt regarding his influence in the decision-making process as evidenced by his influence on the previously referenced Walter Lippmann column.

We need to understand what motivated this otherwise thoughtful, cautious, and responsible public servant to assume a major leadership role in a terribly flawed and misguided decision that harmed the innocent. There can be no mistaking nor minimizing the harm Warren had a direct role in creating.

There is no doubt regarding Warren's fundamental decency and respect for others. I have found no evidence suggesting otherwise. And yet, harm was caused to Japanese Americans as a result of Warren's actions. His words, actions, and concerns were not directed at particular individuals; there was no effort on Warren's part to target specific individuals. That would have been well-nigh impossible because Japanese Americans committed no crime. An entire ethnic class was wrongly targeted, devoid of individual particularization.

Japanese Americans were not beaten, attacked by dogs or worse. The internment camps were not the American version of Auschwitz, Treblinka, or Buchenwald. Japanese Americans were not interrogated. They were removed from their homes, held in internment, and largely allowed to conduct their lives within the confines of internment.[16]

However, the physical hardship of internment in stark, barren camps that provided minimal protection against the weather—in summer and winter—must not be minimized. Those interned were American citizens of all ages. They had committed no crime. This was internment for the sake of internment predicated on racial and ethnic basis exclusively.

No government official was able to provide compelling justification for the decision. That is not to say statements, many of which were incendiary, were not made. Warren,

---

16. For discussion regarding life in internment camps, please see Greg Robinson, *A Tragedy of Democracy: Japanese Confinement in North America* (2009); Jere Takahashi, *Nisei Sansei: Asian American History & Cultu* (1998); Eric K. Yamamoto et al. *Race, Rights and Reparation: Law and the Japanese American Internment* (2nd. ed. 2013); Richard Reeves, *Infamy: The Shocking Story of the Japanese Internment in World War II* (2016); Roger Daniels, *Prisoners without Trial: Japanese Americans in World War II* (Revised ed. 2004).

like others in the aftermath of Pearl Harbor, was firmly convinced *with no cause for so believing* that Japanese Americans posed an extraordinary threat to America. Their words reflect that conviction.

From a remarkable Oral History project about Earl Warren, we gain great insight into Warren; Carey McWilliams was the editor of The Nation; Wlila Baum was an internationally recognized oral historian:

> **Baum**: He makes statements that I found very, very difficult to understand from a man like Warren. For example, he said that the Nisei generation gave him far more concern on the score of loyalty and security than the Issei generation did. Well, if you really honestly believe this, as I 'm sure he did, then you must have concluded that the American education of the Nisei didn't have any impact on them. It was a nonsensical kind of position, really. But that's what he said, and that's what I'm sure he believed.
>
> I remember he put a map on the blackboard, too, in talking to the Tolan Committee. He said that he thought it very significant that beneath these power lines—it was either Southern California Edison, or one of the power lines—that beneath these power lines, you could find, here, there and elsewhere, the small plots of produce farming. And they just happened to be farmed by Japanese. You know, "Very strange, isn't it, gentlemen, that they should be farming here."

Well, in point of fact there wasn't anything strange about it. Nothing whatever was strange about it, because the power companies had to condemn the right of way, you see, when they built a big power line. Nobody else was interested in taking these little pinches of land. Nobody else could do anything with them but the Japanese. It was completely innocent. There was nothing sinister about it, you see. But he seemed to think that there was.

Here again, I think he was entrapped to a certain extent by his own political support, the kind of support that he had, and a kind of political environment out of which he came in California. For example, he was a very active personage in the Native Sons of the Golden West; he was very active in this organization. The Native sons of the Golden West and Daughters were very anti-Japanese and very insistent on this. They always had been anti -Oriental. And Hiram Johnson—great man that Hiram Johnson was—had this same bias. Johnson was very anti -Oriental. Warren greatly respected Johnson, and, I think, from this source, and from the fact that organized labor, particularly the AFL, had always been bitten with this virus, Warren sort of had this point of view.

I'm sure in retrospect that he would probably feel that he had been wrong about it.

He might have been overcome simply by his responsibility to protect the state.

McWilliams: Yes, but you know, It's Interesting. The people that had that situation thoroughly cased and really understood It were the officials of naval intelligence. They had been studying Japanese communities since the turn of the century, because of the connection with the fleet coming into San Diego. They had been watching at San Pedro; they had been studying. They really knew the situation, and they were very much opposed to mass evacuation. They did not want to see this happen. They thought it was a mistake, and they couldn't take a public position, but they were working behind the scenes and they were opposed.

Of course, one thing: while Earl Warren was strongly in favor of the mass evacuation of Japanese, and while he didn't want any of them returned (he took a very strong position against the return) once the decision was made, he did behave very well.[17]

---

17. United States. Congress. House. Select Committee Investigating National Defense Migration, 77th Cong., 2nd sess. *National Defense Migration. Parts 29, 30, 31: Problems of Evacuation of Enemy Aliens and Others from Prohibited Military Zones* (Tolan Committee hearings) (Feb. 21–22, 1942), https://archive.org/stream /viewsepisodes00warrrich/viewsepisodes00warrrich_djvu.txt; http://www.oac .cdlib.org/view?docId=ft9f59p1z7&brand=oac4&doc.view=entire_text.

With that, we turn to Warren's testimony before the Tolan Committee.

The Tolan Committee was officially called the Select Committee Investigating National Defense Migration, House of Representatives. The Committee was chaired by Congressman John H. Tolan (D-California)[18]; its members included Congressman John J. Sparkman (D-Alabama), Congressman Laurence F. Arnold, (D-Illinois), Congressman Carl T. Curtis (R-Nebraska), and Congressman George H. Bender (R-Ohio). Warren testified before the Committee when it convened in San Francisco on February 21 and 22, 1942 to discuss "Problems of Evacuation of Enemy Aliens and Others from Prohibited Military Zones."

Important to note: the Committee met two days *after* President Roosevelt signed Executive Order 9066. While there is, perhaps, a sense of "why convene" after the Order was signed, the Committee addressed a wide range of additional issues. That said, Warren's testimony is telling with respect to the forcefulness of the position he powerfully advocated before the Committee that was, also, reflected in his meeting with Lippmann.

I have chosen to bring before the reader excerpts from Warren's testimony:

Early in February 1942 I requested the district attorneys of those counties of the State having a Japanese

---

18. In a touch of irony, Tolan represented the Congressional district where Warren resided.

population to have prepared maps of their counties showing all land owned, occupied, or controlled by Japanese, including American born Japanese as well as Japanese aliens. . . .

An inspection of these maps shows a disturbing situation. It shows that along the coast from Marin County to the Mexican border, virtually every important strategic location and installation has one or more Japanese in its immediate vicinity. . . .

This list, lengthy though it is, by no means includes all such points. It does not even include all such points on the maps. It is intended to be merely illustrative and not exhaustive. In addition it should be understood that for obvious reasons the maps do not show our coastal defense and very few of our war industries. That there are Japanese in the immediate vicinity of many such establishments is unquestionably the fact.

Notwithstanding the fact that the county maps showing the location of Japanese lands have omitted most coastal defenses and war industries, still it is plain from them that in our coastal counties . . . virtually every feasible landing beach, air field, railroad, highway, powerhouse, power line, gas storage . . . and other points of strategic importance have several—and usually a considerable number—of Japanese in their immediate vicinity. The same situation prevails in all of the interior counties that have any considerable Japanese population.

An additional factor in the danger and one which would probably not be apparent to persons unfamiliar with the California Japanese lies in the fact that the Japanese in this State are very closely organized.

These associations are composed of natives of a particular prefecture living in the locality where the association is located.

We believe that the action that the President took yesterday (signing of Executive Order 9066, ANG) was most wise and that it at least points the way to a real solution of our problem.

For some time I have been of the opinion that the solution of our alien enemy problem with all its ramifications, which include the descendents of aliens, is not only a Federal problem but is a military problem. We believe that all the decisions in that regard must be made by the military command that is charged with the security of this area.

I am convinced that the fifth-column activities of our enemy call for the participation of people who are in fact American citizens, and that if we are to deal realistically with the problem we must realize that we will be obliged in times of stress to deal with subversive elements of our own citizenry.

If that be true, it creates almost an impossible situation for the civil authorities because the civil authorities cannot take protective measures against people of that character. We may suspect their loyalty. We may even have some evidence or, perhaps, substantial evidence of their disloyalty. But until we have the whole pattern of the enemy plan, until we are able to go into court and beyond the exclusion of a reasonable doubt establish the guilt of those elements among our American citizens, there is no way that civil government can cope with the situation.

On the other hand, we believe that in an area such as California, which has been designated as a combat zone, when things have happened such as have happened here on the coast, something should be done and done immediately.

We believe that any delay in the adoption of the necessary protective measures is to invite disaster. It means that we, too, will have in California a Pearl Harbor incident.

I believe that up to the present and perhaps for a long time to come the greatest danger to continental United States is that from well organized sabotage and fifth-column activity.

Unfortunately, however, many of our people and some of our authorities and, I am afraid, many of our people in other parts of the country are of the opinion that because we have had no sabotage and no Fifth Column activities in this State since the beginning of the war, that means that none have been planned for us. But I take the view that this is the most ominous sign in our whole situation. It convinces me more than perhaps any other factor that the sabotage that we are to get, the Fifth Column activities that we are to get, are timed just like Pearl Harbor was timed and just like the invasion of France, and of Denmark, and of Norway, and all of those other countries.

We believe that when we are dealing with the Caucasian race we have methods that will test the loyalty of them, and we believe that we can, in dealing with the Germans and the Italians arrive at some fairly sound conclusions because our of our knowledge of the way they live in the community and have lived for many years. But when we deal with the Japanese we are in an entirely different field and cannot form any opinion that we believe to be sound.

Their method of living, their language, make for this difficulty. Many of them who show you a birth certificate stating that they were born in this State, perhaps, or born in Honolulu, can hardly speak the English language because, although they were born here, when they were 4 or 5 years of age they were sent over to Japan to be educated and they stayed over there through their adolescent period at least, and they came back here thoroughly Japanese.[19]

The testimony is deeply troubling. It is predicated on assumptions devoid of supporting evidence; it reflects stereotypes regarding Japanese Americans; it damns an entire class of loyal American citizens; it carries with it the full gravity of Warren's position and personal prestige. It is clearly intended to convey danger posed to American national security by Japanese Americans. That would be understandable were it true. However, it could not be further from the truth. There was no evidence to support Warren's claims.

Yes, Japanese farms were located as Warren's maps showed; however, they had been there for years. There was no demonstrated correlation between farm land owned by Japanese Americans and the presence of the infrastructure Warren correctly notes in his testimony. Simply put, the extrapolation between two correctly stated facts—location of farms and location of infrastructure—was incorrect.

Similarly, there was no evidence *at all* of Fifth Column activity by Japanese Americans; when Warren testified, there was no proof of sabotage committed by Japanese Americans or indications that such attacks were considered. The testimony reflected conjecture, at best. It was base politics at its worse: connecting individual dots that

---

19. Tolan Committee, *supra* note 84, at 10973–74.

existed but with no basis for linking them together. The testimony was impressive in its scope and breadth; Warren was powerful, compelling and prepared.

He carried himself as one would expect from a highly accomplished, confident, and ambitious politician equipped with maps, charts, and information. It was, frankly, "easy pickings" for a skilled politician: America had just been attacked by Japan, Japanese Americans lived in California, and public safety and national security demanded action. Interning Japanese Americans was a logical measure. The only problem was that they did not pose a threat to America. This is a classic example of the facts be damned in order to fit into an otherwise "neat" narrative that seemed logical and obvious. The wrong imposed on Japanese Americans was profound; it is, without doubt, one of the darkest moments in American history. It is suggestive of xenophobia, racism, and group think devoid of facts and reason.

The argument, proposed by Warren, that the lack of attacks by Japanese Americans was an "ominous" sign is disingenuous. Sly is another word. The argument was not to Warren's credit. It reflected the degree to which he was convinced of the threat posed albeit no proof that one existed. His testimony was powerful, compelling, coherent, and articulate; it was also, false, erroneous, and misleading. It was predicated on an *unwarranted* perception of Japanese Americans. There is no evidence suggesting that Japanese Americans were any less loyal to America than Earl Warren.

When we come to consider the *Miranda* holding, we must recall Warren's actions in February 1942. Regardless of whether President Roosevelt inquired as to the opinion of the Attorney General of California regarding the threat posed by Japanese Americans, Warren's statements speak for themselves. More than that. His conversation with Lippmann, and the resulting article, was a deliberate effort to frame the debate. The Lippmann article was of the greatest importance; Warren was a critical source to the venerated and venerable columnist whose influence was extraordinary. It is not an exaggeration to suggest that Walter Lippmann shaped opinion public because of his influence on decision makers. Warren did not meet with him by chance or randomly.

The Earl Warren of 1942 was a politician and an ambitious one at that. That does not, under any circumstances, suggest his motivations were nefarious. It does, however, suggest that his presentation—including maps and charts—reflected a perspective that, in retrospect, is deeply troubling. The consequences of the Executive Order were tragic; Warren's contribution must be understood in that light.

Prior to his election to Attorney General, Warren was the Alameda County District Attorney. He was widely praised and acclaimed. However, his troubling action on one particular occasion deserves our attention. Its importance, from our perspective, is telling for it highlights the manner in which interrogations were conducted in a different era and the measures DA Warren considered lawful in an effort to secure a confession.

In asking Warren experts whether his actions in the case discussed below impacted the *Miranda* holding, the responses were mixed. Some rejected the possible connection in its entirety, some claimed never to have considered it, and others suggested that, perhaps, but added that self-reflection was not a Warren trait.

That question is equally relevant in the *Point Lobos* murder trial; it is to that case that we turn.

Point Lobos

Earl Warren was an aggressive, ambitious, and determined District Attorney. He was committed to fighting crime; by all accounts, he was tough and demanding, committed to the rule of law. His subordinates respected him, believed in him, and were committed to prosecuting criminals to the fullest extent of the law. There was no coddling of criminals. Warren's tough-on crime-perspective defined the office and his staff responded to the professional standards he demanded. In 1931, Columbia Professor of Law Raymond Moley, on the basis of a national survey, referred to Warren as "the most intelligent and politically independent district attorney in the United States."[20]

---

20. Yale Kamisar. *How Earl Warren's Twenty-Two Years in Law Enforcement Affected His Work as Chief Justice*, 3 Ohio St. J. Crim. L. 11–32 (2005).

This suggests an upright public servant, dedicated to the law, possessing a strong moral code. Warren was a strict District Attorney, committed to forcefully fighting crime within the limits of what was legally acceptable at the time. For example, in 1936, the exclusionary rule did not exist.[21] Similarly, extensive and lengthy interrogations of suspects were acceptable police conduct as was the bugging of rooms without warrants.

As District Attorney, Warren was focused on unions; in particular, the Maritime Federation and the American Federation of Labor (AFL). Whether this reflects efforts to prosecute communist elements is a fair question; it is, however, beyond our purview.[22] However, we cannot gloss over this issue for it is relevant to our inquiry. Its relevance is rooted in the question of how Warren perceived a threat and what measures could be taken in response. As Professor White notes, Warren:

> "was convinced . . . that 'subversives' of all types were a threat to the security of California and that Communists, Fascists, and other 'enemies of democracy'

---

21. The Supreme Court, in *Mapp vs. Ohio* 347 U.S. 643 (1961), held that illegally obtained incriminating evidence may be excluded at trial.

22. Warren's efforts, and concerns, regarding communism have been suggested by others; see Michael R. Belknap, *The Supreme Court Under Earl Warren 1953-1969* (2005); G. Edward White, *Earl Warren: A Public Life* (1987); Jim Newton, *Justice for All, Earl Warren and the Nation He Made* (2007).

were attempting to prey upon the fears and aspirations of the 'average working man.' "[23]

I do not believe Warren was a purist or naïve; perhaps he was a combination of a moralist with a straightforward, traditional understanding of the role and responsibility of a District Attorney: a crime must be thoroughly investigated and prosecuted to the fullest extent tolerated by the law. We must examine Warren's actions in accordance with the law of 1936, and not through the lens of 2017. Our judgment must reflect what the law tolerated when Warren was District Attorney.

On March 22, 1936 when the *Point Lobos* was berthed at Encinal Terminals in Alameda, California, the ship's chief engineer, George Alberts, was murdered on board. It is unclear whether the attackers, who beat and stabbed Mr. Alberts, intended to kill or only injure their victim. Alberts was killed by two men in his quarters while others acted as look-outs. The attackers had previously planned on attacking Alberts; however, the presence of police deterred them. The fact they returned to the ship suggests clear intent to cause physical harm.

The attack must be viewed in the context of the times: unions were aggressive in punishing both union members identified as "scabs" and ship officers considered particularly tough and, therefore, disliked. Union membership

---

23. White, *supra* note 10, at 42.

was loyal, ready to do the organization's bidding, and committed to improving the lot of its members. Unions were an important component of President Roosevelt's coalition, wielding influence locally and nationally.

Power was brought to the fore in multiple manners, including harsh imposition of internal discipline and meting out punishment when deemed appropriate. The activists of the Marine Firemen, Oilers, Watertenders and Wipers Association (MFOW) conducted themselves accordingly. They did so consistently, unwaveringly, and forcefully. Breaking the law was an acceptable manner of imposing their will; shying away from violence was not the way of the unions Warren confronted. The physical attacks were unrelenting.

The targets knew the attackers; the attackers knew the targets. The literature suggests a closed society of men, with violence, or the threat of violence, a constant reality. Escape seems to have not been possible; even those union members who left the Bay Area appeared to have returned. The reasons were varied; regardless of individual motivations, union leadership could count on its membership. The message to strikebreakers was clear: unforgiving violence.

When announcing the indictments, Warren said the murder was a "paid assassin's job, and the basis of the plot was communistic."[24] According to Newton:

---

24. Newton, *supra* note 12, at 64.

"... when Warren elected to prosecute the *Point Lobos* murder as a labor conspiracy—and to link that conspiracy to Communism—he gave strong moral support to employers.... The result: Earl Warren ... now became the enemy of Bay Area unions."[25]

The unions clearly challenged Warren's understanding of society, one that must be subservient to law and order. To a District Attorney who believed punishing wrongdoers was the principle mission of his office, the "why" of the crime was not relevant. Even if the crimes committed by union members were all "internal." Arrest, interrogation, prosecution, and conviction were all that mattered. That would serve the public interest in the context of a public good.

Alberts was married with three small children; his attackers were, according to available evidence, not family men. Mrs. Alberts attended the trial; her emotional presence was in stark contrast to the defendants who had minimal contact with their families and were neither compelling nor sympathetic. They were quite the opposite: tough men whose world view was violent and rough. Warren was of the belief that subversive and communist elements permeated the unions. This, then, was a twofold threat: raw, physical violence and possible connections to communism.

The targets of the union attacks were not outsiders; those unrelated to the conflict between the union and scabs or

---

25. *Id.*

between the union and demanding ship officers were not directly impacted by the union violence. They were not its intended victims. This was violence in a closed world; the broader public was not involved in what was an internal struggle. Nevertheless, Earl Warren was confronted with a significant challenge to his understanding of, and respect for, law and order even if the victims of union strong men were insiders.

Whether Warren could have adopted a tolerant attitude regarding union violence seems incongruent with his uncompromising stance. To not aggressively interrogate, much less prosecute, would reflect acquiescence in the face of violence and communism, regardless of who the intended victims were. For Warren, prosecutorial action was demanded whenever a crime was committed.

Our inquiry regarding Warren's conduct in the *Point Lobos* murder case focuses on one question: whether Warren's efforts to aggressively prosecute union-related crimes reflect the determination of a DA committed to fighting unions or an overzealous DA willing to push the envelope. The line between the two is thin; how we resolve the question is important to our core question.

The Interrogation

The investigation was lengthy; a number of months passed before suspects were identified, arrested, and interrogated. Warren's office was very involved, working closely with local law enforcement in a concerted effort to combat union-related crime. The unions clearly challenged his understanding of a society subservient to law and order, even if the crimes committed were all "internal."

The question, as we shall come to see below, is whether or not his efforts crossed the line. In examining this issue, we need to recall that the rules of Criminal Procedure in 1936 were very different than in 2017. Similar to the complexity of examining Warren's language and conduct regarding Japanese Americans, we need to recognize different eras are characterized by distinct standards pertaining to individual rights and the power and reach of the state. To instinctively criticize actions and comments predicated on contemporary values and principles is tempting, yet problematic.[26]

This requires setting aside what we know now about then; we enjoy the benefit of 20/20 vision. Hindsight is empowering; the extent to which it is helpful is uncertain. In order to extrapolate Earl Warren's conduct in the *Point Lobos* interrogation, we need to understand his perspective, world view, and understanding of the situation. This is not intended to justify or excuse; it is, however, necessary in seeking to understand how Warren would perceive terrorism and what protections, if any, he would extend to suspected terrorists. The importance of the Point Lobos

---

26. In examining Warren's conduct in the *Point Lobos* interrogation process, I relied heavily on Miriam Feingold's unpublished PhD dissertation; I did so at the encouragement of Professor White who wisely recommended reading the two-volume thesis. I found it thoroughly researched, fair, and compelling.

interrogation is the insight it arguably sheds on the question at the core of this book.

1. The relevant issue

Frank Connor was arrested in Seattle and flown to Oakland a couple days thereafter. When arrested, Connor was extremely drunk and limped due to a knee injury. His arrest was the subject of significant media attention in the Bay Area. Connor, accompanied by law enforcement, arrived in Oakland 8 p.m., Wednesday September 22, 1936.

Upon arrival, Connor was taken to the Hotel Whitecotton in Berkley. According to Feingold, as confirmed in the oral history below, the fact Connor was not taken to jail to be booked was common practice at the time. The reason for this is that taking Connor to jail would have prevented further questioning. For Warren's staff, it was important to get information from Connor before defense attorneys were able to meet with him.

Commencing at 9 p.m., Connor was interrogated by members of Warren's office. The interrogation was long, hard, and intense; Connor subsequently accused the interrogators of both applying the third degree and refusing his request to meet with an attorney. The interrogators denied both charges. The interrogation concluded at 2:30 a.m.; while Connor requested he to be transported to the county jail, the DA team chose not to book him.

Therefore, Connor, along with two members of Warren's office, stayed in the hotel room for the reminder of the night. Connor was handcuffed to the hotel bed. At 7 a.m., Connor was awakened; at 7:45 a.m., the handcuffs were removed and he was taken to the District Attorney's office for arraignment that morning.

Connor subsequently confessed to his role in Alberts murder and implicated others. This led to the prosecution and conviction of four of the five assailants; the fifth suspect was never arrested.

2. Interrogation standards

Connor's interrogation was conducted in accordance with the standards of 1936 when Courts admitted confessions taken in questionable circumstances. According to Feingold:

> In practice judges accepted a wide range of circumstances as not being severe enough to cause a defendant to confess falsely. These included where the defendant was ill, injured, or without food, where he had been told he had better tell the truth or ought to come clean, where tricks or fraud had been used, where he had not been advised of his rights or denied counsel, where he had been subjected to prolonged questioning, or where there had been delays in arraignment or the prisoner had been held incommunicado.[27]

---

27. Feingold, Miriam, The King-Ramsay-Connor Case: Labor Radicalism and the Law in California, 1936-1941 235 (2008) (unpublished dissertation, University of Wisconsin) (on file with the Wisconsin University Library).

Below is an excerpt from an Oral History interview between Miriam Feingold and Clarence Severin, chief clerk in the Alameda County District Attorney Office when Warren was the DA. The excerpt sheds light on Warren's office and acceptable police and prosecutorial behavior at the time. While its relevance to the Miranda decision is a matter of interpretation, it adds an addition layer of information to our inquiry.

Feingold

Frank Conner was one of the defendants. He was arrested in Seattle and flown to Whitecotton Hotel in Berkeley and questioned there by a number of the inspectors from the office. . . . I was wondering if this was common practice at the time to use hotel rooms rather than the jail, or wherever, for questioning?

Severin

Oh, yes. We questioned defendants or witnesses wherever it was convenient. We questioned them at the place where they were arrested or any place where we found them. Sometimes in the office itself, any place. There was no particular technique as to that practice. We questioned them anywhere, any time, any place, usually right after they were arrested, wherever that may be.

We took what we call a statement from them right then. We committed them to a story, in other words. Maybe it was not the true story, but at least we had them tied down to what they said was the case, and then they had a hard time changing it. That was a common practice, get them right away and ask them what happened, what they did. They would make up something to go along, to excuse themselves. Nine times out of ten, it was not the true story, and later on they could not change what they had said for the record. They had any number of reasons for so doing. But that practice was one of the first principles of good criminal investigative techniques, in that we would take a statement right away. You cannot do that now any more. You now have to warn them to be careful what they say ahead of time. In those days, we did not have to. We just put it right up to them at the time and we would get all sorts of weird stories.[28]

What Do We Learn from *Point Lobos* and Internment?

Bob Dylan famously wrote, "The Times They Are A-changin'"; that iconic phrase accurately describes the change in the limits of interrogations in the United States. This is a theme we shall address in great detail in later chapters. It is, however, important to pause and consider the *Point Lobos* interrogation with respect to 1936, 1966, 2017 (when these lines are written), and thereafter. In 1936, an

---

28. Interview by Amelia R. Fry, *Attorney, Legislator and Judge: Clarence E. Severin* (1972), http://content.cdlib.org/view?docId=kt2j49n5p1&brand=calisphere&doc.view=entire_text.

aggressive, ambitious, determined District Attorney oversaw an interrogation conducted in accordance with the times.

Warren and his team did not violate the law, were not afoul of relevant criminal procedure rules and regulations, and could not be accused of engaging in excessive conduct as defined in 1936. Holding Frank Connor in a hotel room in 1966, denying him the right to counsel and handcuffing him to a bed, when he was injured, would have violated principles articulated by Earl Warren, Chief Justice of the Supreme Court. Of that, there is no doubt. The language in *Miranda* is unequivocally clear on this point.

I am convinced, beyond a shadow of a doubt, that Warren, as Chief Justice, would apply *Miranda* in 2017 to criminal suspects. He would have seen no reason to alter the language of 1966. The subsequent "tweaks" to *Miranda,* much less the public safety exception established in *NY v. Quarles,*[29] would be met with strong disfavor. Whether that is also true for suspected terrorists is an issue we shall consider in later chapters.

What is clear is that Warren's conduct regarding Frank Connor was the very antithesis of *Miranda.* Connor was under arrest, his movements were restricted, and he was interrogated. There is no doubt that he was in custody and denied the right to counsel. That was the primary reason he was taken to the hotel from the airport rather than to the jail. That was a deliberate decision by Warren's colleagues

---

29. 467 U.S. 649 (1984).

acting in accordance with the times and policy of the DA's office. The conduct was not illegal. It did not lead to investigations, public scrutiny, much less condemnations. There were no calls for Warren's resignation; his public career was not derailed by what Frank Connor was subjected to.

As District Attorney, Warren was confronted with a significant challenge: violent unions that, he believed, were permeated with subversive elements. There was, from his perspective, genuine concern regarding threats—to what degree is unclear—posed by communist elements. I do not believe that he was exaggerating the threat he perceived. The record supports his concern regarding union-based violence; similarly, links between the American labor movement and communism were based on communist infiltration of unions.

That was a legitimate concern on Warren's part; this was not a District Attorney whose actions reflected naked political ambition. However, we cannot dismiss out of hand Warren's ambition; that, too, would be incorrect. His aggressive prosecution of those responsible for union violence was important to his election to Attorney General in 1938.

That is not by any stretch unusual: District Attorneys and Prosecuting Attorneys stand for election, promising aggressive action against criminals and strict enforcement of the law in an effort to protect the public. In addition, many have political aspirations and seek to attain higher office—elected or appointed—based on their prosecutorial record. Reticence and timidity are not viewed with favor; the public expects strong action and the aggressive prosecution of those who threaten and undermine society.

While by today's interrogation standards Warren's office violated Frank Connor's rights, we must judge his actions in accordance with 1936 standards. We cannot fault Warren's actions for they were acceptable in that era. This was standard operating procedure tolerated by courts and the public alike. We are but left to note—in the context of our question—that, at least on one instance, Earl Warren pushed the envelope, albeit within the boundaries of the realm of what was acceptable, relevant to his era.

There are no heroes in the internment tragedy. There are only those who sought to prevent the decision but, ultimately, did not have the political wherewithal to counter the voices determined to do "something" in the aftermath of December 7, 1941. To his credit, US Attorney General Biddle made an honest effort; however, his good intentions were outweighed by his minimal political power and willingness to defer to Secretary of War Stimson. Warren, as California Attorney General, had a very different perspective than Biddle; though both were lawyers, their respective roles could not have been more distinct and dissimilar.

Biddle served at the pleasure of a powerful, dominant, manipulative, charming President on the cusp of being a war-time President. Warren was elected to his position and had an untenable relationship with Governor Olson. However, unlike Biddle, who was appointed, Warren was independent of the chief executive of the State of California, Governor Olson.

Nevertheless, the latter tried to do the right thing, whereas the former aggressively pushed an agenda that resulted in a terrible wrong. The list of those who acted akin to Warren is long. Nevertheless, there is little doubt of Warren's leading role. As previously noted, determining whether it was "the" or "a" role is beyond our capabilities. It is also not important given the clear leadership role he played.

In his memoir, Warren addressed his role in the internment decision. The memoir is neither compelling nor satisfactory; perhaps self-reflection was not in his nature. That is unfortunate. Warren's cursory discussion of the internment decision frustrates our ability to better understand his motivations and impedes our ability to extrapolate his conduct to our question. The explanation Warren offered in his memoir is, frankly, unsatisfactory. Perhaps it was in keeping with his personality: not particularly self-reflective, keeping emotions in check and self-restrained.

"I have since deeply regretted the removal order and my own testimony advocating it, because it was not in keeping with our American concept of freedom and the rights of citizens. Whenever I thought of the innocent little children who were torn from home, school friends, and congenial surroundings, I was conscience-stricken. It was wrong to react to impulsively, without positive evidence of disloyalty, even though we felt we had a good motive in the security of our state."[30]

A careful review of numerous documents, including firsthand accounts, oral histories, congressional testimony, and memoirs paints a clear picture: there was no justification for the internment decision. Those involved, including Earl Warren, committed a terrible and unwarranted wrong. The subsequent apology and compensation provided by Congress was decades long in the making and is reflective of the saying, "dollar short, day late." Perhaps, it was an important gesture for those interned and their families. However, for our purposes that is not the crucial question.

Rather, we ask whether Earl Warren would countenance a similar executive action in the face of terrorist attacks committed by American citizens. The question is, unfortunately, not asked in the abstract. The 2016 presidential election raised the ugly specter of racism and hatred suggesting that particular ethnic groups—not individuals—pose a threat to American national security.[31]

---

30. Earl Warren, *The Memoirs of Earl Warren* (New York: Doubleday & Company, 1977), 149. There have been intimations that Warren's memoirs were "edited" after his death and before their publication, including the paragraph regarding internment. Those with whom I have discussed this issue were unable to shed conclusive light on this issue.

31. Holly Yan et al. *Post-Election Hate Crimes Continue to Grow across U.S.*, CNN WIRE, December 22, 2016, http://kdvr.com/2016/11/14/list-of-post-election -hate-crimes-keeps-growing/.

We would like to believe that Warren, a person of integrity who was committed to public service in the finest tradition, would recoil at the hatred and racism that is an undeniable component of contemporary American life. We learned once again in February, 1942 that the US government has the capability and willingness to punish in a harsh manner, *devoid of due process and right to appeal,* innocent American citizens for the crime of belonging to the "wrong" ethnicity.

Warren was not complicit by silence. He was front and center. Warren was, as the expression goes, "all in."

We are left with a troubling record when reviewing these seminal events from Warren's record in California.

Chapter Three

The 1960s: The Streets Are Burning

The Vietnam Song

Give me an "F!... "F"! give me a "U"!... "U"!
Give me a "C"!... "C" Give me a "K"!... "K"!
WHATS THAT SPELL?... "FUCK!"

Well come on all of you big strong men, Uncle Sam
*   needs your help again,*
he got himself in a terrible jam, way down yonder in
*   Vietnam,*
put down your books and pick up a gun, we're gunna
*   have a whole lotta fun.*

CHORUS
and its 1,2,3 what are we fightin for?
don't ask me i don't give a dam, the next stop is
*   Vietnam,*

and its 5,6,7 open up the pearly gates. Well there aint
no time to wonder why . . . WHOPEE we're all
gunna die!!!![1]

https://www.npr.org/sections/codeswitch/2014/08/24/342170766/50-years-before
-ferguson-a-summer-of-riots-racked-the-u-http://www.dailymail.co.uk/news/
article-2177891/Detroit-Riots-1967-Powerful-TIME-images-aftermath-race-riots
.html

Historical Background

The *Miranda* decision did not occur in a vacuum.

At the very time persistent unrest and urban violence
plagued America, the Warren Court sought to limit police
power. In that sense, the decision was dramatically at odds

---

1. Country Joe and Fish, *Vietnam Song (Live from Woodstock)* (Vanguard Studios, 1967), http://www.lyricsbox.com/country-joe-and-the-fish-vietnam-song
-live-from-woodstock-lyrics-dzgc6jx.html.

with the times. The holding limited police power at the very time that law enforcement was directly challenged in an unprecedented manner. Police departments, under duress, oftentimes responded in a heavy-handed manner, reflecting institutionalized racism, raw brutality, and unrestrained violence.

There is an incongruity between the decision's timing and its impact on law enforcement and the broader public. The dissonance is undeniable. While public opposition to the decision was clear, Warren's determination to address how interrogations were conducted was equally powerful. Warren was convinced, as made clear in the holding's language, that "enough was enough": how police departments conducted interrogations had to radically change, immediately.

Earl Warren's era as Chief Justice was a particularly turbulent time in American history.

The America that emerged victorious, powerful, and seemingly invincible from the Second World War had given way to an America marked by turmoil, uncertainty, and violence. Racism was not new to America: Jim Crow, slavery, lynchings, *Dred Scott,* and *Plessey v. Ferguson* are but examples of massive injustices imposed on black America.

Racism did not abate even when black soldiers gave their lives on the battlefields in foreign lands, fighting on behalf of a nation that institutionalized racism in a relentless and unforgiving manner. Blacks and whites alike paid the price for demanding equal rights for all. "Justice" was meted out to those who sought to ensure the Constitution be upheld and that "all men are created equal" truly be extended to *all* men.

The assassinations of President John F. Kennedy, Senator Robert F. Kennedy, and Dr. Martin Luther King, Jr. in the span of five years were deeply traumatic to the American public. However, violence was not limited to public figures. Americans felt threatened; their senses of safety and security were shaken. The fear of violence was undeniable. Fear is a powerful motif; it impacts politicians, society, and law enforcement. If exaggerated, it potentially results in significant violations of individual rights. The role of the judiciary is to protect the vulnerable members of society and to uphold the law.

The streets were dangerous; crime was rampant. White flight became a byword; the term was tinged with racism. Coded language ruled the day. More importantly, there was a sense of violence run amok, with no clear sense of a government in control that was able to provide answers to a deeply concerned public.

While President Lyndon B. Johnson (LBJ) was wedded to the Great Society and firmly believed in civil rights, he was unable to assuage an increasingly anxious public. By 1968, LBJ's 1964 landslide victory over Senator Goldwater (R-ARIZ) was long forgotten. Liberals never quite felt comfortable with Johnson; conservatives took advantage of white middle-class fear and anxiety.

Johnson's commitment to the Vietnam War—regardless of the endless historical discussion regarding the War's genesis—ultimately led those who supported him in 1964 to abandon him in 1968. Senator Eugene McCarthy (D-WI) and Senator Robert F. Kennedy (D-NY) were but short-term beneficiaries of growing disenchantment with Johnson, the former because of political realities, the latter because he was felled by a bullet after winning the California primary.

Johnson, who was firmly committed to changing how Americans lived, was hesitant to link race and crime. To do so would undermine the principles that he truly believed in. While the Johnson presidency will be forever linked to the overwhelming failure in Vietnam, there is little doubt regarding Johnson's deep belief in equal rights for all Americans. That, however, does not translate into, or equate to, safety in the streets, or at the very least the perception of safety and the belief that one could comfortably and confidently walk the streets of America.

The story that the visuals told was grim. It was violent. Streets were burning. People were dying. Stores were looted. The power of television was extraordinary. The scenes were brought to America's living rooms on a nightly basis. It was well-nigh impossible to deny that anger, frustration, and, ultimately, violence were the reality. Society was challenged by young voices demanding swift, violent change. Violence was not a new phenomenon in America; what made this different was the advent of television and the images conveyed. Turning off the television was possible with a flick of the switch; however, the reality was there whether one chose to ignore it or not.

Barry Goldwater, George Wallace, and Richard M. Nixon were right to highlight crime; riots reinforced fear that the nation's streets were unsafe, particularly for white Americans. The unspoken message was that white America was under threat from blacks; in particular, white women were vulnerable to attacks by black males. This was fearmongering at its most basic level.

These politicians aggressively articulated the argument that, by imposing limits on those entrusted with our safety, the Court fostered crime. It was an easy argument to make: riots in urban areas, violence in our communities, and attacks on our women. What could be an easier picture to paint than this? If only the courts would support law enforcement and give them the tools to protect us.

The argument, although simplistic, proved convincing. It paints a black and white picture reinforced by the reality of violence. President Johnson's Great Society was an extraordinary idea; at its core, it intended to right a historical wrong, to undo injustice to America's black population. The civil rights movement reflected Johnson's vision. That is not to suggest that President Johnson and Dr. Martin Luther King, Jr. saw eye to eye or that their political tactics and strategies meshed seamlessly.

Of course, they did not because both men had different audiences, interests, and stakes. Nevertheless, the overriding principle was shared: enable America's blacks to be fully invested in America and to share the same opportunities afforded whites. This was the liberal ideal of the 1960s. The vision never materialized; the majestic words uttered by Dr. King, President Johnson, and Senator Kennedy did not come to fruition. The tragedies were compounded in that not only were dreams not realized but the price paid in human life was significant.

How police departments interrogated blacks is deeply embedded in the troubled racial history of the United States. That is not to suggest whites were not interrogated; it is, however, to highlight the deeply troubling reality of how police departments treated black suspects. Contrary to popular belief, the much-documented mistreatment did not occur exclusively in the Deep South.

Police departments throughout the country regularly applied interrogation measures defined as the third degree. Coercion, denial of rights, and violence were staples of interrogations. It took the Supreme Court decades to address the reality of police interrogations. The failure to do so insured suspects were vulnerable to injustice and endless beatings. This was an oft-repeated pattern. It would result in the *Miranda* decision. It also, undoubtedly, played a role in America's burning streets in the 1960s. Whether it played a direct or indirect role is a matter of historical conjecture.

It is also not important what degree of contribution is assigned to the mistreatment of suspects. The reality is that certain events, such as riots, reflect pent-up emotions, angers, and frustrations. The burning streets were a result of many factors; they did not happen "just like that." The historical mistreatment of black suspects was one factor. Were there others? Of course.

Nevertheless, the contribution of the continued denial of rights to young black men had a cumulative effect; to suggest otherwise is folly. Black people had grown accustomed to a system that perpetuated their mistreatment and the denial of their rights. This was the reality both of the street and interrogations. Earl Warren focused on the latter in *Miranda*.

For Warren, protecting the suspect's rights was of paramount importance. In a series of landmark cases, the Court extended individual rights and protections while the national landscape was pockmarked with flames, shootings, and riots. Anger was rampant, protest was daily, and distrust of the government replaced the halcyon days of the 1950s. The chant, heard throughout college campuses: "Hey, hey, LBJ how many kids did you kill today," captured the mood of millions. Similarly, the black power phrase, "Burn, baby, burn," was on the lips of many blacks. Traditional values, norms, and mores were under daily challenge. The challenge was vocal, angry, and often violent. The confluence of opposition to the Vietnam War and racial tension was combustible.

While the 1960s began with the promise of John F Kennedy's election—the first President born in the twentieth century—they ended with hundreds of thousands of young people singing the Vietnam Song at the Woodstock Music Festival in July 1969.[2] Country Joe McDonald captured the mood of young people; his stark and powerful words expressed anger, bewilderment, cynicism, and despair.[3]

This picture captures the spirit and crowd of Woodstock:

http://www.lhsva.org/images/timeline/1969-woodstock.gif

---

2. https://www.youtube.com/playlist?list=PLx2gag3c36fiiOd_kbgB7V_udcUm-xHqp

3. https://www.nytimes.com/2017/10/10/opinion/country-joe-vietnam-woodstock.html?emc=edit_vm_20171010&nl=&nlid=59030603&te=1

The most popular song was against the Vietnam War. Just as it finished, an Army helicopter flew over. The whole crowd—all those hundreds of thousands—looked up and waved their forefingers in the peace sign, and then gave a cheer for themselves. It was an extraordinary thing.[4]

However, an extraordinary music festival notwithstanding, deep frustration at injustice boiled over.

Wherever one looked, the streets were burning: Watts; Harlem; Newark; Detroit; and Washington, DC. The years 1964 to 1968 were marked by unprecedented violence in America. This was not the first time Americans had either taken to the streets or been attacked for their race, political beliefs, or ethnic background. However, there was something different about this time period. Perhaps that reflects the deep discontent across ethnic, racial, and generational lines. As much as urban America was burning, college campuses were battle zones. The University of Michigan; the University of Wisconsin; University of California—Berkeley; and Columbia University are but the most prominent examples of university campuses marked by student activism and violence.

Much of this tension and anger came to a head at the Democratic National Convention in Chicago, August 1968:

---

4. *The 60s: The Story of a Decade*, The New Yorker, Random House, 2016, at 234.

"The 1968 Chicago convention became a lacerating event, a distillation of a year of heartbreak, assassinations, riots and a breakdown in law and order that made it seem as if the country were coming apart. In its psychic impact, and its long-term political consequences, it eclipsed any other such convention in American history, destroying faith in politicians, in the political system, in the country and in its institutions. No one who was there, or who watched it on television, could escape the memory of what took place before their eyes."[5]

The combination of police brutality, the intensity of the vitriol, and hatred directed at the "establishment" gave rise to deep concerns regarding the nation's future path. As is inevitable, politicians quickly seized the moment seeking electoral advantage.

Barry Goldwater's 1964 presidential campaign was the first to highlight the theme of "law and order." While Goldwater was defeated by President Lyndon B. Johnson, "law and order" proved very effective for Richard M. Nixon in 1968 when he defeated Vice President Hubert H. Humphrey. Nixon's campaign did not focus on uniting a fractured America; rather, Nixon highlighted the dangers posed to the "Silent Majority" by a Supreme Court endangering the public by protecting criminals and weakening

---

5. http://www.smithsonianmag.com/history/1968-democratic-convention-931079/.

law enforcement. Law enforcement in shackles concisely captures the Nixon's "law and order" campaign. The term is, of course, imbued with racism: it is an insidious suggestion that white America must be protected from blacks.

George Wallace, the Democratic Governor of Alabama, ran as an Independent in 1968. While finishing last in the race, his campaign of racism struck a deep chord among many white voters. After all, it was Wallace as Governor who famously declared, "segregation today, segregation tomorrow, segregation forever" in seeking to prevent integration of Alabama public schools.

The 1968 campaign—coming on the heels of the 1966 *Miranda* decision—enabled Nixon subtly, and Wallace crudely, to highlight the campaign as one between the forces of good and the forces of evil. The latter were, largely, middle-class whites; the former, criminals threatening the safety and security of white America. Humphrey had no compelling sound bite; no powerful response that would enable him to regain the offensive until the campaign was in its very late stages. By then, it was too late. The framing of Miranda as the embodiment of a Supreme Court soft on crime was—at its core—racist, stoking fears and anxieties of middle-class white Americans.

Nixon's negative portrayal and comments regarding the Supreme Court were important to his successful campaign. *Miranda* was the focal point of Nixon's displeasure with the Supreme Court. The decision to protect the criminal suspect—oftentimes a young African American male—at the cost of protecting society (white) was a theme Nixon brilliantly exploited. The historical animosity between Nixon and Warren was not the issue; rather, the question was who deserved protection: the criminal or society? Law and order was the answer.

Those fears had been, doubtlessly, exacerbated by the urban riots. Television graphically brought the unrest to white America's living rooms. Whether they lived near major urban centers or not, the sense of unrest, danger, and violence was pervasive and powerful.

P.F. Sloan's words[6] as sung by Barry McGuire powerfully captured the mood of anxiety, fear, and anger felt by many; although written in 1965, it was relevant in the years to come:

> *The eastern world it is explodin',*
> *violence flarin', bullets loadin',*
> *you're old enough to kill but not for votin',*
> *you don't believe in war, what's that gun you're totin',*
> *and even the Jordan river has bodies floatin',*
> *but you tell me over and over and over again my*
> *   friend,*
> *ah, you don't believe we're on the eve of destruction.*
>
> *Think of all the hate there is in Red China!*
> *Then take a look around to Selma, Alabama!*

---

6. http://www2.gol.com/users/davidr/sloan/aboutsongs.html.

Ah, you may leave here, for four days in space,
but when your return, it's the same old place,
the poundin' of the drums, the pride and disgrace,
you can bury your dead, but don't leave a trace,
hate your next-door-neighbour, but don't forget to say
grace,
and you tell me over and over and over and over again
my friend,
ah, you don't believe we're on the eve of destruction."[7]

Urban Riots

The immediate cause of urban riots was invariably routine: a traffic stop by a white policeman of a black driver quickly spun out of control:

The Watts Riot, which raged for six days and resulted in more than forty million dollars worth of property damage, was both the largest and costliest urban rebellion of the Civil Rights era. The riot spurred from an incident on August 11, 1965 when Marquette Frye, a young African American motorist, was pulled over and arrested by Lee W. Minikus, a white California Highway Patrolman, for suspicion of driving while

---

7. Barry McGuire, *Eve of Destruction* (Dunhill, 1965), https://www.youtube .com/watch?v=ntLsElbW9Xo Barry McGuire's "Eve of Destruction" compellingly captures the tragedy of the 1960s.

intoxicated. As a crowd on onlookers gathered at the scene of Frye's arrest, strained tensions between police officers and the crowd erupted in a violent exchange. The outbreak of violence that followed Frye's arrest immediately touched off a large-scale riot centered in the commercial section of Watts, a deeply impoverished African American neighborhood in South Central Los Angeles. For several days, rioters overturned and burned automobiles and looted and damaged grocery stores, liquor stores, department stores, and pawnshops. Over the course of the six-day riot, over 14,000 California National Guard troops were mobilized in South Los Angeles and a curfew zone encompassing over forty-five miles was established in an attempt to restore public order. All told, the rioting claimed the lives of thirty-four people, resulted in more than one thousand reported injuries, and almost four thousand arrests before order was restored on August 17. Throughout the crisis, public officials advanced the argument that the riot was the work of outside agitators; however, an official investigation, prompted by Governor Pat Brown, found that the riot was a result of the Watts community's longstanding grievances and growing discontentment with high unemployment rates, substandard housing, and inadequate schools. Despite the reported findings of the gubernatorial commission, following the riot, city

leaders and state officials failed to implement measures
to improve the social and economic conditions of African Americans living in the Watts neighborhood.[8]

http://hubpages.com/politics/Stereotyping-is-Inevitable-Racism-is-Optional

The impetus for the Detroit riot that began on July 23,
1967 was a police raid on an illegal after-hours drinking
club. There was, according to the available evidence, no
intent on the part of either the Detroit Police Department
or the city's residents to turn the streets of Detroit into a
war zone. Nevertheless, that is what happened. The consequences were terrible.

---

8. Civil Rights Digital Library, *Watts Riots*, Digital Library of Georgia (Feb.
10, 2017), http://crdl.usg.edu/events/watts_riots/?Welcome.

The immediate cause of the riot was a police raid at an illegal after-hours drinking club, the site of a welcome-home party for two returning Vietnam War veterans. The police arrested all patrons in attendance, including 82 African Americans. Local residents who witnessed the raid protested, and several of them vandalized property, looted businesses, and started fires. Police responded by blockading the surrounding neighbourhood, but outraged local residents drove through the blockade. The protests and violence spread to other areas of the city as police lost control of the situation.[9]

There was nothing out of ordinary in this; it was routine police activity in any American city. However, as instance after instance demonstrated, these were anything but ordinary times. What might have been shrugged off as irritating, perhaps aggressive police activity, quickly exploded into something very different.

What happened in the immediate aftermath was predictable. Angry blacks gathered in the wake of rumors about police brutality. Ill-trained, scared, and undermanned police forces responded. Words were exchanged. Rocks were thrown. Bullets were fired. The aftermath was inevitable:

---

9. Traqina Quarks Emeka, *Detroit Riot of 1967*, Encyclopedia Britannica (Feb. 10, 2015), https://www.britannica.com/event/Detroit-Riot-of-1967.

An hour passed before the last prisoner was taken away, and by then about 200 onlookers lined the street. A bottle crashed into the street. The remaining police ignored it, but then more bottles were thrown, including one through the window of a patrol car. The police fled as a riot erupted. Within an hour, thousands of people had spilled out onto the street. Looting began on 12th Street, and some whites arrived to join in. Around 6:30 a.m., the first fire broke out, and soon much of the street was set ablaze. By midmorning, every policeman and fireman in Detroit was called to duty. On 12th Street, officers fought to control the mob. Firemen were attacked as they tried to battle the flames.

Detroit Mayor Jerome P. Cavanaugh asked Michigan Governor George Romney to send in the state police, but these 300 more officers could not keep the riot from spreading to a 100-block area around Virginia Park. The National Guard was called in shortly after but didn't arrive until evening. By the end of the day, more than 1,000 were arrested, but still the riot kept growing. Five people were dead.

On Monday, 16 people were killed, most by police or guardsmen. Snipers fired at firemen, and fire hoses were cut. Governor Romney asked President Lyndon Johnson to send in US troops. Nearly 2,000 army paratroopers arrived on Tuesday and began patrolling the street in tanks and armored carriers. Ten more people died that day, and 12 more on Wednesday. On Thursday, July 27, order was finally restored. More than 7,000 people were arrested during the four days of rioting. A total of 43 were killed. Some 1,700 stores were looted and nearly 1,400 buildings burned, causing $50 million in property damage. Some 5,000 people were left homeless.[10]

Sending in the Army was dramatic, necessary, and ultimately effective. Local police departments were not always able to restore order; the intensity and anger of rioters and looters proved overwhelming. National Guard units were insufficiently trained, quick to pull the trigger and not the answer to the burning streets. The Army's presence gave a sense of a war zone. The political, social, and cultural ramifications were obvious: sending in the Army was a clear message of a situation out of control.

On April 4, 1968, James Earl Ray assassinated Dr. King in Memphis, Tennessee. Immediately thereafter riots broke out in more than sixty US cities; two blocks from the White House, Washington, DC burned. President Johnson had no choice, his deep reluctance notwithstanding, but to call in the US Army.

Public opinion polls taken during these times provide insight into the clashing viewpoints present in America of

---

10. http://www.history.com/this-day-in-history/the-12th-street-riot.

the demonstrations and race riots taking place throughout the nation.

HARRIS

What do you think are the two or three main reasons riots have broken out in this country? Any other reasons?

1967: August 9	Nationwide	Whites	Negroes
Outside agitation	40%	45%	10%
Prejudice, promises not kept, bad treatment	19	16	36
Poverty, slums, ghetto conditions	16	14	28
Lack of jobs, unfair employment	12	10	29
Negroes are too lazy to work for their rights	11	13	5
Uneducated people, don't know what they are doing	11	11	9
Teenagers looking for trouble	7	7	7

	Nationwide	Whites	Negroes
Law has been too lax	6	7	*
Negroes want to control whites	4	4	1
Crazy people, addicts	3	3	3
Gotten too much too fast	3	3	—
Negroes love violence	3	3	1
Don't know	9	8	19

* Less than half of 1 per cent.

Tough on crime meant strengthening law enforcement. Tough law enforcement would return order to what had become a lawless culture. There was, for the political right, a powerful dissonance that could be exploited. The liberal judiciary was disconnected from the fears of decent, hard-working Americans who desired nothing more than to enjoy their families, leisure time, and, of course, safety from the jungle the streets had become.

HARRIS

Now I want to ask you about some things some people have said are the causes of riots such as those we've had this summer. Do you feel (read list) *is a major cause of riots?*
1967: August 9

	Nation-wide	Whites	Negroes	Negro-White Difference
Lack of good education for Negroes	48%	46%	61%	+15%
Lack of decent housing for Negroes	41	39	68	+29
Lack of jobs for young Negroes	36	34	67	+33
Lack of firmness by local mayors and governors	35	37	24	−13
Lack of progress in giving Negroes equality	34	30	72	+42
Hatred of whites by Negroes	32	33	20	−13
Desire of Negroes to loot stores	24	26	9	−17
Desire of Negroes for violence	22	23	13	−10
Police brutality against Negroes	12	8	49	+41

	College	High School	Grade School
Lack of good education for Negroes	60%	44%	40%
Lack of decent housing for Negroes	52	37	36
Lack of jobs for young Negroes	45	32	33
Lack of firmness by local mayors and governors	40	34	33
Lack of progress in giving Negroes equality	43	30	31
Hatred of whites by Negroes	33	32	30
Desire of Negroes to loot stores	21	26	24
Desire of Negroes for violence	14	25	28
Police brutality against Negroes	12	10	15

Hazel Erskine, *The Polls: Demonstrations and Race Riots*, The Public Opinion Quarterly, Vol. 31, No. 4, The Historical Study of Public Opinion (Winter, 1967–1968), at 655–77.

Coded language was rampant. While Johnson was determined to avoid linking crime with race, the effort was futile. The two terms became synonymous. The "War on Poverty" and "War on Crime" were two of three wars Johnson fought; the third was the Vietnam War. All three were abject failures, resulting in deep fissures that haunt America to this day.

On July 29, 1967, President Johnson signed Executive Order 11365, which established the National Advisory Commission on Civil Disorders. Chaired by former Illinois Governor, Otto Kerner, the Commission was mandated by Johnson to answer three questions regarding the riots: what happened; why did it happen; what can be done to prevent such riots from happening again. Johnson's words were "As best you can, find the truth and express it in your report."[11]

Johnson refused to meet with Commission members when they wished to submit their report; however, its importance and contribution cannot be minimized.[12] Johnson's refusal was based on his belief that Commission members, particularly New York City Mayor, John Lindsay, were politically motivated rather than engaged in an objective assessment. The report made clear that there were two America's: one white, one black.[13]

That is the phrase most remembered from the Commission's extraordinary efforts; it is an exhaustive, thoughtful, and important document, as relevant today as it was when written. While Johnson mandated the Commission in the aftermath of the 1967 Detroit and Newark riots, the report goes well beyond the events of that summer. The

---

11. The National Advisory Commission on Civil Disorders, *The Kerner Report* (2016).

12. Johnson's refusal has been thought to reflect his anger with the Commission's findings, which he perceived to be a denunciation of the Great Society and because his belief that John Lindsey would be a future political opponent.

13. That phrase has been credited to New York City Mayor John Lindsay who served as Vice Chairman.

report examines the tragic history of blacks in the United States and the inherent racism that defines their relationship with white America.

The Commission's report argues that the black community's primary interaction with white America, particularly with "official" America, was the local police department. According to the report that relationship was beyond troubled; that is very obvious from all accounts of the riots. The riots, while described as "race riots," were primarily violent interactions between blacks and law enforcement. The civilian white population was largely not involved; the riots overwhelmingly took place in ghettos almost exclusively populated by African Americans.

The interaction, time after time, was fraught with tension, misunderstanding, and violence. The causes of police versus black violence have been much studied; in some cases, violence was deliberately provoked. More often than not, however, the situation that quickly spun out of control was an ordinary interaction between a black civilian and white law enforcement.

Were that not enough, in writing about the Detroit riots, the Commission wrote the following about the judicial process:

"In the cities shaken by disorders during the summer of 1967, there were recurring breakdowns in the mechanisms for processing, prosecuting, and protecting arrested persons."

The Vietnam War

The Vietnam War is a tragic and dark chapter in American history. While the origins are a matter of endless historical conjecture and dispute, the cost and consequence are undeniable. More than 50,000 American soldiers died in a war that made very little sense at the time and makes even less sense fifty years later. One of its most disturbing realities is the manner in which American generals and politicians lied to the American public from start to finish.

As historical documents have made abundantly clear, those lying were well aware of the reality: the war was unwinnable and American soldiers were needlessly dying. That, obviously, is equally true and tragic with respect to North and South Vietnamese alike. The price paid by those who served thousands of miles away from home in a land of which they knew next to thing, whose culture was alien to them, and whose language was beyond comprehension is a permanent stain on America.

While those drafted were fighting, killing, and dying in a strange land, those fortunate enough to receive a deferment—or resist the draft—stayed home. Many of them took to the streets to protest the war. The scenes at Woodstock, demonstrations on college campuses, and the 1968 Democratic convention capture draft age young people opposed to the war, but benefiting from the privilege of not being drafted.

There is a long list of draft dodgers; those whose fathers knew who to call took full advantage of that. John Fogerty of Creedence Clearwater Revival captured this reality in his song, "Fortunate Son":

"Fortunate Son"

Some folks are born made to wave the flag
Ooh, they're red, white and blue
And when the band plays "Hail to the chief"
Ooh, they point the cannon at you, Lord
It ain't me, it ain't me, I ain't no senator's son, son
It ain't me, it ain't me; I ain't no fortunate one, no
Yeah!
Some folks are born silver spoon in hand
Lord, don't they help themselves, oh
But when the taxman comes to the door
Lord, the house looks like a rummage sale, yes
It ain't me, it ain't me, I ain't no millionaire's son, no
It ain't me, it ain't me; I ain't no fortunate one, no[14]

Fogerty's song highlights an important reality regarding Vietnam. While there was a draft, the war was primarily fought by those who either could not get a deferment or chose to serve. Some referred to the war as the "black man's war." In other words, there was significant inequity

---

14. Creedence Clearwater, *Fortunate Son* (Fantasy, 1969), https://www.youtube.com/watch?v=ec0XKhAHR5I.

regarding *who fought* 9,000 miles from the United States. In broad strokes, those fighting came from urban areas; those not fighting were demonstrating, whether on college campuses or in Washington, DC.

As the Chicago police made clear during the Democratic convention, demonstrators were held in total contempt, dismissed as long-haired college students challenging America and disrespecting authority. Because they were in college, the demonstrators, unlike those unable to secure a deferment, were largely protected from the draft.

The riots in America's large urban centers were compounded by the loud, sometimes very loud, anti-war demonstrations. The confluence of the two—riots and anti-war demonstrations—taxed law enforcement and challenged mainstream, middle-class America. The challenge was not peaceful.

The American public was largely ignorant of the conflict until the January, 1968 Tet Offensive, which brought the war home. Television networks captured the reality of the war in a manner unlike any other medium. Even though the Tet Offensive did not result in a US military defeat, the visuals were too overwhelming. The false bravado of the military and of the Johnson Administration was irreversibly destroyed. Pictures were essential to understanding the brutal reality of Vietnam.

The shocking picture of a young Vietnamese girl running in horror in the immediate aftermath of a napalm attack; the close-up picture of a Vietnamese security official murdering a prisoner; the burning village of My Lai after Charlie Company, under the command of Lieutenant William Calley, committed a war crime massacring hundreds of innocent Vietnamese. All were powerful images of something gone terribly wrong. The media spin of the Johnson Administration was eviscerated by the pictures.

South Vietnamese forces follow after terrified children, including nine-year-old Kim Phuc, center, as they run down Route 1 near Trang Bang after an aerial napalm attack on suspected Vietcong hiding places on June 8, 1972. Nick Ut—AP[15]

15. http://time.com/4485344/napalm-girl-war-photo-facebook/.

Johnson's "whiz kid" Secretary of Defense Robert McNamara—a Kennedy appointee—emphasized the deceitful "body counts,"[16] intended to convince the public America was winning the war.

It could not have been further from the truth.

The Animal's classic song, "We Gotta Get Out of This Place" captured the mood of those fighting in Vietnam even if the songs' original meaning was of a couple hoping to get out of an industrial English town for a better life:

In this dirty old part of the city
Where the sun refuse to shine
People tell me there ain't no use in trying
Now my girl you're so young and pretty
And one thing I know is true
You'll be dead before your time is due
We gotta get out of this place
If it's the last thing we ever do
We gotta get out of this place
'Cause girl, there's a better life
For me and you;[17]

16. http://www.washingtonpost.com/wp-dyn/content/article/2005/10/23/AR2005102301273.html; http://articles.latimes.com/1991-02-09/news/mn-675_1_vietnam-war.

17. The Animals, *We Gotta Get Out of This Place* (ABKCO 1965), https://www.youtube.com/watch?v=W5ueEVlUUgk&list=RDW5ueEVlUUgk&index=2.

Radical Movements and Civil Rights

"Black day in July
Black day in July
Motor City madness has touched the countryside
And the people rise in anger
And the streets begin to fill
And there's gunfire from the rooftops
And the blood begins to spill";[18]

Warren's era was marked by radical movements, unrest on college campuses, and urban violence. Law enforcement, whether federal or state, perceived the actors as criminals. There was no attempt to create a special paradigm suggesting otherwise; existing laws were considered sufficient to confront the challenge posed. Many of those involved perceived themselves as revolutionaries; in particular, the vanguard of the revolution.

To their way of thinking, they were not common criminals. Their motivation was not pecuniary gain, rather a deep desire, based on ideology, to confront the ills of American society. Some clearly were intent on changing America; at the very least, they challenged American political leadership and society.

In large part, they were young, educated, and determined. In 1960, half the population was under the age of

---

18. Gordon Lightfoot, *Black Day in July* (1968), https://www.youtube.com/watch?v=DPXL3iEVnCM.

eighteen. This surplus of youth, coupled with unpopular political decisions, both domestic and abroad, led to the rapid rise of protest groups warring against establishment practices in the 1960s, 1970s, and 1980s.

The depth of their commitment and resolve to achieve stated goals recalls contemporary terrorist organizations. Similar to terrorists willing to impose hardships on themselves and their families, many members of radical movement groups went underground, moving from hiding place to hiding place. Some were married and had children, financial resources were not always plentiful, much less available, and logistics were complicated and burdensome.

However, their dedication to the "cause" was uppermost and absolute. While rhetoric was important, many of these groups were violent. Peaceful revolution was not their way. They saw themselves as participating in an armed struggle against society in general and law enforcement in particular. Bombings and shootings were their tactics of choice.

To a contemporary ear, many of these radical groups "sound" like today's terrorists. Insert different names, replace mantras and slogans, and the groups of fifty years ago could be today's terrorists. Commitment to the cause—and the willingness to self-impose significant hardship—always struck me as critical to understanding terrorist DNA. In endless interactions with terrorists, in a variety of circumstances and settings, I learned that physical discomfort and sacrifice were integral to their lives and experiences.

Reading accounts of the radical movements contours up very similar images and perceptions.

Collectively, these groups constituted "The Movement" or the "New Left"; the summaries below are intended to give the reader a glimpse into the groups of the 1960s, 1970s, and 1980s. This is important not only for historical purposes but also to remind that in the face of urban riots, anti-war demonstrations, and campus unrest, Miranda rights were extended to suspects. That fact is of great significance in considering whether Warren would similarly protect the rights of suspected terrorists. While the activists of previous decades were not called "terrorists," their actions, today, would, in all probability, be defined as "domestic terrorism."

STUDENTS FOR A DEMOCRATIC SOCIETY

We are people of this generation, bred in at least modest comfort, housed now in universities, looking uncomfortably to the world we inherit.

First line of The Port Huron Statement, Oct. 15, 1962.

Students for a Democratic Society was a radical student activist organization founded in 1960. Originally, the group's purpose was to engage students in establishing "participatory democracies" in which people take part in making decisions that affect their own lives. The group's first convention, which was held in Port Huron, Michigan, had fewer than one hundred participants. It was then that the group officially adopted the Port Huron Statement, a political manifesto advocating for "participatory democracies." The idea of owning your own politics gained a great deal of popularity, and by the mid-1960s, SDS was assembling protests of more than 25,000 people. A 1968 protest sponsored by SDS at Columbia University led to the arrest of over 700 protesters; by that time, SDS had more than 50,000 members. Factional disputes led to the group's dissolution in 1969, but a small faction of the collapsed organization that advocated more violent revolutionary action, known as the Weathermen, survived from SDS.

THE WEATHERMEN/THE WEATHER UNDERGROUND

"When you feel you have right on your side, you can do some pretty horrific things."
—*Former Weathermen member Brian Flanigan*

Believing peaceful protests to be ineffective, the Weathermen were not above utilizing violence to promote social and political change. The Weathermen would conduct a series of bombings, riots, and jailbreaks throughout the 1970s. The Weathermen's first public demonstration on October 8, 1969, known as the "Days of Rage," was a riot in Chicago coinciding with the trial of the Chicago Seven, seven defendants charged by the federal government for various antigovernment actions. A premature nail bomb detonation at a safe house in Greenwich Village resulted in the deaths of three Weathermen members in 1970, and the organization became known as the Weather Underground. The Weather Underground would go on to conduct a series of bombings in protests of various actions taken by the government abroad, including a bombing of the New York City police headquarters in 1970, the US Capitol in 1971, the Pentagon in 1971, and the Department of State Building in 1975.

The Weather Underground began to dismantle after the United States conducted a peace accord with Vietnam, and became defunct in 1970, as the New Left movement was losing steam. The Weathermen strongly sympathized with another radical group, the Black Panthers. The police killing of Black Panther chairman of the Illinois chapter, Fred Hampton, Jr., prompted the Weatherman to issue a declaration of war upon the US government.

THE BLACK PANTHERS

https://fusion.net/story/188909/the-black-panthers-were-fighting-for
-exactly-the-same-rights-as-black-lives-matter-protesters-new
-documentary-proves/

The Black Panther Party for Self-Defense ("The Black Panthers") was founded in October 1966 by Huey Newton and Bobby Seale. The Panthers fought to establish revolutionary socialism through mass organizing and community-based programs, enforced by militant self-defense practices by minorities oppressed by the government. In addition to those protesting against Vietnam and US political action abroad, the Black Panthers represented one of the first groups to militantly struggle for ethnic minorities and the working class, in an attempt to establish social, political, and gender equality for all in America. The party established a unified platform in a ten-point plan that included demands for freedom, education, and employment. In 1967, founding member Huey Newton was charged in the fatal shooting of a twenty-three–year-old police officer during a traffic stop, leading to a nationwide campaign to "Free Huey." The twenty-one–year-old Black Panther chairman of the Illinois chapter, Fred Hampton, Jr., and his guard, Mark Clark, were shot and killed in a raid orchestrated by the police in conjunction with the FBI. An investigation revealed that he was drugged with barbiturates and shot more than eighty times.

J. Edgar Hoover, then the director of the FBI, feared that black nationalist groups were the greatest threat to the security of America and created a counterintelligence program in 1967 specifically to discredit black nationalist groups. Hoover would continuously send letters to police officers, encouraging them to find new ways to cripple the Black Panthers. The increased attacks by the government, coupled with various mistakes and corruption by the Party, and an inability to fulfill all of the claims it made to the media, would lead to the Black Panther's downfall in the early 1980s.

THE SYMBIONESE LIBERATION ARMY

http://landsendthebook.com/finding-the-symbionese-liberation-army
-hideout/

Death to the fascist insect that preys upon the life of the people.
                    —Slogan of the Symbionese Liberation Army

The Symbionese Liberation Army ("SLA") was a group of radicals from Berkeley led by an escaped convict, Donald deFreeze in 1973. The rhetoric employed by the group was derived from Communist and South American revolutionary groups, and their loosely Marxist priorities included ending racism, monogamy, and the prison system. The most famous act of the group was the kidnapping of nineteen-year-old heiress, Patricia "Patty" Hearst, in 1974. The kidnapping led to a media frenzy across the nation, largely because Patty denounced her family and sympathized with her abductors. The group disbanded in 1975, after members of the group, including Patty Hearst were tried and convicted following their arrest from a shootout in California Patty was sentenced to seven years in prison, but was released after twenty-two months in a commuted sentence action by President Jimmy Carter.

THE BLACK LIBERATION ARMY

http://www.esquire.com/news-politics/a53648/nypd-undercover-black
-radical-groups/

The Black Liberation Army ("BLA") was a militant black Marxist organization that developed as a splinter group of the Black Panthers in the 1970s, after certain members of the Panthers felt that the organization was "selling out" under the leadership of Huey Newton. The group was most notorious for killing police officers in the 1970s, but also made attempted jailbreaks and bank robberies. Although purporting a mission to advance equality and civil rights for oppressed groups in America, the violent actions of groups like the Black Liberation Army and the Symbionese Liberation Army led many to question whether such groups were politically or purely criminally motivated.

THE FUERZAS ARMADAS DE LIBERACIÓN NACIONAL

http://www.latinamericanstudies.org/puertorico/

The FALN, Fuerzas Armadas de Liberación Nacional (also known as the Armed Forces of National

Liberation), was a secret Puerto Rican paramilitary organization committed to the political independence of Puerto Rico from the United States. Founded in the 1960s under the leadership of Filiberto Ojeda Rios, the organization's purpose was to draw attention to Puerto Rico's political relationship with the United States, and object to increased influence of US-based corporate and financial institutions on the island. Between 1974 and 1983, the FALN claimed responsibility for more than 120 bombings of military and government buildings, financial institutions, and corporate headquarters in Chicago, New York, and Washington, DC. These bombings lead to the deaths of six people and left dozens more injured.

On April 4, 1980, police arrested eleven FALN members in Evanston near Northwestern University's campus. These members, as well as others arrested in Chicago in the early 1980s, were charged and found guilty of seditious conspiracy and sentenced to extensive prison terms in federal prisons throughout the United States.

When activists were arrested, there was no discussion regarding denial of basic constitutional protections; in the aftermath of the *Miranda* ruling, I have found no documentation of instances where law enforcement considered denying suspects their Miranda rights. That is not to suggest those arrested were treated with kid gloves; that would be an unwarranted exaggeration. That has been documented and discussed elsewhere.

Nevertheless, regardless of their actions, the word *terrorist* was rarely used; there was little, if any, serious discussion suggesting law enforcement perceived these groups as committing acts of terrorism. While the actions of groups such as the Weathermen and the Black Panthers might be defined as terrorism today, that was not the terminology applied then. While the radical movements were violent, angry and determined, the public did not perceive them as terrorists.

The FBI approach to those responsible for violent actions in the 1960s to 1980s reflected traditional law enforcement methods and measures. That is not to suggest that the FBI did not apply controversial measures, some borderline illegal, while others were in violation of the law. That reflects the FBI under J. Edgar Hoover. There is little doubt Hoover's FBI was a very different FBI than today's. Some of that reflects a more mature society and a more aggressive and skeptical media, including social media. The blind faith placed in Hoover would be all but impossible to recreate today.

The FBI's efforts, legal and illegal, reflect the extraordinary challenge of tracking leaders and members of groups numbering in the tens, at the most in the hundreds. In some cases, cells comprised a mere handful of individuals, having no contact with other group members, much less knowledge of their activities. While New York City Mayor Abraham Beame defined a FALN bombing "as an outrageous act of terrorism,"[19] few used similar terminology.

Whether public officials deliberately chose not to use the term *terrorism* or believed terrorism to be international, rather than domestic, is an interesting point of inquiry. What is clear is that the language of today is not the language of previous decades. This is not insignificant for language reflects social and cultural mores and norms.

There is great importance in labeling and terminology. Politicians and media are particularly sensitive to this; perhaps the public is less focused on nuance in the face of threats, violence, and physical harm. What is important is how law enforcement, police, and prosecutors perceived the threats posed and whether respect for individual rights articulated by the Supreme Court were honored.

The troubling reality was a powerful clash between angry young people—black and white—and local police departments and the FBI. It is fair to state that there was mutual loathing: excessive police power was the response to the deliberate targeting of police officers. It did not take much to "set" police officers off; some, clearly, were looking to beat protestors and rioters. Of that, there is no doubt. However, there were no innocents in this struggle; the adage "it

---

19. Bryan Burrough, *Days of Rage: America's Radical Underground, the FBI, and the Forgotten Age of Revolutionary Violence* 401 (Reprint ed. 2016).

takes two to tango" undoubtedly applies to the violent interactions between police and civilians.

Were groups such as the Black Panthers or Black Liberation Army to specifically target policemen today, as they did decades ago, it is reasonable to assume that they would be defined as terrorists. In contrast to contemporary discussion regarding the rights of suspected terrorists, public debate focused neither on the granting of Miranda rights nor the appropriate judicial forum for those involved.

In the aftermath of the Supreme Court's ruling, those arrested received their Miranda warnings and were brought to trial akin to any "traditional" criminal suspect. I have found no indication that an alternative judicial system was considered, despite the violence and revolutionary ethos that characterized many of the groups.

This was a criminal action; the invariable response was implementation of the criminal justice system, from investigation to arrest to interrogation to trial.

Perhaps that reflects the composition of many of the actors: American citizens, living "among us" who were, at least with respect to the SDS and Weatherman, white college students.

The violence in America's streets reflected three critical realities: *street crime, urban riots, and opposition to the war.* The question of interrogation was relevant to all three; suspects were arrested for involvement in all three. The protections they were to be extended were the essence of the *Miranda* decision despite the violence.

Yet, the US Supreme Court held, violence notwithstanding, that the rights of those protesting, demonstrating, and engaging in violence must be protected. Nixon used this to his political advantage. However, Earl Warren was determined to protect the rights of the vulnerable, even if the vulnerable individual was responsible for the crime at hand.

In a turbulent time, marked by violence, direct challenges to mainstream society and clear anger from young blacks, the role of the Supreme Court took on greater meaning and significance. The Warren Court emphasized individual rights regardless of the violence in America's streets. It is, on some level, counterintuitive: why would a Court extend rights to suspects at the very time that law enforcement was in pitched battle and larger—meaning white—society felt vulnerable and under attack? Nevertheless, the Court, in the face of this overwhelming tension, rearticulated the balance of power and established clear limits on how police could interrogate suspects.

The response from the political right was clear and unequivocal: The judiciary must stop coddling the criminals among us. Politicians, particularly but not exclusively Nixon, pointed an accusatory finger at the Supreme Court. The Court was seen as "soft on crime," depriving law enforcement the means necessary to restore order in what had become a disorderly time. It was incongruous from the perspective of the right to weaken law enforcement at the very time strong, tough measures were necessary to protect a society endangered from within.

This, for politicians on the right, made no sense: why protect those responsible for violence, thereby increasing the vulnerability of crime victims? Casting the Court as blind to the dangers of mainstream White society was good politics: the Court could not respond to the criticism and politicians presented themselves as protecting the vulnerable.

This was J'accuse personified: Earl Warren was seen as the primary protector of criminals. More than any other decision, the 1966 *Miranda* decision was the lightning rod because it imposed clear, specific limits on law enforcement. The Miranda warning left nothing to the imagination. The guiding principle was that interrogations of the past could not be the interrogations of the present, much less of the future.

The holding was announced on June 13, 1966. Earl Warren read the decision in its entirety. This was considered most unusual, given its length. In doing so, Warren signaled its significance. This was a momentous event in American jurisprudential history.

At that very moment, the US Supreme Court informed the public and law enforcement agencies that, regardless of the crime committed, a suspect's Fifth Amendment rights must be protected. This was a blanket protection. The various exceptions created in its aftermath reflect a "chipping away" from the absolutism that Warren intended.

We now turn to the Warren Court's Criminal Procedure Revolution.

Chapter Four

The Warren Court's Criminal Procedure Revolution

"The Warren Court was the right court at the right time . . . and that is rarely the case. This was a nice pairing."

—Dr. Hugh Roberts, Former Criminal Defense
Attorney (2014 Interview)

The Warren Court

As the chapter title suggests, the emphasis in the pages ahead is on the Warren Court's criminal procedure revolution. While the Warren Court's opinions were of profound importance, touching upon innumerable aspects of life in America, for many, the highlight of the Warren years is *Brown v. Board of Education*,[1] whereas Warren pointed to

---

1. 347 U.S. 483 (1954).

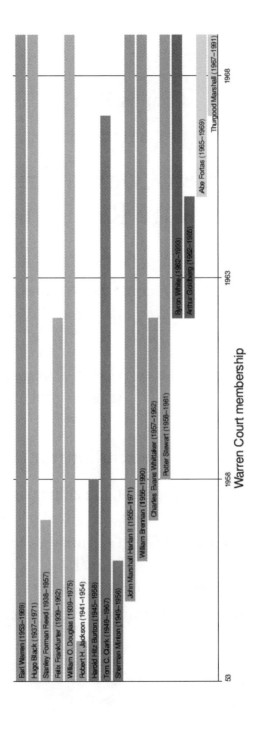

Warren Court membership

Earl Warren (1953–1969)
Hugo Black (1937–1971)
Stanley Forman Reed (1938–1957)
Felix Frankfurter (1939–1962)
William O. Douglas (1939–1975)
Robert H. Jackson (1941–1954)
Harold Hitz Burton (1945–1958)
Tom C. Clark (1949–1967)
Sherman Minton (1949–1956)
John Marshall Harlan II (1955–1971)
William Brennan (1956–1990)
Charles Evans Whittaker (1957–1962)
Potter Stewart (1958–1981)
Byron White (1962–1993)
Arthur Goldberg (1962–1965)
Abe Fortas (1965–1969)
Thurgood Marshall (1967–1991)

53   1958   1963   1968

Baker v. Carr[2] as his most important decision; of particular importance and relevance to us are criminal law cases. The impact of the opinions discussed below was monumental.

It is hard to overstate the extent to which the Warren Court fundamentally changed the relationship between law enforcement and the individual. The word *revolution* may sound overdrawn and exaggerated; however, I am of the opinion that the word choice correctly describes the consequences of the decisions. The Warren Court, over the course of sixteen years, engaged in judicial activism in a determined effort to protect the individual. As discussed in the previous chapter, this was not received with open arms in all quarters. Nevertheless, political and public criticism notwithstanding, the Court articulated clear limits on government power and reach.

The *Miranda* opinion represents the zenith; however, to be fully understood and appreciated, it must be viewed in a broader context. The decision was not "out of the blue"; rather, it reflected the culmination of a steady path and determined course by the Court under Warren's strong leadership. While the Supreme Court is comprised of nine Justices, all with one vote, Warren's unique background greatly facilitated his role in the criminal procedure revolution.

---

2. 369 U.S. 186 (1962).

The fact that Warren had been both an extraordinarily popular governor and a greatly respected District Attorney and Attorney General provided him the "credibility" to advance the rights of the individual. It is not far-fetched to suggest this revolution could not have taken place under a different Chief Justice who did not possess Warren's law enforcement background.

In addition, there was a growing realization that individual rights had, for decades, taken a clear backseat to the power of the state. While this was particularly true with respect to blacks, whites had also suffered at the hands of law enforcement. However, the cost was particularly paid by minorities. In order to address what was clearly a wrong, the Warren Court, in a series of landmark decisions, forever altered the American landscape.

The Warren Court was composed of individual justices with an array of background experiences and influences. Some of the most prominent members of the Warren Court who were on the bench during the "revolution" included:

Justice Hugo Black

In 1937, Justice Hugo Black became President Franklin D. Roosevelt's first appointment to the Court. Black had previously served as US Senator, a part-time police court judge and a county prosecuting attorney. After his Senate confirmation, it was revealed that Justice Black had once, for two years, been a member of the Ku Klux Klan.

Black repudiated his Klan membership and vocally and fiercely supported the view that the Court's earlier decisions allowing for segregation should be overruled. Black was often quoted as saying that "[The] Constitution is my legal bible," and he carried a copy of it in his pocket at all times.

Justice William J. Brennan, Jr.

Formerly a New Jersey Supreme Court Justice, Brennan was appointed to the Supreme Court by President Eisenhower. Brennan grew up in a Catholic household in New Jersey, graduated from Harvard Law School, and served in the Army during World War II. As a member of the New Jersey Supreme Court, Brennan risked his future judicial advancements by regularly making speeches against Senator McCarthy's increasing abuse of the government's investigative powers.

Brennan would eventually become the Court's most formidable liberal influence. Brennan was a devout Catholic; this was a source of criticism throughout his years as a Supreme Court Justice, both by those who felt his religious holdings negatively impacted his ability to uphold the law, and others who criticized his decisions on the Court as not "Catholic" enough, particularly his decision to uphold a ban on school prayer. Brennan staunchly maintained that the Constitution, and his obligation to uphold it, superseded all other considerations.

Justice Tom C. Clark

Justice Clark was appointed by President Harry S. Truman in 1949; prior to that, Clark had served as Truman's Attorney General. Clark was the father of Ramsey Clark who President Johnson named as Attorney General in 1967. In order to avoid possible conflicts of interest, Justice Clark resigned. It has been suggested that Johnson named Ramsey Clark Attorney General in order to force Justice Clark to resign so that Johnson could appoint Abe Fortas (see below) to the Court. While Truman's biographer, Merle Miller, quoted Truman speaking disparagingly of Clark, that has been refuted by others.

Clark surprised and angered Earl Warren on the morning the *Miranda* decision was to be announced: Warren believed that Clark would vote with the majority, making the decision 6-3; however, Clark wrote a dissent and also concurred. As a result, the decision is understood to be 5-4.

Justice William O. Douglas

William O. Douglas was appointed to the Supreme Court at the age of forty-one in 1939 by President Roosevelt—the second-youngest person ever nominated to the Court. Previously, Douglas had been a professor at Yale Law School and Chairman of the Securities and Exchange Commission.

Douglas' advocacy for outcasts and the poor was strongly influenced by his childhood early adult life, during which he was known to travel around the country on railroad box-cars with hobos. Justice Douglas, whose opinions reflect his liberal political outlook was considered a loner, who loved the West and the outdoors. He was viewed by many as the most brilliant Justice albeit not particularly interested in Court politics or swaying his Brethren on opinions he wrote.

Justice Arthur J. Goldberg

Justice Goldberg was appointed in 1962 by President Kennedy to replace Justice Felix Frankfurter; Goldberg had previously served as Kennedy's Secretary of Labor after having been a prominent labor lawyer. Goldberg would serve only three years on the Supreme Court, before President Johnson persuaded him to become the US Ambassador to the United Nations in order to appoint his close friend and advisor Abe Fortas to the Court. Johnson evidently promised Goldberg involvement in peace efforts seeking to resolve the Vietnam War; this never came to fruition. Goldberg returned to private practice after Richard Nixon's election in 1968.

Justice Abe Fortas

Justice Fortas was born in Memphis, Tennessee, the son of Russian Orthodox Jews. As a child, he attended public schools and graduated from Yale Law School. During his time in Law School, Fortas was greatly influenced by his professor, William O. Douglas. Fortas represented Lyndon Johnson in legal battles in a hotly contested Democratic primary runoff victory.[3] Thereafter, Fortas formed a deep, long-standing political connection with Johnson. In the landmark case of *Gideon v. Wainwright*, involving the right to counsel, Fortas represented Clarence Earl Gideon before the Court. Johnson viewed Fortas as an invaluable political advisor and one who would, as a Justice, provide him "inside information" on matters relevant to the Great Society.

In 1968, Johnson named Fortas to replace Warren; however, during the confirmation hearings, reports of financial

---

3. http://www.nytimes.com/1990/02/11/us/how-johnson-won-election-he-d -lost.html.

improprieties led Fortas to request that Johnson withdraw the nomination and to resign from the Court.

Warren Burger replaced Warren in 1969 as Chief Justice.

Justice John Marshall Harlan II

Justice Harlan was appointed to the Court in 1955 by President Eisenhower following the death of Justice Robert H. Jackson. He would serve on the Court until 1971. Harlan was a former Rhodes Scholar who studied at Princeton and Oxford before attending law school New York University Law School. He would later serve as Assistant US Attorney for the Southern District of New York and as Special Assistant Attorney General of New York. In 1954, Harlan was appointed to the US Court of Appeals for the Second Circuit, one year before his nomination to the Supreme Court.

Harlan has been characterized the "Great Dissenter" of the Warren Court.

Justice Marshall, admitted to the Court in 1967, was the first African American appointed to the Supreme Court. A descendant of slaves, Marshall had spent the majority of his legal career as counsel to the National Association for the

Justice Thurgood Marshall

Advancement of Colored People (NAACP). In his role as counsel for the NAACP, Marshall successfully developed the legal strategy that led to the Court's holding in *Brown v. Board of Education.*

As a Supreme Court Justice, a position he would hold for twenty-four years, Marshall was a strong advocate for the protection of individual rights, especially in the areas of civil rights and criminal procedure. In the years after

Justice Potter Stewart

Warren retired from the Court, Marshall and Brennan were considered the Court's great liberals.

President Eisenhower appointed Justice Stewart in 1958. Temperamentally, he was inclined to more moderate positions. As a strict adherent to intentionalism, the practice of applying the Constitution to questions of law that would supposedly reflect the intention of the framers of the Constitution, Stewart was often a dissenter to Warren Court's liberal majority. Justice Stewart dissented in *Miranda*.

Justice Byron White

Justice White was appointed to the Court in 1962 by President Kennedy. White was the Colorado state chair of Kennedy's 1960 presidential campaign; after the election, White was named Deputy Attorney General. White attended law school at Yale while playing for the Detroit Lions football team in the National Football League (NFL). White served in the Navy in World War II.

White's ideologies have been difficult for legal scholars to pin down; he is largely understood to be a practitioner of judicial restraint, consistently voting against the liberal majority. In that sense, White is considered to have been a disappointment to liberals in the same sense that Warren was perceived to have been a disappointment to President Eisenhower. Justice White dissented in *Miranda*.

Warren as Chief Justice

The Justices of the 1960s respected Warren; it was suggested to me in the course of my research that Brennan, more than any other, was deferential to the Chief Justice. That assessment is not shared by all who I interviewed for this book. Others with whom I spoke suggested sensitivity to Justice Black's resentment of the label the "Warren Court." According to those who spoke to me on this matter, Black perceived himself as Warren's mentor and felt that this was not fully appreciated or recognized. Of the differences between Frankfurter and Warren, we have already alluded to. These matters are interesting; to what extent they are important is a different question.

There is, as Bob Woodward and Scott Armstrong's book, *The Brethren: Inside the Supreme Court*, makes clear, inevitable tension among Supreme Court Justices.[4]

---

4. Bob Woodward and Scott Armstrong, *The Brethren: Inside the Supreme Court* (Simon and Schuster Paperbacks, 1979).

The Warren Court was no different than its predecessors or successors. Nevertheless, tensions notwithstanding, Chief Justice Warren was able to steer the Court in an extraordinary manner. He was truly first among equals. That became very clear to me in the many interviews I conducted in the course of writing this book. That also stands out in the numerous books written about Earl Warren and the Warren Court.

The "revolution" this chapter suggests is a direct result of Warren's background and force of character. This was his Court. Warren's determination to steer the Court in a particular manner, especially regarding individual rights, is reflected in the decisions highlighted above. It is, frankly, an extraordinary legacy. That, in spite of subsequent decisions that created exceptions to the strong positions he articulated. Nevertheless, in spite of opportunities to do so, the Burger, Rehnquist, and Roberts Courts have not overturned *Miranda*, in spite of clear opportunities to do so.

Before turning our attention to the *Miranda* decision, we take stock of what we have learned through the first half of our journey. In doing so, we are reminded that our goal is to assess whether Earl Warren would apply *Miranda* to the terrorism of today. To enable answering this question, we have examined, in detail, Earl Warren's extraordinary career, the turbulent era in which he served as Chief Justice and the Warren Court. This detailed three-part analysis facilitates competently coping with the query we have posed.

The Warren Court and the Criminal Procedure Revolution

The *Miranda* decision reflects the Warren Court's commitment to individual rights, especially in criminal procedure cases. In addition to *Miranda*, of particular importance are the Court's holdings in *Mapp v. Ohio*,[5] *Gideon v. Wainwright*,[6] and *Escobedo v. Illinois*.[7]

Terry v. Ohio[8] is an exceptionally important case, although it represents a stepping back from the expansive individual protections the Court had established in *Mapp, Gideon, Escobedo,* and *Miranda*.

Mapp v. Ohio (1961)

In *Mapp*, the Court ruled that all evidence discovered as a result of a search and seizure conducted in violation of the Fourth Amendment of the US Constitution shall be inadmissible in state court proceedings.[9]

Cleveland police officers forced their way into Dollree Mapp's house without a proper search warrant. When Mapp demanded to see a search warrant, the police officers left her home only to return with what they claimed was a search warrant.

---

5. 367 U.S. 643, 660 (1961).
6. 372 U.S. 335 (1963).
7. 378 U.S. 478, 84 S. Ct. 1758, 12 L. Ed. 2d 977 (1964).
8. 392 U.S. 1 (1968).
9. *Mapp v Ohio*, 367 U.S. 643 (1961).

After a struggle ensued between Mapp and the police over physical custody of the search warrant (which was not actually a search warrant), the police arrested Mapp and forced her to her bedroom while conducting a widespread search of the residence.

Police discovered a trunk of obscene pictures in Mapp's basement. Mapp was ultimately convicted in an Ohio court for possession of the pictures. Mapp argued that her Fourth Amendment rights had been violated by the search. Prior to the Court's holding in *Mapp*, unlawfully seized evidence was banned from federal courts, but not state courts.[10]

Justice Tom Clark wrote the majority opinion,[11] expanding the exclusionary rule, applying the rule to evidence obtained in violation of the Fourth Amendment's search and seizure clause in all state prosecutions. Justices Black and Douglas wrote concurring opinions.

Justice Harlan wrote a dissenting opinion joined by Justice Frankfurter and Justice Charles; the dissent referenced a recent study that showed that half of the states still adhered to the common-law non-exclusionary rule. Their primary concern was using the Judiciary to force states to alter their criminal law enforcement mechanisms.

---

10. *Wolf v. Colorado*, 338 U.S. 25 (1949).

11. Warren referenced Clark's majority opinion in the Miranda decision; he did this—at the last moment and on the spur of the moment—when he learned that Clark would not be joining the majority opinion. Warren did this in a deliberate effort to embarrass Clark.

Gideon v. Wainwright (1963)

Gideon v. Wainwright[12] is a landmark Supreme Court case, holding that a defendant must have the right to counsel during any federal or state felony cases involving robbery, murder, or other major crimes.

Clarence Earl Gideon was charged with breaking and entering with the intent to commit a misdemeanor, which was a felony under Florida law. At trial, Gideon, a man with an eighth grade education who spent much of his adult life in and out of prison for committing nonviolent crimes, chose to represent himself after his request for an attorney was denied. At the time, Florida law only permitted counsel to be appointed for poor defendants who had committed capital crimes; accordingly, the trial judge denied Gideon's request. Despite Gideon's best effort to represent himself, including making an opening statement to the jury, cross-examining and presenting witnesses, and declining to testify against himself, Gideon was found guilty and sentenced to five years in prison.

After conviction, Gideon sought relief by filing a petition for writ of habeas corpus in the Florida Supreme Court, challenging the conviction on the grounds that the judge's denial of right to counsel was a violation of his

---

12. *Gideon v. Wainwright*, 372 U.S. 335. (1963); to read more about the case, see Anthony Lewis, *Gideon's Trumpet: How One Man, a Poor Prisoner, Took his Case to the Supreme Court and Changed the Law of the United States* (Vintage Books, 1964).

constitutional rights.[13] After the petition was denied, Gideon handwrote a petition to the Supreme Court of the United States. The Supreme Court agreed to hear the case to resolve the question of whether the right to counsel guaranteed under the Sixth Amendment of the Constitution applies to defendants in state court.

Prior to *Gideon*, in 1942, the Supreme Court had decided *Betts v. Brady*, holding that the refusal to appoint counsel for an indigent defendant charged with a felony in state court did not necessarily violate the Due Process Clause of the Fourteenth Amendment.[14] The Supreme Court's decision to consider Gideon's case would determine whether or not the ruling in *Betts* should be reconsidered.

On March 18, 1963, the Court, in a unanimous decision, overruled *Betts v. Brady*. In an opinion written by Justice Hugo Black,[15] the Court held that the Sixth Amendment's guarantee of counsel is a fundamental right essential to a fair trial and, as such, applies to the states through the Due Process Clause of the Fourteenth Amendment.

In overturning *Betts*, Justice Black stated that "reason and reflection require us to recognize that in our adversary system of criminal justice, any person haled into court, who is too poor to hire a lawyer, cannot be assured a fair trial unless

---

13. A *writ of habeas corpus* is a legal recourse whereby a person can report unlawful detention or imprisonment before a court.

14. *Betts v. Brady*, 316 U.S. 455 (1942).

15. Black had written a dissent in *Betts*.

counsel is provided for him." Black further wrote that the "noble ideal" of "fair trials before impartial tribunals in which ever defendant stands equal before the law . . . cannot be realized if the poor man charged with crime has to face his accusers without a lawyer to assist him."[16]

Escobedo v. Illinois (1964)

In a trial where a "particular suspect in police custody . . . has been refused an opportunity to consult with his counsel and . . . has not been warned of his constitutional right to keep silent, the accused has been denied the assistance of counsel in violation of the Sixth and Fourteenth Amendments . . ."[17]

Escobedo, decided a year after *Gideon v. Wainwright*, held suspects have a right to counsel during police interrogations under the Sixth Amendment, but only when they become THE suspect.[18] The tables below illustrate the warning practices that occurred before and after the *Escobedo* decision.

---

16. *Id.*
17. *Escobedo*, 378 U.S. 478 (1964).
18. *Id.* -

TABLE 2A: WARNING BEGUN BEFORE *ESCOBEDO*—SILENCE

Question 3: During what year and month was this policy begun?

	Percentage Starting Silence Warning Before *Escobedo*					
	City Police		Small City Police		Prosecution	
At least 10 yrs. ago	40*	(20)†	26*	(27)†	40*	(21)†
From 10 yrs. ago to May 30, 1961	10	(5)	17	(17)	22	(12)
June 1, 1961 *(Mapp)* to December 31, 1962	28	(14)	17	(17)	9	(5)
January 1, 1963 to December 31, 1963	13	(6)	0	(0)	22	(12)
January 1, 1964 to June 1, 1964	8	(4)	4	(4)	9	(5)
Total percentage warning before *Escobedo*††	51		71		57	

* Percentage of the total who began warning before *Escobedo* during each time period.

† Numbers in parenthesis represent percentages of the total of before *and* after *Escobedo* responses in the designated time period.

†† This percentage includes responses which indicated they began warning before *Escobedo*, but could not be included in the categories because no time period was given.

Escobedo v. Illinois, decided two years before the Miranda decision, was a far-reaching decision, which held *for the first time* that defendants had a right to counsel even before they were indicted for a particular crime. Although later decisions by the courts would indicate that the application of *Escobedo* was to be limited to the facts, the Supreme Court has never directly overturned *Escobedo.*

Danny Escobedo was arrested on the night of January 19, 1960 for the murder of his brother-in-law but was released after contacting his lawyer. The lawyer told him not to answer any more questions if the police rearrested him. Ten days later, Escobedo was arrested a second time and made repeated requests to contact his attorney, all of which were denied.

TABLE 2B: WARNINGS BEGUN BEFORE *ESCOBEDO*—COUNSEL

Question 9: When was this policy begun?

Time Warning Policy	Percentage Starting Counsel Warning Before *Escobedo*					
	City Police		*Small City Police*		*Prosecution*	
At least 10 yrs. ago	36*	(16)†	36*	(23)†	22*	(11)†
From 10 yrs. ago to May 30, 1961	18	(8)	30	(19)	22	(11)
June 1, 1961 *(Mapp)* to December 31, 1962	34	(15)	27	(17)	5	(2)
January 1, 1963 to December 31, 1963	8	(5)	0	(0)	27	(13)
January 1, 1964 to June 1, 1964	6	(4)	6	(4)	22	(11)
Total percentage warning before *Escobedo*††	46		71		45	

---

* Percentage of the total of those who began warning before *Escobedo* during each time period.

† Numbers in parentheses represent percentages of the total of before *and* after *Escobedo* responses in the designated time period.

†† This percentage includes responses which indicated they began warning before *Escobedo* but could not be included in the categories because no time period was given.

At the police station, Escobedo's attorney was denied permission to see his client. The police interrogated Escobedo and claimed that his alleged coconspirator had confessed and implicated Escobedo. Despite previously denying he had committed the crime, the police were finally able to extract a written confession, leading to Escobedo's eventual conviction for murder. Escobedo appealed the decision to the Supreme Court, arguing that the confession had been obtained after his requests to see his attorney were denied.

TABLE 2C: WARNING BEGUN AFTER *ESCOBEDO*—SILENCE

Question 3: During what year and month was this policy begun?

Time Warning Policy Begun	Percentage Starting Silence Warning After *Escobedo*					
	City Police		Small City Police**		Prosecution	
At the time of *Escobedo*, June, 1964	25*	(13)†	5*	(2)†	15*	(7)†
July—August, 1964	24	(12)	17	(6)	20	(9)
September 1—December 31, 1964	25	(13)	34	(12)	32	(13)
January 1, 1965 to June 30, 1965	18	(9)	44	(16)	26	(12)
July 1, 1965 to December 31, 1965	2	(0)	0	(0)	5	(5)
After January 1, 1966	6	(3)	0	(0)	0	(0)
Total Percentage Beginning Warning After *Escobedo*††	49		29		43	

* Percentage of the total of those who began warning after *Escobedo* during each time period.

** Because of the large percentage of small city police who had already begun warning before *Escobedo*, the numbers which remain for post-*Escobedo* study have limited statistical significance.

† Numbers in parentheses represent percentages of the total of before *and* after *Escobedo* responses in the designated time period.

†† This percentage includes responses which indicated they began warning *after Escobedo* but could not be included in the categories because no time period was given.

The violation of his right to counsel, Escobedo claimed, should result in reversal of the conviction.

Just six weeks before, the Court decided *Massiah v. United States,* holding that the Sixth Amendment right to counsel attaches once an individual has been indicted.[19] The Court held that the defendant's Sixth Amendment rights were violated when the police used an accomplice to

---

19. *Massiah v. United States,* 377 U.S. 201, 84 S. Ct. 1199, 12 L.Ed.2d 246 (U.S.N.Y. 1964).

elicit an incriminating statement from the defendant after he had been granted a right to counsel.[20]

The Supreme Court in *Escobedo* reached a similar result in a 5-4 decision. Justice Arthur Goldberg, writing for the majority, held Escobedo's right to counsel did not depend on whether, at the time of interrogation, the authorities have secured a formal indictment. Wrote Goldberg:

> We hold, therefore, that where, as here, the investigation is no longer a general inquiry into an unsolved crime but has begun to focus on a particular suspect, the suspect has been taken into police custody, the police carry out a process of interrogations that lends itself to eliciting incriminating statements, the suspect has requested and been denied an opportunity to consult with his lawyer, and the police have not effectively warned him of his absolute constitutional right to remain silent, the accused has been denied "The Assistance of Counsel" in violation of the Sixth Amendment to the Constitution as "made obligatory upon the States by the Fourteenth Amendment," and that no statement elicited by the police during the interrogation may be used against him at a criminal trial.[21]

---

20. *Id.*
21. *Escobedo,* 378 U.S. 478.

Terry v. Ohio (1968)

Terry v. Ohio represents the beginning of the end of the Warren Court criminal procedure revolution. In Terry— with Warren writing for the draft—the Court ruled that the Fourth Amendment permits a law enforcement officer to stop and frisk persons suspected of criminal activity without first obtaining their consent, even though the officer may lack a warrant to conduct a search or probable cause to make an arrest.[22]

The case stemmed from an incident in Cleveland, Ohio. Police officer Martin McFadden observed two men, including Terry, talking on a street corner while repeatedly walking up and down the same street. The men would occasionally peer into a store window and talk some more, and they were eventually joined by a third man. Based on his extensive career in law enforcement, the officer believed that the three men were "casing" the store to rob it. McFadden then approached the men to question them, but initially decided to search them.

The search, or "frisk," of Terry revealed a concealed weapon; Terry was charged with carrying a concealed weapon without a permit. At trial, Terry argued (unsuccessfully), the weapons were inadmissible because they were discovered as a result of an unlawful search conducted without probable cause or a search warrant. After the Supreme

---

22. Terry v. Ohio, 392 U.S. 1 (1968).

Court of Ohio affirmed the conviction, Terry appealed the decision to the Supreme Court.

The Supreme Court held a search is reasonable when an officer performs a cursory limited search on a person the officer reasonably believes could be armed.

Ernesto Miranda and the Path to the Supreme Court

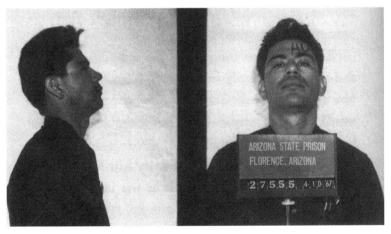

http://djiaran.tk/miranda-vs-arizona-essay.html

On March 13, 1963, officers of the Phoenix Police Department knocked on Ernesto Arthur Miranda's door. Miranda had become the sole suspect in a series of two attempted rapes, and the successful rape and kidnap of an eighteen-year-old woman. At the time, the police had very little by way of physical evidence. However, a report of a suspicious vehicle had led officers to identify the car of Twila Hoffman, whose boyfriend, Ernesto Miranda, previously had a few run-ins with law enforcement. Miranda did not seem concerned by the officers at his door; when one of the officers informed him that he did not have to talk to them, he said he did not mind talking and would accompany them to the police station.

When they arrived at the station, the police escorted Miranda to Interrogation Room #2, dubbed the "sweat room." There the officers immediately began to confront Miranda with selective details from the crimes. Initially, Miranda expressed his innocence, stating he was working the night of the crime. Later, Miranda was asked to participate in a lineup; Detective Carroll Cooley assured Miranda that once the victims cleared him he would be driven home. The victims tentatively picked Miranda from the lineup, but stated that they could not be sure.

When they returned to the interrogation room, Miranda was told he did not do well during the lineup. He then stated, "I guess I'd better tell you about it then." An officer gave Miranda a standard statement form, which he completed and signed, detailing his perpetration of the crime.

At the time, Miranda was twenty-three years old, "indigent" (though during my personal interviews with those involved and who knew Miranda, that was not the case), and had not completed ninth grade. Miranda was then placed under arrest; until then, he had been "in custody."

At the trial, Miranda's court-appointed defense moved to suppress the written confession on the grounds the suspect had not been made aware of his Fifth Amendment right against self-incrimination. However, the confession was admitted into evidence and Miranda was convicted of rape and kidnapping and sentenced to twenty to thirty years imprisonment on each charge, with sentences to run concurrently.

Ernesto Miranda's story should have ended there. No one involved with the case had any doubt that Miranda was a serial rapist. At no time was Miranda subjected to overly coercive police tactics; most of the evidence used to convict him came from his own confession. There has never been a claim by any attorney representing Miranda that Detective Cooley conducted the interrogation in violation of accepted methods at the time. A careful reading of the interrogation record reflects, without doubt, that Cooley was respectful of Miranda and of his rights as understood at the time. There is no hint, much less suggestion, of coercive methods that led to Miranda's confession.

The case would later be appealed to the Arizona Supreme Court, which affirmed the trial court's decision.

In 1966, the Warren Court heard four different cases involving custodial interrogations, including *Miranda v. Arizona*. All four cases resulted in convictions obtained after the defendants had admitted guilt.

With that, we undertake a very detailed discussion and analysis of the *Miranda* decision. A word of warning to the reader: to truly understand the decision, it is necessary to "get into the weeds." Otherwise, it is impossible to both fully appreciate the decision's importance and to robustly answer our question.

Chapter Five

The Essence of *Miranda*

You have the right to remain silent. Anything that you say or do can be used against you in a court of law. You have the right to an attorney. If you cannot afford an attorney, one will be provided to you. Do you understand these rights as I have read them to you?

Miranda

Miranda is arguably the most recognized Supreme Court decision in US jurisprudence. TV has popularized the Miranda warning; an evening spent watching "cop shows" makes that very clear. Whether or not the viewing public knows the facts of *Miranda v. Arizona* is an open question. Whether or not Warren intended for the *Miranda* opinion to become part of popular culture is unknown.

Casual conversation with people from different walks of life reinforces the extent to which Miranda impacts American society. The familiarity I repeatedly encountered is not dependent on personal or familial interaction with law enforcement. The Miranda warning is part of the American culture; many people I met while writing this book could recite the warning in full; none were unacquainted with it.

Whether or not they agree with its consequences is a different question. Earl Warren sought to protect the vulnerable; he clearly understood the realities of the interrogation paradigm. Warren, based on his experiences as a District Attorney, was fully cognizant of the inherent imbalance between the interrogator and the suspect. Furthermore, Warren understood that suspects with limited resources, financial and otherwise, were at even greater disadvantage and that protecting them was essential. As the opinion made clear, Warren recognized that interrogations were inherently coercive.

His motivations were simultaneously simple and profound: simple in that he wanted to protect suspects; profound in that he imposed limits on how the nation-state interacted with vulnerable individuals. That is, in protecting those suspected of criminal activity, Warren sent a clear message to law enforcement and society. That message, while focusing on the specific individual, also had powerful consequences regarding larger society.

The opinion was not written in a vacuum; as discussed throughout this book, America in 1966 was in turmoil. The Harlem and Watts riots of 1964 and 1965 dramatically and violently highlighted profound anger, resentment, and social injustice. The Detroit and Newark riots in 1967 and the riots that followed the assassination of Dr. King in 1968 were extremely violent, resulting in significant loss of life, requiring intervention by the US military. In between those two "book ends," Earl Warren's Supreme Court imposed limits on law enforcement.

While law enforcement loudly complained that the decision "handcuffed" police officers, Earl Warren believed that protecting the individual was paramount. The tension between these two perspectives must be acknowledged; that was clearly conveyed when meeting with law enforcement officials. It would not be an exaggeration to use the phrase "necessary evil" in describing how *Miranda* is perceived in certain quarters.

I do not share that highly negative view. However, I understand that it must be accounted for. Out-of-hand dismissal of positions articulated by law enforcement is gratuitous and counterproductive. Their criticism, candid and direct, is relevant for our inquiry. One of the most interesting interviews I conducted was with a former Supreme Court clerk.[1] In his opinion, Warren "pushed" on *Miranda* and "went over the line"; the clerk noted that Miranda was not subject to a violent, physical interrogation conjured up in images of sheriff deputies beating black suspects in the back seat.

There is no indication that Detective Carroll Cooley pressured or coerced Miranda during the course of the interrogation. Arguably, that was a strategic decision by

---

1. I interviewed a number of Supreme Court clerks while writing this book; notes from those interviews are in my records.

Warren: there was nothing unusual or extraordinary in how Miranda was interrogated; it was a run-of-the-mill interrogation conducted in the aftermath of a crime with nothing to indicate its uniqueness. Cooley did not coerce Miranda; there was never any indication of that. This was not an interrogation whose visual images were particularly dramatic or remarkable.

Viewing the case in that context increases the power of the holding; were Miranda the victim of a backseat beating then it would be possible to dismiss the opinion by suggesting, "of course the suspect has to be protected; otherwise, he'll come within a whisker of a brutal death." That dismissiveness cannot be applied given how Cooley interrogated Miranda. The facts of Miranda's interrogation lent themselves to Warren's decision to "use" Miranda as the platform to extend *Escobedo*. Interviews with clerks from the 1965 to 1966 Supreme Court term confirm that Warren fully intended to protect the interrogated suspect. That conviction was premised on a twofold conviction: the interrogation setting is inherently coercive and the right to an attorney must be guaranteed.

It is not by chance that Warren penned the opinion himself. Unlike his fellow justices, Warren had been elected to serve as district attorney and had intimate knowledge of the interrogation paradigm.[2] As previously noted, Warren

---

2. Justice Tom Clark served as an assistant district attorney, https://www .oyez.org/justices/tom_c_clark.

was not a jurisprudential scholar and he made no pretensions of being one. Warren was guided by a strong sense of right and wrong with a clear understanding of what, for him, must be the correct decision in every case. In addition to a powerful moral compass, Warren had been a remarkably successful politician. Those two attributes, more than other qualities, are the basis of his judicial philosophy. More than anything, the word *practical* can be used to describe Warren's approach to cases before the Court. That is what uniquely positioned him to write the opinion and to ensure that a majority, albeit a slim majority, would support the specific limitations imposed on law enforcement.

The word *slim* is not randomly chosen for it reflects the reality of a majority of five Justices, three dissenters, and one Justice, Clark, both dissenting and concurring. Whereas Warren believed that he had forged a majority of six Justices, Clark's decision to not join the majority was, for Warren, both surprising and significant—it was surprising in that he believed Clark would cast his vote with the majority; it was significant because it turned a 6-3 (which he assumed) decision into a 5-4 ruling.[3]

The opinion is neither complex nor sophisticated; it is written in a manner that any member of the public and law enforcement can easily understand. That was a direct result of Warren's style and intent: for the opinion to have its

---

3. I am grateful to Mr. Ken Ziffren, C.J. Warren's clerk in the 1965 term, for patiently explaining the nuances and gravity of Clark's decision and actions.

desired impact, clarity, and directness. That conciseness is felt throughout the opinion, which is devoid of "feint here, jab there" that characterizes many Supreme Court holdings.

There is no hidden ball and no "between the lines" analysis required to comprehend its full import. For Warren, the most effective way to protect the suspect was to inform him clearly that he had the right to remain silent and that, if need be, an attorney will be provided. The obligation imposed on the interrogator was twofold: to read the suspect the warning and to ensure that the suspect understood the rights granted. Whether the suspect chose to exercise the right or to "waive" was a personal decision. The decision represents recognition of the mistreatment of suspects throughout history. That is an extraordinarily important acknowledgment both for the specific suspect and for the relationship between the state and the individual. The decision is powerful on a micro and macroscale alike.

From Warren's perspective, protecting the suspect was essential. There is no doubt that he was fully aware of the injustices that had been visited upon suspects over the years. In establishing a rights-based interrogation regime, Warren was also protecting larger society from the consequences of confessions elicited from mistreated suspects. Warren was concerned about the lack of professionalism among police departments; he believed that coerced confessions reflected laziness among police officers. In addition, coerced confessions resulted in wrongful convictions. The consequences from all perspectives were, for Warren, deeply troubling.

In establishing the Miranda warnings, Warren and the four justices who joined him took a clear and bold stand regarding interrogations. Simply stated, they said "enough is enough." The decision was not born in a vacuum; it reflects a logical progression of increasing rights for the individual. In *Escobedo's* aftermath, there was much anticipation regarding what the Court would do next.

Warren's majority opinion, brought below, is a model of clarity, directness, and practicality. Admittedly long, the opinion explains the core issue in a manner that left no doubt as to the writer's intention. Those reading the opinion, easily accessible in its language and meaning, were left with no doubt as to what Warren meant. Warren meant what he wrote and wrote what he meant. The opinion must be read in that spirit. To attach additional meanings, interpretations or "spin" is to miss its import and to purpose. The words must be read at their face value.

Rereading Warren's text, the sense of a seasoned member of law enforcement speaking directly to colleagues permeates throughout the passages. Perhaps some felt Warren was "lecturing" rather than "talking." There is strength in the tone. It is unapologetic; there can be no mistaking its purpose and goal. There is also a clear sense of Warren reflecting back on his career and using the "bully pulpit" to right the wrongs that he was fully aware of. I do not know if the term *magnum opus* is appropriate in describing the relationship between Warren and the opinion he drafted. There is a strong sense that this decision was both special and different. Warren clearly "knew of what he wrote"; of that there is no doubt.

His in-depth understanding of interrogations, law enforcement, the vulnerability of the suspect, and deep concern for the integrity of confessions is integral to the decision. One cannot—must not—read the decision without recognizing that Warren was uniquely positioned to write it. That is not to suggest that other Justices did not have the ability to do so; it is, however, to posit that Warren had a perspective, understanding, and history that positioned him, like no other Justice, to write the opinion.

It was, in many ways, a perfect confluence when historical circumstances join together in a truly remarkable fashion. The line of criminal procedure cases of the Warren Court reached their apex on June 13, 1966. There must be no mistaking the extraordinary importance and power of Warren's words. That is conveyed in direct simplicity; the opinion is neither sophisticated nor nuanced.

The language is neither soaring nor particularly elegant. The prose is not of a poet; Warren was neither bard nor man of letters. The directness conveys a powerful message to interrogators: **ENOUGH**. There is a tone of reproach that could only come from someone who knew, who had been there, and who understood, and recoiled from, the consequences of how interrogations were conducted in the United States.

A careful reading suggests every word in the opinion was carefully weighed and measured; while long, it is not wordy.

There is an important difference: wordy suggests lack of clarity and words merely for the sake of words. A fair number of Supreme Court opinions leave the reader unsure of what the writer intended; that was not the case with Warren's decision. Critics and supporters alike understood the opinion's meaning and consequences. The loud and sustained criticism reflected an accurate read of what Warren intended. Law enforcement may well have resented the rebuke conveyed in the opinion. It is fair to surmise that was the author's intention.

Emphasizing the suspects Fifth Amendment privilege against self-incrimination was the cornerstone of the decision; the "right to remain silent" is the practical, jurisprudential, and existential core of the opinion. For Warren, protecting that constitutionally guaranteed privilege was of the essence. It is not an exaggeration to suggest for Warren it was sacrosanct. The opinion must be read accordingly.

Perhaps, were the opinion penned by a Justice not deeply invested in law enforcement, one who had not "been around the block," critics would suggest the writer was sanctimonious, what might be termed a "bleeding heart liberal." Obviously, Warren was not that. For Warren, the centerpiece of the decision was ensuring that the suspect be protected from state agents.

That does not mean, as some have suggested, that Warren minimized harm caused to the victim of a crime. I believe that to be a spurious charge. One must not forget that Warren well understood the victim's pain: his own father had been murdered, a murder which is to this day, unsolved. Warren was sympathetic to the victim; however, he differentiated between the victim's unquestioned harm and suffering and the individual suspected of having committed the crime in question.

The difference is significant: the victim was clearly identified, the suspect but a suspect. Protecting the rights of the latter does not, in any way, trivialize or disrespect the suffering of the former. To suggest that Warren preferred one over the other or was more sympathetic to suspects than to victims is erroneous. It also significantly misses the point of the opinion and what was of grave concern to the majority. The opinion was neither victim "unfriendly" nor suspect "friendly." That is to miss the point. Rather, Earl Warren, as Chief Justice of the US Supreme Court sought to ensure that basic constitutional rights were protected in the interrogation setting and that law enforcement respected the rights of the suspect.

I have questioned what is the most effective and compelling way to bring the opinion to life. There is no easy and "right" answer to the dilemma. I have considered various options and alternatives with the primary question being how will the reader best understand the opinion in the context of the question at the core of this book? To resolve what is, admittedly, speculative history, we must have Earl Warren's words fully in front of us. However, as the reader will see in the pages ahead, examining *only* his words is insufficient for our purposes. That is why I have chosen to include both the dissents and oral arguments.

Below are excerpts from the opinion intertwined with commentary and analysis, which Warren read in its entirety on June 13, 1966.

The Majority Opinion

THE MAJORITY OPINION: WARREN, C.J., JOINED BY JUSTICES BRENNAN, DOUGLAS, BLACK, FORTAS

The cases before us raise questions, which go to the roots of our concepts of American criminal jurisprudence: the restraints society must observe consistent with the Federal Constitution in prosecuting individuals for crime. More specifically, we deal with the admissibility of statements obtained from an individual who is subjected to custodial police interrogation and the necessity for procedures, which assure that the individual is accorded his privilege under the Fifth Amendment to the Constitution not to be compelled to incriminate himself.[4]

Our holding will be spelled out with some specificity in the pages that follow, but, briefly stated, it is

---

4. *Miranda v. Arizona*, 384 U.S. 436, 439 (1966).

this: the prosecution may not use statements, whether exculpatory or inculpatory, stemming from custodial interrogation of the defendant unless it demonstrates the use of procedural safeguards effective to secure the privilege against self-incrimination. By custodial interrogation, we mean questioning initiated by law enforcement officers after a person has been taken into custody or otherwise deprived of his freedom of action in any significant way. As for the procedural safeguards to be employed, unless other fully effective means are devised to inform accused persons of their right of silence and to assure a continuous opportunity to exercise it, the following measures are required. Prior to any questioning, the person must be warned that he has a right to remain silent, that any statement he does make may be used as evidence against him, and that he has a right to the presence of an attorney, either retained or appointed. The defendant may waive effectuation of these rights, provided the waiver is made voluntarily, knowingly and intelligently. If, however, he indicates in any manner and at any stage of the process that he wishes to consult with an attorney before speaking, there can be no questioning. Likewise, if the individual is alone and indicates in any manner that he does not wish to be interrogated, the police may not question him. The mere fact that he may have answered some questions or volunteered some statements on his own does not deprive him of the right to refrain from answering any further inquiries until he has consulted with an attorney and thereafter consents to be questioned.[5]

The constitutional issue we decide in each of these cases is the admissibility of statements obtained from a defendant questioned while in custody or otherwise deprived of his freedom of action in any significant way. In each, the defendant was questioned by police officers, detectives, or a prosecuting attorney in a room in which he was cut off from the outside world. In none of these cases was the defendant given a full and effective warning of his rights at the outset of the interrogation process. In all the cases, the questioning elicited oral admissions, and, in three of them, signed statements as well that were admitted at their trials. They all thus share salient features—incommunicado interrogation of individuals in a police-dominated atmosphere, resulting in self-incriminating statements without full warnings of constitutional rights.

An understanding of the nature and setting of this in-custody interrogation is essential to our decisions today. The difficulty in depicting what transpires at such interrogations stems from the fact

5. *Id.* at 444–45.

that, in this country, they have largely taken place incommunicado. From extensive factual studies undertaken in the early 1930s, including the famous Wickersham Report to Congress by a Presidential Commission, it is clear that police violence and the "third degree" flourished at that time. In a series of cases decided by this Court long after these studies, the police resorted to physical brutality—beating, hanging, whipping—and to sustained and protracted questioning incommunicado in order to extort confessions. The Commission on Civil Rights in 1961 found much evidence to indicate that "some policemen still resort to physical force to obtain confessions." The use of physical brutality and violence is not, unfortunately, relegated to the past or to any part of the country. Only recently in Kings County, New York, the police brutally beat, kicked, and placed lighted cigarette butts on the back of a potential witness under interrogation for the purpose of securing a statement incriminating a third party.[6]

Again, we stress that the modern practice of in-custody interrogation is psychologically, rather than physically, oriented.

---

6. *Id.* at 445–46.

Interrogations

Interrogations reflect an imbalance between the interrogator and suspect, a nitty-gritty confluence of fear, anxiety, and control.

"If he's a meek kind of guy, and you send in a 6ft-tall,
football-player-type interrogator, screaming, 'A year
from now you're going to have a needle in your arm,
and you're going to be dead,' he might just melt and
tell you everything."[7]

"It was very hard, because you don't know why you
are in there and the only person you speak to is either
yourself, or the wall, or when you go to the restroom
or when you go to the torture place," said Mr. Fikre,
who was held for 106 days. . . .[8]

"When the FBI interviews you, it is their word against
yours. Why? Because they in most cases will not

---

7. "Spike" Bowman former general counsel for the FBI and an "anonymous
source" dated April 24, 2013.

8. *Report: The FBI Has Been Beating, Torturing and Threatening to Kill American Citizens if They Will Not Become Snitches (Informants),* The Judiciary Report
(April 25, 2012), http://www.aishamusic.com/Judiciary_Report/report_the_fbi_
has_been_beating_torturing_threating_to_kill_americans_if_they_will_not_
become_snitches.htm. (19 April 2012—US citizen Yonas Fikre claimed he was
detained in the United Arab Emirates last year and tortured by FBI agents.
Mr. Fikre, a Muslim seeking asylum in Sweden, told a press conference in Stock-
holm that he was beaten, threatened with death and kept in solitary confinement
for over three months. . . .)

record the interview/interrogation, because this way they can write a summary and claim that in the summary is the evidence about what you said to them in the interview and show this as evidence in court. A jury will more likely believe an FBI agent's summary about what you said than to trust your own testimony. They will twist the truth and will lie. This is what they are trained to do."[9]

My term *nitty-gritty* is intended to convey the essence of interrogations: two or three people in one room—physical discomfort, power disparity, anxiety, and a loss of liberty and freedom. Control is in the hands of one party. There is a distinct lack of control for the other party. That is the reality of interrogation.[10]

One party wants information it believes the other party has. That information may significantly harm that party. That information may save lives. Perhaps, the party that wants the information has pieces of that information and is looking to corroborate what he or she knows. Maybe this is nothing but a fishing expedition intended to disarm the other side. The two parties are engaged in trying to gauge what the other knows. There is an element of a cat and mouse game.

---

9. Michael J. Macabe, *Do Not Talk to the FBI without an Attorney even if You Have Nothing to Hide.* San Diego Criminal Defense (Aug. 2, 2011), http://www.mccabelawyer.com/2011/08/02/do-not-talk-to-the-fbi-with-out-an-attorney-even-if-you-know-you-have-nothing-to-hide/.

10. For more on interrogations, see Wrongful Convictions, *Rights Violated during Police Interrogation*, YouTube (Nov. 16, 2014), https://www.youtube.com/watch?v=rM1bVvPTL6g; https://www.youtube.com/watch?v=Z-VW8Ldw6YI.

The roles are clear: the interrogator wants information; the interrogatee is not necessarily inclined to provide the information. More than anything else, the two parties are together in the same room for one primary reason: the interrogator, acting on behalf of the nation-state, wants information the interrogatee possesses, or at least information he or she believes the interrogatee possesses.

This means that the information may incriminate the suspect. That information may well incriminate others. The interrogatee may be fearful of providing information that may result in personal harm: a confession leading to an indictment and possible conviction with incarceration in the offing, depending on the severity of the crime.

That is what has brought the two parties together. That is the only reason they occupy the same space. There is significant gamesmanship; on some level, it is a chess match combined with poker. The stakes can be very high with significant consequences and ramifications. However, as the *Miranda* ruling made clear, *protecting the suspect is of prime importance.*

The protection is from the other person in the room. Two people are sharing a common space and one person needs protection from the other. One is at risk, the other not. The lack of symmetry is essential to understanding the essence of the relationship.

However, while protection is an important concept, we must recall who the two actors are: one a state agent,

entrusted with public safety; the other an individual suspected of having committed a crime. The state agent is mandated with gathering information about criminal conduct
that either led to the commission of a crime or was intended
to result in one. It is assumed by the state agent that the
suspect has information that will result in solving or pre-
venting the crime in question.

To solve the crime, the interrogator needs information.
The essence of police work is gathering information, col-
lecting evidence, connecting various dots, and then determining who is responsible for violating the law. There is
nothing magical about this. While contemporary methods
are more sophisticated, more scientifically based, and, hopefully, more objective than in years past, the critical interaction is between the two individuals. As Earl Warren fully
understood, *that* relationship is at the epicenter of criminal
law and procedure. The interrogator wants the truth. That is
the purest form of law enforcement in the ideal. What Warren feared was an interrogator who wants a confession and
for the suspect to incriminate himself and say, "I did it"
regardless of the truth. That is an interrogator who coerces a
confession from the suspect.

If there is one word that captures the interrogation
paradigm, it is "coercive." While the environment is not
intended to resemble comfort and leisure, the question is
to what degree does the suspect have to be coerced before
confessing.

A table demonstrating the **legally permissible** techniques the Department of Justice High Value Interrogation teams may employ during their interrogation of a suspect[11]

General Method	Effects (Purposes)	Variants
1. Isolation	Deprives victim of all social support of his ability to resist. Develops an intense concern with self. Makes victim dependent upon interrogator.	Complete solitary confinement. Complete isolation. Semi-isolation. Group isolation.
2. Monopolization of Perception	Fixes attention upon immediate predicament. Fosters introspection. Eliminates stimuli competing with those controlled by captor. Frustrates all action not consistent with compliance.	Physical isolation. Darkness or bright light. Barren environment. Restricted movement. Monotonous food.
3. Induced Debilitation and Exhaustion	Weakens mental and physical ability to resist.	Semi-starvation. Exposure. Exploitation of wounds. Induced illness. Sleep deprivation. Prolonged interrogation. Forced writing. Overexertion.

(continued)

11. *Dzhokhar Tsarnaev: The FBI, Interrogations and a Crash Course in Coerced Confessions*, The Boston Marathon Bombings: What Happened? http://thebostonmarathonbombings.weebly.com/dzhokhar-tsarnaev-the-fbi-interrogations-and-a-crash-course-in-coerced-confessions.html.

General Method	Effects (Purposes)	Variants
4. Threats	Cultivates anxiety and despair.	Threats of death. Threats of non [return?] Threats of endless interrogation and isolation. Threats against family. Vague threats. Mysterious charges of treatment.
5. Occasional Indulgences	Provides positive motivation for compliance. Hinders adjustment to deprivation.	{Occasional?} favors. Fluctuations of interrogator's attitudes. Promises. Rewards for partial compliance. Tantalizing.
6. Demonstrating "Omnipotence" and "Omniscience"	Suggests futility of resistance.	Confrontation. Pretending cooperation taken for granted. Demonstrating complete control over victim's fate.
7. Degradation	Makes cost of resistance more damaging to self-esteem than capitulation. Reduces prisoner to "animal-level" concerns.	Personal hygiene prevented. Filthy infested surrounds. Damaging punishments. Insults and taunts. Denial of privacy.
8. Enforcing Trivial Demands	Develops habits of compliance.	Forced writing. Enforcement of minute rules.

At the crux of that question is what does society desire from law enforcement: *a confession to stop an interrogation or a confession that is the truth.* A false confession, after all, results in conviction of the innocent and leaves the guilty on the street. On the one hand, not all suspects willingly provide information that would seal their fates. On the other hand, society wants to be safe, to feel comfortable to walk the streets at night, to not have to look over their shoulders, wondering whether or not they are vulnerable. That same anxiety extends to worries over their family members.[12]

That is understandable; many of us can well relate to these common concerns. Whether those concerns are exaggerated or justified is a matter of personal opinion and predilection. Different people have different understandings of danger and threats. Racial prejudices, prior experiences, and contemporary events impact how we perceive the question of crime and what measures are legitimate to protect us.

This question goes well beyond the specific interaction between a detective and a suspect regarding a particular crime. It is a question that defines how society perceives duties owed, to whom are those duties owed, and the dangers emanating from failure to protect the vulnerable. Answering that obviously requires defining who is the vulnerable and whether there are different categories of vulnerabilities and vulnerable members of society.

---

12. Important to recall that racism is integral to this discussion: in the Deep South of previous decades, the primary fear was that black men would attack white women. In many ways, the law enforcement paradigm focused on this; in order to protect the white woman, all methods were acceptable. American history is permanently stained by the actions of law enforcement and society, facilitated by the public and politicians deliberately turning a blind eye. While we do not know to what extent Warren was aware of society's actions, we know he was deeply concerned by the lack of law enforcement professionalism.

While law enforcement is mandated to keep the streets safe, it is unrealistic to expect that all members of society can be protected at all times. Crime is a reality. Criminal conduct and criminals are an unfortunate reality of human conduct, nature, and society. Criminal conduct is as old as mankind. The efforts to reduce crime have had varying degrees of success. Crime rates, the politicization of crime and crime-fighting, the inevitable finger-pointing, and grandstanding are as common as the crime itself. Discussions regarding crime touch upon particularly sensitive questions that society faces including race, poverty, socio-economic influences, discrimination, and prejudices.

Political candidates invariably promise to fight crime, to clean the streets and to punish the wrongdoers. Those seeking election for prosecutorial positions or judgeships promise the voter to be tough on crime. The subtext is clear: punish the wrongdoer and ensure significant periods of incarceration. No candidate runs on the "I will protect suspect's rights" ticket. Such an election slogan would guarantee defeat at the polls. Actually, it would guarantee a landslide.

The public wants assurances regarding its safety; safeguarding of protections for the criminal does not score points for political candidates. Rehabilitation of the convicted is perhaps a public interest; nevertheless, it is not politically expedient in a campaign to emphasize this issue. The phrase "throw away the key" captures public sentiment regarding criminals. It is for that reason that protecting the suspect is critical notwithstanding that from the public's perspective: those arrested are guilty, deserving significant punishment for their actions.

Whether one's perspective is to blame the individual for criminal behavior or to blame society for not providing economic and educational opportunities to break the cycle of crime, crime is an inherent component of the human condition.

While tragic, that reality does not justify mistreating those suspected of committing a crime. That does not mean the suspected criminal must be awarded a prize or patted on the back. It does, however, mean that protecting the suspected criminal is the essence of a democracy. Even if the individual is accused of a heinous crime, guaranteeing protections is essential. Simply put, the vulnerable suspect is in need of protection. That has not always been the case in the United States.

Miranda continued . . .

Since *Chambers v. Florida,* this Court has recognized that coercion can be mental as well as physical, and that the blood of the accused is not the only hallmark of an unconstitutional inquisition.

Interrogation still takes place in privacy. Privacy results in secrecy, and this, in turn, results in a gap in our knowledge as to what, in fact, goes on in the interrogation rooms. A valuable source of information about present police practices, however, may be found in various police manuals and texts, which document procedures employed with success in the past, and which recommend various other effective tactics. These texts are used by law enforcement agencies themselves as guides. It should be noted that these texts professedly present the most enlightened and effective means presently used to obtain statements through custodial interrogation. By considering these texts and other data, it is possible to describe procedures observed and noted around the country.

The officers are told by the manuals that the principal psychological factor contributing to a successful interrogation is *privacy*—being alone with the person under interrogation.

The efficacy of this tactic has been explained as follows:

> If at all practicable, the interrogation should take place in the investigator's office or at least in a room of his own choice. The subject should be deprived of every psychological advantage. In his own home, he may be confident, indignant, or recalcitrant. He is more keenly aware of his rights and more reluctant to tell of his indiscretions or

criminal behavior within the walls of his home. Moreover his family and other friends are nearby, their presence lending moral support. In his own office, the investigator possesses all the advantages. The atmosphere suggests the invincibility of the forces of the law.

To highlight the isolation and unfamiliar surroundings, the manuals instruct the police to display an air of confidence in the suspect's guilt and, from outward appearance, to maintain only an interest in confirming certain details. The guilt of the subject is to be posited as a fact. The interrogator should direct his comments toward the reasons why the subject committed the act, rather than court failure by asking the subject whether he did it. Like other men, perhaps the subject has had a bad family life, had an unhappy childhood, had too much to drink, and had an unrequited desire for women. The officers are instructed to minimize the moral seriousness of the offense, to cast blame on the victim or on society. These tactics are designed to put the subject in a psychological state where his story is but an elaboration of what the police purport to know already—that he is guilty. Explanations to the contrary are dismissed and discouraged.[13]

---

13. *Id.* at 450.

My IDF Service

For twenty years, I served in the Israel Defense Forces, Judge Advocate General's Corps. I had a seat at the table of operational counter-terrorism decision making. I have been involved in complex, complicated, and controversial matters. Relevant to this book are three postings in particular. I served as a Military Court Judge in the Gaza Strip.[14] In addition, I served as a Military Prosecutor in the West Bank[15] and as the Legal Advisor to the Gaza Strip[16] I had command responsibility for the Gaza Strip Military Prosecution.

As a Judge, I convicted and sentenced Palestinians accused by the Military Prosecutor of having committed serious offenses. In a number of cases, I conducted suppression hearings in which defense counsel argued that the confessions were illegally obtained. In one instance, I ruled the confession inadmissible. In another, I limited the scope of a confession that could be admitted.

My decisions reflected an assessment that interrogators crossed the line and the confession was not of the suspect's "free will and volition."[17] In other cases, I denied the suppression request. As part of the suppression hearing, I invited the defense counsel to visit the jail with me. I felt it important to the case and my decisions.

---

14. 1992–1994.
15. 1986–1989.
16. 1994–1997.
17. Israeli jurisprudential terms of art.

I do not know if my decisions were influenced, consciously or otherwise, by the Supreme Court's holding in *Miranda*. On a personal note: I was raised in the United States, graduated from Kenyon College and Case Western Reserve Law School before moving to Israel. This is why I raise this possibility, though it may be a stretch, to draw a direct line between my US education and my IDF decision making. My focus was on assessment of guilt in a difficult situation: Palestinians living under Israeli occupation were committing what Israel defined as acts of terrorism against Palestinians and Israelis.

I did not approach my positions in the IDF from the perspective of an American liberal, but rather as a military officer whose postings were central to the preservation of the rule of law in the context of Palestinian terrorism and Israeli counterterrorism. While undoubtedly influenced by my background, particularly regarding the protection of individual rights, I was similarly aware that the state had an obligation to act forcefully, albeit subject to limits and restraints.

Remand hearings—police or prosecutorial requests to extend detention of suspects—were often held in jails. This gave me unique insight into the interrogation setting. Conducting remand hearings in jail, rather than a courtroom, is controversial and ill-advised. Not only is the setting physically uncomfortable but it also suggests an intimacy between the Court and prison that is inappropriate from the detainee's perspective.

Nevertheless, the countless hours, over a number of years, I spent in prisons gave me a front row seat, and unique insight, into the physicality of jail and the complicated relationship between interrogators, interrogations, and interrogatees. I was able to engage interrogators and suspects alike in informal conversation; we were, after all, sharing a space that bred a certain intimacy. I gained a better understanding of interrogations from the suspect's perspective.

However, I did not delude myself. When a hearing ended, an interrogation would resume that I could neither see nor hear. In the overwhelming majority of cases, detainees confessed. That is akin to the United States. According to available statistics, 80% of suspects confess. That is *after* they have been given the Miranda warning.

These postings shaped my understanding of interrogations, confessions, questions of admissibility, and the complicated relationship between the interrogator and interrogatee. I was confronted on a regular basis with the reality of the interrogation setting.

Of particular importance is my understanding of the physicality of the interrogation setting. While that does not make me an expert on the actual art of interrogation—a unique skill set—my interaction with both participants enables my understanding of both. While I developed great respect for Israeli interrogators, I was not blind to their complicated reality and the need to receive information essential for Israeli national security.

The Landau Commission, convened in the aftermath of an unjustified killing of a Palestinian detained in the aftermath of a terrorist attack and its subsequent cover-up, shed disturbing light on the how the General Security Services[18] conducted interrogations. It was not, to say the least, a positive picture. Quite the opposite. It painted a deeply troubling picture. It brought to light the dark side of interrogations of Palestinians suspected of committing terrorist attacks.

It is fair to assume that the majority of the Israeli public was surprised. The public was caught off guard both by the interrogation methods used and the cover-up, which sought to "frame" a Brigadier General. The assumption, in retrospect unwarranted, was that all Palestinians were interrogated in accordance with acceptable standards of the rule of law. In certain instances, that was incorrect. For some Israelis, akin to some Americans, protecting the public from those wishing to harm innocent members of society justified harsh and coercive interrogation measures. Public commentary in the aftermath of 9/11 made that very clear. That, however, does not translate into legal measures. Rather, that only means the public—or certain elements of the public—are willing to tolerate what Earl Warren held illegal. That was the case in both Israel and the United States.

The Commission's Report led to significant changes in how interrogations were conducted. There was recognition

---

18. In Hebrew, Sherut Bitachon Clali (SHABAK); for years, the English language translation was General Security Services (GSS) later changed to Israel Security Agency (ISA).

of the need to impose limits on interrogators. Establishing clear boundaries was deemed essential on three distinct levels: for the interrogators, for the detainees, and for the liberal democratic values that Israel espouses in the face of Palestinian terrorism.

In the years thereafter, petitions were filed to the Israeli Supreme Court, sitting as the High Court of Justice,[19] on behalf of Palestinians claiming that interrogators had tortured them. While the Supreme Court regularly denied requested relief, the importance of active and robust judicial review cannot be minimized. It forced the intelligence service to explain its methods; it served as notice that limits articulated by the Landau Commission and adopted by the Supreme Court were binding. The principle of imposing limits on interrogators, even in the face of terrorism, is essential to preserving democratic values.

Miranda Continued and Interrogations in the Deep South

Miranda continued . . .

In the cases before us today, given this background, we concern ourselves primarily with this interrogation atmosphere and the evils it can bring. In No. 759,

---

19. In Hebrew: Bet HaMeshpat HaGavoha LeTzedek (BAGATZ).

Miranda v. Arizona, the police arrested the defendant and took him to a special interrogation room, where they secured a confession. In No. 760, *Vignera v. New York,* the defendant made oral admissions to the police after interrogation in the afternoon, and then signed an inculpatory statement upon being questioned by an assistant district attorney later the same evening. In No. 761, *Westover v. United States,* the defendant was handed over to the Federal Bureau of Investigation by local authorities after they had detained and interrogated him for a lengthy period, both at night and the following morning. After some two hours of questioning, the federal officers had obtained signed statements from the defendant. Lastly, in No. 584, *California v. Stewart,* the local police held the defendant five days in the station and interrogated him on nine separate occasions before they secured his inculpatory statement.

In these cases, we might not find the defendants' statements to have been involuntary in traditional terms. Our concern for adequate safeguards to protect precious Fifth Amendment rights is, of course, not lessened in the slightest. In each of the cases, the defendant was thrust into an unfamiliar atmosphere and run through menacing police interrogation procedures. The potentiality for compulsion is forcefully apparent, for example, in *Miranda,* where the indigent Mexican defendant was a seriously disturbed individual with pronounced sexual fantasies, and in *Stewart,* in which the defendant was an indigent Los Angeles Negro who had dropped out of school in the sixth grade. To be sure, the records do not evince overt physical coercion or patent psychological ploys. The fact remains that in none of these cases did the officers undertake to afford appropriate safeguards at the outset of the interrogation to ensure that the statements were truly the product of free choice.

For innumerable decades, blacks were victims of violence facilitated by complicity of local law enforcement officials.[20] This was exacerbated by mistreatment in local jails. The history of black inmates in southern jails has been well documented.[21] The complacency of local communities

---

20. See Mark Curriden & Leroy Phillips, Jr., Contempt of Court, the Turn-of-the-Century Lynching that Launched 100 Years of Federalism 354–55 (2001) (stating that there were 3385 documented mob lynchings of African Americans in the United States between 1882 and 1935); see also W. Fitzhugh Brundage, Lynching in the New South: Georgia and Virginia, 1880–1930, at 262 (1993) (noting that of the 460 lynching victims in Georgia between 1880 and 1930, 441 were African Americans).

21. See generally John C. Knechtle, When to Regulate Hate Speech, 110 Penn St. L. Rev. 539 (2006) (discussing the different approaches taken by the United States and the rest of the international community in dealing with hate speech); Seth F. Kreimer, "Torture Lite," "Full Bodied" Torture, and the Insulation of

contributed to mistreatment. More troubling, many abuses involved the active or passive participation of local law enforcement.[22] In the Deep South, blacks were often rounded up and accused without evidentiary justification.[23] The accusation by a white woman that a black man had sexually assaulted her guaranteed his arrest, regardless of proof; an accusation that he was merely "looking" may have doomed him to "mob rule."[24] In the same vein, many of the detainees in the ill-defined "war on terror" have been detained, devoid of Miranda rights, on a "roundup" basis.[25] The classic

---

Legal Conscience, 1 J. Nat'l Security L. & Pol'y 187 (2005) (discussing the changing legal landscape on torture in the War on Terror); Rutledge, *supra* note 32; Mitchell P. Schwartz, *Compensating Victims of Police-Fabricated Confessions*, 70 U. Chi. L. Rev. 1119 (2003) (discussing the problems with forced confessions).

22. See Brundage, *supra* note 49, at 18; Sherrilyn A. Ifill, *Creating a Truth and Reconciliation Commission for Lynching*, 21 Law & Ineq. 263, 281 (2003).

23. As one example, the 1831 case of Nat Turner involved thousands of slaves acting in rebellion. The response was not to search out the guilty parties for trial, but rather to hang all African American men who either participated or were thought to have done so. Further, night riders were organized with police authority to put down any groupings they determined to be secret meetings. See Herbert Aptheker, A Documentary History of the Negro People in the United States 119 (1951); John A. Davis, *Black, Crime, and American Culture*, 423 Annals Am. Acad. Pol. & Soc. Sci. 89–98 (1976).

24. The Scottsboro Case, which has become the exemplar for "black on white" rapes, was a case where the accuser's "whiteness" overrode any other evidentiary consideration. The accused were convicted and sentenced to death, despite evidence of the accuser's involvement in prostitution and adultery. One spectator told a reporter that the "victim might be a fallen woman, but by God she is a white woman." Lisa Lindquist Dorr, *White Women, Rape, and the Power of Race in Virginia 1900-1960* 2 (2004).

25. Of the 760 detainees brought to Guantanamo Bay in 2002, the military has released 180 without ever charging any of them. Further, 55% of detainees are not charged with having committed any hostile acts against the United States, only 8% of the detainees were characterized as Al-Qaeda fighters, numerous

line from Casablanca—"roundup the usual suspects"—is unfortunately apt.

In 1931, Wickersham Commission Report on Lawlessness in Law Enforcement[26] was established by President Herbert Hoover. Commission's members concluded that suspects had been regularly subjected to "the third degree," defined as "the employment of methods which inflict suffering, physical or mental, upon a person, in order to obtain from that person information about a crime."[27]

The Commission determined willful infliction of pain on criminal suspects was widespread and pervasive. The investigation also revealed that the abusers were not only those interrogating suspects; police officers, judges, magistrates, and other officials of the criminal justice system were also implicated. The Commission found violations in the form of illegal arrests, bribery, coercion of witnesses,

---

individuals have been detained based merely on affiliations with large groups not on the Department of Homeland Security watchlist, and only 5% of detainees were even captured by U.S. forces. See Mark Denbeaux et al., The Guantánamo Detainees during Detention: Data from Department of Defense Records (2006), http://law.shu.edu/news/guantanamo_third_report_7_11_06.pdf.

26. One of fourteen reports published by the National Commission on Law Observance and Enforcement, or "The Wickersham Commission." See Samuel Walker, Records of the Wickersham Commission on Law Observance and Enforcement (Dec. 1977), http://www.lexisnexis.com/academic/guides/jurisprudence/wickersham.asp.

27. National Commission on Law Observance and Enforcement, Report on Lawlessness in Law Enforcement (1931).

fabrication of evidence, and the aforementioned "third degree."[28]

There are significant similarities between the mistreatment in the Deep South and abuses in modern detainee interrogations. Beyond similarities in interrogation methods,[29] there is an unfortunate parallel in the tragedies that result from employing these methods. Just as blacks in the Deep South often died as a result of physical mistreatment, such tragedies have also occurred in detainee interrogations. With respect to ill-treatment in the Deep South, the Supreme Court finally entered the mix. In a series of monumental decisions predicated on the Fifth and Fourteenth Amendments, the Court held that interrogation methods in the Deep South were unconstitutional, and government must immediately extend constitutional protections and due process to remedy the situation.

While *Bram v. United States*[30] did not involve a black person, the Court's holding was critical in subsequent race-based cases. Bram, a first officer, was accused of committing murder on board an American vessel sailing from Boston to

---

28. *Id*. at 3.

29. Techniques authorized by U.S. Secretary of Defense Rumsfeld include the use of stress positions, isolation, hoods over head, removal of comfort items, forced grooming, removal of clothing, and using detainees' phobias to induce stress. See, e.g., Human Rights Watch, Getting Away with Torture? Command Responsibility for the U.S. Abuse of Detainees 29–48 (2005), http://www.hrw.org/reports/2005/us0405/us0405.pdf.

30. *Bram v. United States*, 168 U.S. 532 (1897).

South America.[31] The crew overpowered Bram and placed him in irons until the vessel reached Halifax, where Bram was brought to jail and interrogated by a detective from the Halifax Police Department.[32] Bram's subsequent confession led to his conviction for murder.[33]

Bram appealed, claiming the confession was coerced; the interrogator testified Bram had confessed without undue influence or coercion.[34] Bram's counsel argued Bram had been brought to the detective's private office where he was stripped and interrogated, and that "no statement made by the defendant while so held in custody and his rights interfered with to the extent described was a free and voluntary statement, and no statement as made by him bearing upon this issue was competent."[35] The Court's decision to reverse Bram's conviction established a bright-line rule with respect to threats made during interrogation:

> A confession can never be received in evidence where the prisoner has been influenced by any threat or promise; for the law cannot measure the force of the influence used, or decide upon its effect upon the

---

31. *Id.* at 534.

32. *Id.* at 536–37 (noting that the American consul eventually requested that Bram be brought to Boston where he was formally charged with murder).

33. *Id.* at 540.

34. *Id.* at 538–39.

35. *Id.* at 539.

mind of the prisoner, and therefore excludes the declaration if any degree of influence has been exerted.[36]

The *Bram* rule has never been overturned.[37] Rather, it has been affirmed through incorporation into broader tests, including the "totality of the circumstances" test articulated by the Court in *Ashcraft v. State of Tennessee*,[38] which then morphed[39] into the "shocks the conscience" test in *Rochin v. California* determining whether an interrogation violated a suspect's Fifth and Fourteenth Amendments

---

36. *Id.* at 543.

37. See Mark A. Goodsey, *The New Frontier of Constitutional Confession Law—The International Arena: Exploring the Admissibility of Confessions Taken by U.S. Investigators From Non-Americans Abroad*, 91 Geo. L.J. 851 (2003); Alan Hirsch, *Threats, Promises, and False Confessions: Lessons of Slavery*, 49 How. L.J. 31 (2005); Marvin Zalman, *The Coming Paradigm Shift on Miranda: The Impact of Chavez v. Martinez*, 39 Crim. L. Bull. 4 (2003).

38. *Ashcraft v. Tennessee*, 322 U.S. 143, 148 (1944); see also *Arizona v. Fulminante*, 499 U.S. 279, 285–86 (1991) (holding a jailhouse confession coerced where defendant confessed to a government agent posing as a fellow prisoner, and noting the continued appropriateness of the Bram standard).

39. See David Aram Kaiser, *Note, United States v. Coon: The End of Detrimental Reliance for Plea Agreements?* 52 Hastings L.J. 579 (2001) (noting that for the middle third of the twentieth century, the Court based the rule against admitting coerced confessions primarily, if not exclusively, on notions of due process); MaryAnn Fenicato, *Miranda Upheld by U.S. Supreme Court*, Law. J., Sept. 2000, at 2, available at Westlaw 2 No. 19 LAWYERSJ 2 (explaining that "the due process test was utilized in approximately thirty different cases . . . and continually refined into an inquiry examining whether a defendant's will was overborne by 'weighing the circumstances of pressure against the power of resistance of the person confessing.'"); Edward L. Fiandach, Miranda Revisited, Champion, Nov. 2005, at 22 (describing the Court's return to the rationale of Bram, with a focus on the motivation to make the statement and whether the decision to testify against one's self was "free and voluntary").

rights.[40] Bram's bright-line rule specifically acknowledged that:

> [T]here can be no doubt that long prior to our independence the doctrine that one accused of crime could not be compelled to testify against himself had reached its full development in the common law . . . as resting on the law of nature, and was imbedded in that system as one of its great and distinguishing attributes.[41]

The Supreme Court's initial Deep South interrogation case was in *Brown v. Mississippi*.[42] Brown posed the question as to whether or not convictions based solely on confessions extorted by state officers through brutality and violence were consistent with the Fourteenth Amendment's due process requirement.[43] The holding was, and still is, of particular importance because the "due process doctrine for police interrogations began its life with the Court's dramatic creation of a Fourteenth Amendment exclusionary rule in Brown."[44]

---

40. See *Rochin v. California*, 342 U.S. 165 (1952) (finding that the "shocks the conscience" test stands for the proposition that the police cannot procure evidence for a criminal prosecution in a particularly offensive manner, here a forced stomach pump to look for drugs in defendant's stomach).

41. *Bram v. United States*, 168 U.S. 532, 545 (1897).

42. *Brown v. Mississippi*, 297 U.S. 278 (1936).

43. *Id.* at 279.

44. Catherine Hancock, *Due Process before Miranda*, 70 Tul. L. Rev. 2195, 2203 (1996).

The petitioners in Brown, all of whom were black, were convicted of the murder of a white man and were arrested, indicted, tried, convicted, and sentenced to death in just one week.[45] Upon the discovery of a dead body, local sheriffs retrieved one of the petitioners and took him to the house of the deceased, where a mob had gathered to accuse him of the crime.[46] When the petitioner denied his guilt, the mob seized him and, with the sheriff's assistance, hung him, then let him down before hanging him a second time as Brown repeatedly proclaimed his innocence.

The mob then tied the petitioner to a tree and whipped him, then finally released him to stagger home. The sheriff later returned to Brown's home to arrest him, and while transporting Brown to jail, stopped and severely whipped him, threatening that he would continue until the defendant confessed. Brown finally acceded to the demands and confessed, yet the whippings continued until the confession's specific language was in accordance with that desired by the officers.[47]

The Court held that the trial court should have disallowed the confessions because of the brutality used to procure them. Specifically, the Court used the "totality of the circumstances" approach:

---

45. *Brown*, 297 U.S. at 279.
46. *Id*. at 280–82.
47. *Id*.

There was thus enough before the court when these confessions were first offered to make known to the court that they were not, beyond all reasonable doubt, free and voluntary; and the failure of the court then to exclude the confessions is sufficient to reverse the judgment, under every rule of procedure that has heretofore been prescribed, and hence it was not necessary subsequently to renew the objections by motion or otherwise.[48]

These two watershed cases, *Bram* and *Brown*, extended protections through the use of two constitutional principles: the Fifth Amendment right against self-incrimination in *Bram,* and the Fourteenth Amendment due process clause in *Brown*.[49] In *White v. Texas*, a black farmhand was convicted of rape and subsequently sentenced to death.[50] White was taken to a local jail, where armed officers took him into the woods, asked him to confess, whipped him, and warned him not to tell anyone what transpired.[51] White, who was illiterate, eventually signed a written confession.[52]

---

48. *Id.* at 463.

49. See generally Fenicato, *supra* note 75; Laura Magid, *Deceptive Interrogation Practices: How Far Is Too Far?* 99 Mich. L. Rev. 1168, 1172–73 (2001) ("In 1936 . . . with Brown v. Mississippi, the Court turned to the Due Process Clause of the Fourteenth Amendment as the basis for examining the voluntariness of confessions in dozens of state cases. The Court held that police use of violence was 'revolting to the sense of justice,' stating that '[t]he rack and torture chamber may not be substituted for the witness stand.'").

50. *White v. Texas*, 310 U.S. 530 (1940).

51. *Id.* at 532.

52. *Id.*

In reversing the defendant's conviction, the Court held that "due process of law, preserved for all by our Constitution, commands that no such practice as that disclosed by this record shall send any accused to his death."[53]

Two years later in *Ward v. Texas*, a black man accused of killing a white man appealed his murder conviction, arguing that it was based on a coerced confession.[54] Upon arrest, the police told the defendant that mobs were waiting for him in various towns, and took him from town to town under the cover of night, not allowing him to sleep.[55] Ward contended that he only offered a confession after:

> [He] had been arrested without a warrant, taken from his home town, driven for three days from county to county, placed in a jail more than 100 miles from his home, questioned continuously, and beaten, whipped, and burned by the officer to whom the confession was finally made.[56]

The Ward Court held that accepting the defendant's confession into evidence was a denial of his due process rights because of the cumulative mistreatment[57] to which he was subjected:

---

53. *Id.* at 533 (citing *Chambers v. Florida*, 309 U.S. 227, 241 (1940)).

54. *Ward v. Texas*, 316 U.S. 547 (1942).

55. See *Id.* at 549, 553–55.

56. *Id.* at 549.

57. See infra Part V.C (defining the term and explaining that finding cumulative mistreatment depends on particular circumstances such as amount of

[W]e must conclude that this confession was not free and voluntary but was the product of coercion and duress, that petitioner was no longer able freely to admit or to deny or to refuse to answer, and that he was willing to make any statement that the officers wanted him to make. This Court has set aside convictions based upon confessions extorted from ignorant persons who have been subjected to persistent and protracted questioning, or who have been threatened with mob violence, or who have been unlawfully held incommunicado without advice of friends or counsel, or who have been taken at night to lonely and isolated places for questioning. Any one of these grounds would be sufficient cause for reversal. All of them are to be found in this case.[58]

In *Ashcraft v. Tennessee*, the petitioners claimed their convictions had been improperly extorted by law enforcement officials.[59] Ashcraft was questioned continuously for more than thirty-six hours by a relay of police officers.[60] In reversing the convictions, the Ashcraft Court held that, under the "totality of the circumstances" test, the confessions were

---

movement, specific length of time, number of people, etc., to make a determination of when the "continuousness" breaks the individual's will).

58. *Ward*, 316 U.S. at 555.

59. *Ashcraft v. Tennessee*, 322 U.S. 143, 145 (1944).

60. *Id.* at 153.

compelled through cumulative mistreatment, which was a violation of the Fourteenth Amendment.[61]

Ashcraft is of particular importance because the conviction was overturned on the grounds of cumulative mistreatment, where ". . . Ashcraft from Saturday evening at seven o'clock until Monday morning at approximately nine-thirty never left this homicide room of the fifth floor."[62] The *Ashcraft* dissent, however, was concerned that the majority's position could be construed to mean that any lengthy interrogation was "inherently coercive," and they argued that there still needed to be a focus on the actual coerciveness of the interrogation.[63]

The Bram–Brown progeny's litany of violent and coercive interrogations typifies the treatment of African Americans in the Deep South. African Americans were arrested with little evidentiary cause, subjected to threats of violence and cumulative mistreatment and physically tortured to induce confessions. In each of these cases, the Court took great measures to demand that citizens previously not extended constitutional protections now receive constitutional guarantees afforded to the rest of society.

Akin to black suspects in the cases described above, post-9/11 detainees have, in many instances, been rounded up and detained predicated on vague and unarticulated suspicion

---

61. *Id.* 153–55.
62. See *Id.* at 149.
63. See *Id.* at 157.

of guilt, subjected to violent and degrading interrogations, and held until their will is broken, resulting in unreliable confessions.

Miranda continued . . .

It is obvious that such an interrogation environment is created for no purpose other than to subjugate the individual to the will of his examiner. This atmosphere carries its own badge of intimidation. To be sure, this is not physical intimidation, but it is equally destructive of human dignity. The current practice of incommunicado interrogation is at odds with one of our nation's most cherished principles—that the individual may not be compelled to incriminate himself. Unless adequate protective devices are employed to dispel the compulsion inherent in custodial surroundings, no statement obtained from the defendant can truly be the product of his free choice.

From the foregoing, we can readily perceive an intimate connection between the privilege against self-incrimination and police custodial questioning.[64]

---

64. *Id.* at 458.

The Gatehouse

What Professor Yale Kamisar calls the "gatehouse" shuts the interrogated suspect off from larger society the moment the jailhouse door is slammed.[65] The interrogation begins at *that* moment; the actual interrogation is but a part of the process. Individual liberty and freedom are minimized well before the interrogator asks the initial question.

While the actual interrogation is central to the question this book poses, protection of the individual must not await the encounter between the interrogator and the suspect. Protection is an important word; one must never forget that a vulnerable individual is sitting across from the interrogator.

Unless one has been in the setting, as a participant or an observer, it is impossible to fully appreciate the profound inequality between the two parties. The suspect is as vulnerable as an individual can be. It reflects the reality of an interrogation, whether it be of suspected criminals or suspected terrorists.

As often as the scenes are depicted on the screen, they rarely capture the suspect's vulnerability. More than anything else, it is the suspect's vulnerability, regardless of the crime, that is at the core of the *Miranda* decision. Earl

---

65. Yale Kamisar, *A Look Back at the "Gatehouses and Mansions" of American Criminal Procedure*, 12 Ohio St. J. Crim. L. 645–58 (2015).

Warren came to understand that protecting the suspect was of paramount importance.

The interrogator is in full control of the setting; he represents the full power of the state. The fight is not a contest between equals. Every aspect of the conflict is dictated by the interrogator. The suspect wants a glass of water? The interrogator will decide. The suspect wants to go to the bathroom? The interrogator will decide. The suspect is tired and wishes to rest? The interrogator will decide.

The entire prison infrastructure reinforces the disparity between the interrogator, acting on behalf of the state, and the suspect. When the jail door closes behind the suspect, the state assumes full control. I have seen the reaction of many suspects when they hear that "clang." They understand that it signifies a loss of power and free will. The sound goes well beyond the physical closing of the door; the symbolism is no less powerful. That is true regardless of the nature of the crime in question. Even a seasoned suspect understands the message and its consequences.

I believe Chief Justice Earl Warren clearly recognized this. However, his conduct in a 1936 California murder case raised legitimate questions regarding District Attorney Earl Warren's respect for suspect rights. That is important to recall when we come to address this book's question with the caveat that D.A. Warren's conduct differed significantly from C.J. Warren's opinion.

Miranda continued . . .

Today, then, there can be no doubt that the Fifth Amendment privilege is available outside of criminal court proceedings, and serves to protect persons in all settings in which their freedom of action is curtailed in any significant way from being compelled to incriminate themselves. We have concluded that, without proper safeguards, the process of in-custody interrogation of persons suspected or accused of crime contains inherently compelling pressures that work to undermine the individual's will to resist and to compel him to speak where he would not otherwise do so freely. In order to combat these pressures and to permit a full opportunity to exercise the privilege against self-incrimination, the accused must be adequately and effectively apprised of his rights, and the exercise of those rights must be fully honored.

It is impossible for us to foresee the potential alternatives for protecting the privilege, which might be devised by Congress or the states in the exercise of their creative rule-making capacities. Therefore, we cannot say that the Constitution necessarily requires adherence to any particular solution for the inherent compulsions of the interrogation process as it is presently conducted. Our decision in no way creates a constitutional straitjacket that will handicap sound efforts at reform, nor is it intended to have this effect. We encourage Congress and the States to continue their laudable search for increasingly effective ways of protecting the rights of the individual while promoting efficient enforcement of our criminal laws. However, unless we are shown other procedures that are at least as effective in apprising accused persons of their right of silence and in assuring a continuous opportunity to exercise it, the following safeguards must be observed.

At the outset, if a person in custody is to be subjected to interrogation, he must first be informed in clear and unequivocal terms that he has the right to remain silent. For those unaware of the privilege, the warning is needed simply to make them aware of it—the threshold requirement for an intelligent decision as to its exercise. More important, such a warning is an absolute prerequisite in overcoming the inherent pressures of the interrogation atmosphere. It is not just the subnormal or woefully ignorant who succumb to an interrogator's imprecations, whether implied or expressly stated, that the interrogation will continue until a confession is obtained or that silence in the face of accusation is itself damning, and will bode ill when presented to a jury. Further, the warning will show the individual that his interrogators are prepared to recognize his privilege should he choose to exercise it.

The Fifth Amendment privilege is so fundamental to our system of constitutional rule, and the expedient of giving an adequate warning as to the availability of the privilege so simple, we will not pause to inquire in individual cases whether the defendant was aware of his rights without a warning being given. Assessments of the knowledge the defendant possessed, based on information as to his age, education, intelligence, or prior contact with authorities, can never be more than speculation; a warning is a clear-cut fact. More important, whatever the background of the person interrogated, a warning at the time of the interrogation is indispensable to overcome its pressures and to ensure that the individual knows he is free to exercise the privilege at that point in time.

The warning of the right to remain silent must be accompanied by the explanation that anything said can and will be used against the individual in court. This warning is needed in order to make him aware not only of the privilege, but also of the consequences of forgoing it. It is only through an awareness of these consequences that there can be any assurance of real understanding and intelligent exercise of the privilege. Moreover, this warning may serve to make the individual more acutely aware that he is faced with a phase of the adversary system—that he is not in the presence of persons acting solely in his interest.

The circumstances surrounding in-custody interrogation can operate very quickly to overbear the will of one merely made aware of his privilege by his interrogators. Therefore, the right to have counsel present at the interrogation is indispensable to the protection of the Fifth Amendment privilege under the system we delineate today. Our aim is to assure that the individual's right to choose between silence and speech remains unfettered throughout the interrogation process. A once-stated warning, delivered by those who will conduct the interrogation, cannot itself suffice to that end among those who most require knowledge of their rights. A mere warning given by the interrogators is not alone sufficient to accomplish that end. Prosecutors themselves claim that the admonishment of the right to remain silent, without more, "will benefit only the recidivist and the professional." Even preliminary advice given to the accused by his own attorney can be swiftly overcome by the secret interrogation process. Thus, the need for counsel to protect the Fifth Amendment privilege comprehends not merely a right to consult with counsel prior to questioning, but also to have counsel present during any questioning if the defendant so desires.[66]

If an individual indicates that he wishes the assistance of counsel before any interrogation occurs, the authorities cannot rationally ignore or deny his request on the basis that the individual does not have or cannot afford a retained attorney. The financial ability of the individual has no relationship to the scope of the rights involved here. The privilege against self-incrimination secured by the Constitution applies to all individuals. The need for counsel in order to protect the privilege exists for the indigent as well as the affluent. In fact, were we to limit these constitutional rights to those who can retain an attorney, our decisions today would be of little significance. The cases before us, as well as the vast majority of confession cases with which we have dealt in the past, involve those unable to retain counsel. While authorities are not required to relieve the accused of his poverty, they have the obligation not to take advantage of indigence in the administration of justice. Denial of counsel to the indigent at the time of interrogation while allowing an attorney to those who can afford one would be no more supportable by reason or logic than the similar situation at trial and on

---

66. *Id.* at 469–70.

appeal struck down in *Gideon v. Wainwright* and *Douglas v. California*.

In order fully to apprise a person interrogated of the extent of his rights under this system, then, it is necessary to warn him not only that he has the right to consult with an attorney, but also that, if he is indigent, a lawyer will be appointed to represent him. Without this additional warning, the admonition of the right to consult with counsel would often be understood as meaning only that he can consult with a lawyer if he has one or has the funds to obtain one. The warning of a right to counsel would be hollow if not couched in terms that would convey to the indigent—the person most often subjected to interrogation—the knowledge that he too has a right to have counsel present. As with the warnings of the right to remain silent and of the general right to counsel, only by effective and express explanation to the indigent of this right can there be assurance that he was truly in a position to exercise it.

Once warnings have been given, the subsequent procedure is clear. If the individual indicates in any manner, at any time prior to or during questioning, that he wishes to remain silent, the interrogation must cease. At this point, he has shown that he intends to exercise his Fifth Amendment privilege; any statement taken after the person invokes his privilege cannot be other than the product of compulsion, subtle or otherwise. Without the right to cut off questioning, the setting of in-custody interrogation operates on the individual to overcome free choice in producing a statement after the privilege has been once invoked. If the individual states that he wants an attorney, the interrogation must cease until an attorney is present. At that time, the individual must have an opportunity to confer with the attorney and to have him present during any subsequent questioning. If the individual cannot obtain an attorney and he indicates that he wants one before speaking to police, they must respect his decision to remain silent.

This does not mean, as some have suggested, that each police station must have a "station house lawyer" present at all times to advise prisoners. It does mean, however, that, if police propose to interrogate a person, they must make known to him that he is entitled to a lawyer and that, if he cannot afford one, a lawyer will be provided for him prior to any interrogation. If authorities conclude that they will not provide counsel during a reasonable period of time in which investigation in the field is carried out, they may refrain from doing so without violating the person's Fifth Amendment privilege so long as they do not question him during that time.

If the interrogation continues without the presence of an attorney and a statement is taken, a heavy burden rests on the government to demonstrate that the defendant knowingly and intelligently waived his privilege against self-incrimination and his right to retained or appointed counsel. This Court has always set high standards of proof for the waiver of constitutional rights, and we reassert these standards as applied to in-custody interrogation. Since the state is responsible for establishing the isolated circumstances under which the interrogation takes place, and has the only means of making available corroborated evidence of warnings given during incommunicado interrogation, the burden is rightly on its shoulders.[67]

The principles announced today deal with the protection that must be given to the privilege against self-incrimination when the individual is first subjected to police interrogation while in custody at the station or otherwise deprived of his freedom of action in any significant way. It is at this point that our adversary system of criminal proceedings commences, distinguishing itself at the outset from the inquisitorial system recognized in some countries. Under the system of warnings we delineate today, or under any other system that may be devised and found effective, the safeguards to

---

67. *Id*. at. 475.

be erected about the privilege must come into play at this point.

Our decision is not intended to hamper the traditional function of police officers in investigating crime. When an individual is in custody on probable cause, the police may, of course, seek out evidence in the field to be used at trial against him. Such investigation may include inquiry of persons not under restraint. General on-the-scene questioning as to facts surrounding a crime or other general questioning of citizens in the fact-finding process is not affected by our holding. It is an act of responsible citizenship for individuals to give whatever information they may have to aid in law enforcement. In such situations, the compelling atmosphere inherent in the process of in-custody interrogation is not necessarily present.

In dealing with statements obtained through interrogation, we do not purport to find all confessions inadmissible. Confessions remain a proper element in law enforcement. Any statement given freely and voluntarily without any compelling influences is, of course, admissible in evidence. The fundamental import of the privilege while an individual is in custody is not whether he is allowed to talk to the police without the benefit of warnings and counsel, but whether he can be interrogated. There is no requirement that police stop a person who enters a police station and states that he wishes to confess to a crime, or a person who calls the police to offer a confession or any other statement he desires to make. Volunteered statements of any kind are not barred by the Fifth Amendment, and their admissibility is not affected by our holding today.

To summarize, we hold that when an individual is taken into custody or otherwise deprived of his freedom by the authorities in any significant way and is subjected to questioning, the privilege against self-incrimination is jeopardized. Procedural safeguards must be employed to protect the privilege, and unless other fully effective means are adopted to notify the person of his right of silence and to assure that the exercise of the right will be scrupulously honored, the following measures are required. He must be warned prior to any questioning that he has the right to remain silent, that anything he says can be used against him in a court of law, that he has the right to the presence of an attorney, and that, if he cannot afford an attorney one will be appointed for him prior to any questioning if he so desires. Opportunity to exercise these rights must be afforded to him throughout the interrogation. After such warnings have been given, and such opportunity afforded him, the individual may knowingly and intelligently waive these rights and agree to answer questions or make a statement. But unless and until such warnings and waiver are demonstrated by the prosecution at trial, no evidence obtained as a result of interrogation can be used against him.[68]

---

68. *Id.* at 478–79.

Chapter Six

The Dissents, Oral Arguments, and Controversy of *Miranda*

Miranda Decision Said to End the Effective Use of Confessions

Special to The New York Times
BOULDER, Colo., Aug. 20—
The Supreme Court's decision in
Miranda v. Arizona virtually
puts an end to the effective use
of criminal confessions, a former president of the American
Trial Lawyers Association said
today.

He spoke at the University of
Colorado during a daylong session of lawyers and law enforcement officers from the Rocky
Mountain area.

The speaker, Jacob Fuchs-
berg of New York, said he construed the Miranda decision to
mean that no statement may be
taken by the police unless a
lawyer is present.

And a lawyer would not permit a defendant to say anything, he added.

Mr. Fuchsberg noted that
many defendants, when they
come to trial, repudiate confes-

sions they are alleged to have
made.

"The fact that they do this,"
he said, "is proof the defendant
did not do what he wanted to do
when he supposedly waived his
rights."

Anyone who refuses the presence of an attorney, Mr. Fuchsberg said, is either stupid or if
he cannot afford a lawyer,
uneducated and therefore not in
a position to waive his rights.

Mr. Fuchsberg was one of
several authorities on criminal
law who spoke at the session,
which was aimed at familiar-
izing lawyers and law enforcement officers with the effects
of the Miranda decision and
other recent Supreme Court
decisions.

The Miranda decision, which
was handed down last June 13,
placed rigid restrictions on interrogation of suspects in police
custody.

The Court held, in an opinion
written by Chief Justice Earl
Warren, that the police must
warn a suspect of his right to
remain silent, must warn him
that anything he says may be
used against him in court, must
advise him of his right to counsel, and must inform him that
the state will appoint one for
him.

Panelists here agreed that
the Miranda decision was a
giant step toward the ultimate
demise of the confession as a
law enforcement tool.

Judge Horace W. Gilmore, of
the Michigan Circuit Court,
said the only chance the police
have of proving that a suspect
waived his rights is either by
the use of videotape or tape
record, or by allowing a magistrate to inform the defendant
of his rights.

Detective Chief Vincent Pier-

sante of the Detroit Police Department told the audience that
confessions were not as vital as
they used to be.

He said that in 1961 confessions in his department were
considered essential in 23.6 per
cent of the cases prosecuted. In
1965, he said, the figure had
dropped to 15.2 per cent.

Mr. Piersante said his officers
had been putting together better cases, cases that do not depend on the defendant's own
statement.

Duane Nedrud, executive director of the National District
Attorneys Association Founda-
tion, cited reports by police officials that confessions had been
apparently decreased si

HIGH COURT PUTS NEW CURB ON POWERS OF THE POLICE TO INTERROGATE SUSPECTS

gated a suspect without giving
him the warning prescribed in
Miranda, can the evidence obtained as a result of such an interrogation be admitted as evidence during the trial?

Prof. B. J. George Jr. of the
University of Michigan Law
School said the Miranda case
did not answer that question.
However, he said, one paragraph in the decision hinted
that the Court would not allow
such evidence.

Prof. Yale Kamisar, also of
the University of Michigan,
contended that the Court
clearly indicated it would not

said, means only that these
partments are apparently
Where police have inter-

The New York Times
Published: August 21, 1966
Copyright © The New York Times

DISSENTERS BITTER

Four View Limitation
on Confessions as
Aid to Criminals

The Dissents

Justices Harlan and White dissented; Justice Clark dissented in part and concurred in part; Justice Stewart
joined the Harlan and White dissents. The dissents were
clear and emphatic. They expressed strong criticism of the
majority opinion and grave concern regarding its practical

consequences. Justice Harlan's opening sentence, *"I believe the decision of the Court represents poor constitutional law and entails harmful consequences for the country at large,"* summarizes the concern and criticism.

Harlan was particularly concerned that suspects will not confess in the future and the subsequent impact on society and law enforcement in the face of such a development. Harlan's concluding sentence decisively summarizes his opposition: *"This Court is forever adding new stories to the temples of constitutional law, and the temples have a way of collapsing when one story too many is added."*[1]

Justice White's dissent is particularly forceful; this sentence highlights his dismay: *"I have no desire whatsoever to share the responsibility for any such impact on the present criminal process."* That is as clear a repudiation as can be articulated by a dissenting Supreme Court Justice, particularly of an opinion authored by the Chief Justice. White's concerns regarding the practical consequences of the decision are articulated in these two sentences:

> *"The rule announced today will measurably weaken the ability of the criminal law to perform these tasks. It is a deliberate calculus to prevent interrogations, to reduce the incidence of confessions and pleas of guilty, and to increase the number of trials."*

---

1. Yale Kamisar, *A Look Back at the "Gatehouses and Mansions" of American Criminal Procedure*, 12 Ohio St. J. Crim. L. 526 (2015).

The "battle lines" were clearly demarcated: the majority opinion and dissents articulated two distinct paradigms regarding the interrogator–suspect relationship. The differences between the majority and dissents were great; there was no middle ground that could bridge the distinct approaches. Clark's dissent–concurrence does not bridge the gap. Warren's emphasis on the Fifth Amendment right of the suspects was an anathema to the four Justices who opposed him.

His emphasis on preserving the privilege against self-incrimination was unacceptable to them, jurisprudentially and practically alike. The dissents focused on larger societal considerations and cast doubt whether the Fifth Amendment privilege extended to the interrogation setting. Their practical concern was that the majority's holding would significantly reduce the number of confessions, thereby harming law enforcement directly and society indirectly.

The two—the majority and the dissent—viewed the issue before the Court from two distinct perspectives, of that there is no doubt. The majority focused on the suspect; the dissent questioned Warren's jurisprudence and emphasized its negative impact on society.

Akin to including excerpts from Warren's majority opinion, I have chosen to share with the reader excerpts from the three dissents.

I do so with the hope that the reader will benefit from reading these passages.

Miranda continued . . .

JUSTICE HARLAN

I believe the decision of the Court represents poor constitutional law and entails harmful consequences for the country at large. How serious these consequences may prove to be, only time can tell. But the basic flaws in the Court's justification seem to me readily apparent now, once all sides of the problem are considered.

Introduction

At the outset, it is well to note exactly what is required by the Court's new constitutional code of rules for confessions. The foremost requirement, upon which later admissibility of a confession depends, is that a fourfold warning be given to a person in custody before he is questioned, namely, that he has a right to remain silent, that anything he says may be used against him, that he has a right to have present an attorney during the questioning, and that, if indigent, he has a right to a lawyer without charge. To forgo these rights, some affirmative statement of rejection is seemingly required, and threats, tricks, or cajolings to obtain this waiver are forbidden. If, before or during questioning, the suspect seeks to invoke his right to remain silent, interrogation must be forgone or cease; a request for counsel brings about the same result until a lawyer is procured. Finally, there are a miscellany of minor directives, for example, the burden of proof of waiver is on the state, admissions and exculpatory statements are treated just like confessions, withdrawal of a waiver is always permitted, and so forth.

While the fine points of this scheme are far less clear than the Court admits, the tenor is quite apparent. The new rules are not designed to guard against police brutality or other unmistakably banned forms of coercion. Those who use third-degree tactics and deny them in court are equally able and destined to lie as skillfully about warnings and waivers. Rather, the thrust of the new rules is to negate all pressures, to reinforce the nervous or ignorant suspect, and ultimately to discourage any confession at all. The aim, in short, is toward "voluntariness" in a utopian sense, or, to view it from a different angle, voluntariness with a vengeance.

To incorporate this notion into the Constitution requires a strained reading of history and precedent and a disregard of the very pragmatic concerns that alone may on occasion justify such strains. I believe that reasoned examination will show that the Due Process Clauses provide an adequate tool for coping with confessions, and that, even if the Fifth Amendment privilege against self-incrimination be invoked, its precedents, taken as a whole, do not sustain the present rules. Viewed as a choice based on pure policy, these new rules prove to be a highly debatable, if not one-sided, appraisal of the competing interests, imposed over widespread objection, at the very time when judicial restraint is most called for by the circumstances.[2]

In conclusion: nothing in the letter or the spirit of the Constitution or in the precedents squares with the heavy-handed and one-sided action that is so precipitously taken by the Court in the name of fulfilling its constitutional responsibilities. The foray that the Court makes today brings to mind the wise and farsighted words of Mr. Justice Jackson in *Douglas v. Jeannette:*

> This Court is forever adding new stories to the temples of constitutional law, and the temples have a way of collapsing when one story too many is added.[3]

JUSTICE WHITE

The proposition that the privilege against self-incrimination forbids in-custody interrogation without the warnings specified in the majority opinion and without a clear waiver of counsel has no significant

2. *Id.* at 505.
3. *Id.* at 526.

support in the history of the privilege or in the language of the Fifth Amendment. As for the English authorities and the common law history, the privilege, firmly established in the second half of the seventeenth century, was never applied except to prohibit compelled judicial interrogations. The rule excluding coerced confessions matured about one hundred years later,

> [b]ut there is nothing in the reports to suggest that the theory has its roots in the privilege against self-incrimination. And, so far as the cases reveal, the privilege, as such, seems to have been given effect only in judicial proceedings, including the preliminary examinations by authorized magistrates.[4]

Criticism of the Court's opinion, however, cannot stop with a demonstration that the factual and textual bases for the rule it propounds are, at best, less than compelling. Equally relevant is an assessment of the rule's consequences measured against community values. The Court's duty to assess the consequences of its action is not satisfied by the utterance of the truth that a value of our system of criminal justice is "to respect the inviolability of the human personality" and to require government to produce the evidence against the accused by its own independent labors. More than

---

4. *Id.* at 526.

the human dignity of the accused is involved; the human personality of others in the society must also be preserved. Thus, the values reflected by the privilege are not the sole desideratum; society's interest in the general security is of equal weight.

The obvious underpinning of the Court's decision is a deep-seated distrust of all confessions. As the Court declares that the accused may not be interrogated without counsel present, absent a waiver of the right to counsel, and as the Court all but admonishes the lawyer to advise the accused to remain silent, the result adds up to a judicial judgment that evidence from the accused should not be used against him in any way, whether compelled or not. This is the not so subtle overtone of the opinion—that it is inherently wrong for the police to gather evidence from the accused himself. And this is precisely the nub of this dissent. I see nothing wrong or immoral, and certainly nothing unconstitutional, in the police's asking a suspect whom they have reasonable cause to arrest whether or not he killed his wife, or in confronting him with the evidence on which the arrest was based, at least where he has been plainly advised that he may remain completely silent, see *Escobedo v. Illinois*. Until today, "the admissions or confessions of the prisoner, when voluntarily and freely made, have always ranked high in the scale of incriminating evidence." Particularly when corroborated, as where the police have confirmed the accused's disclosure of the hiding place of implements or fruits of the crime, such confessions have the highest reliability and significantly contribute to the certitude with which we may believe the accused is guilty. Moreover, it is by no means certain that the process of confessing is injurious to the accused. To the contrary, it may provide psychological relief, and enhance the prospects for rehabilitation. This is not to say that the value of respect for the inviolability of the accused's individual personality should be accorded no weight, or that all confessions should be indiscriminately admitted. This Court has long read the Constitution to proscribe compelled confessions, a salutary rule from which there should be no retreat. But I see no sound basis, factual or otherwise, and the Court gives none, for concluding that the present rule against the receipt of coerced confessions is inadequate for the task of sorting out inadmissible evidence, and must be replaced by the *per se* rule, which is now imposed. Even if the new concept can be said to have advantages of some sort over the present law, they are far outweighed by its likely undesirable impact on other very relevant and important interests.[5]

---

5. *Id.* at 537–39.

The rule announced today will measurably weaken the ability of the criminal law to perform these tasks. It is a deliberate calculus to prevent interrogations, to reduce the incidence of confessions and pleas of guilty, and to increase the number of trials. Criminal trials, no matter how efficient the police are, are not sure bets for the prosecution, nor should they be if the evidence is not forthcoming. Under the present law, the prosecution fails to prove its case in about 30% of the criminal cases actually tried in the federal courts. But it is something else again to remove from the ordinary criminal case all those confessions that heretofore have been held to be free and voluntary acts of the accused, and to thus establish a new constitutional barrier to the ascertainment of truth by the judicial process. There is, in my view, every reason to believe that a good many criminal defendants who otherwise would have been convicted on what this Court has previously thought to be the most satisfactory kind of evidence will now, under this new version of the Fifth Amendment, either not be tried at all or will be acquitted if the state's evidence, minus the confession, is put to the test of litigation.

I have no desire whatsoever to share the responsibility for any such impact on the present criminal process.

In some unknown number of cases, the Court's rule will return a killer, a rapist, or other criminal to the streets and to the environment that produced him, to repeat his crime whenever it pleases him. As a consequence, there will not be a gain, but a loss, in human dignity. The real concern is not the unfortunate consequences of this new decision on the criminal law as an abstract, disembodied series of authoritative proscriptions, but the impact on those who rely on the public authority for protection, and who, without it, can only engage in violent self-help with guns, knives, and the help of their neighbors similarly inclined. There is, of course, a saving factor: the next victims are uncertain, unnamed, and unrepresented in this case.[6]

JUSTICE CLARK

It is with regret that I find it necessary to write in these cases. However, I am unable to join the majority because its opinion goes too far on too little, while my dissenting brethren do not go quite far enough. Nor can I join in the Court's criticism of the present practices of police and investigatory agencies as to custodial

---

6. *Id.* at 542–43.

interrogation. The materials it refers to as "police manuals" are, as I read them, merely writings in this field
by professors and some police officers. Not one is shown
by the record here to be the official manual of any police
department, much less in universal use in crime detection. Moreover, the examples of police brutality mentioned by the Court are rare exceptions to the thousands
of cases that appear every year in the law reports. The
police agencies—all the way from municipal and state
forces to the federal bureaus—are responsible for law
enforcement and public safety in this country. I am
proud of their efforts, which, in my view, are not fairly
characterized by the Court's opinion.

Introduction

The *ipse dixit* of the majority has no support in our
cases. Indeed, the Court admits that "we might not
find the defendants' statements [here] to have been
involuntary in traditional terms." In short, the Court
has added more to the requirements that the accused
is entitled to consulting with his lawyer and that he
must be given the traditional warning that he may
remain silent and that anything that he says may be
used against him. *Escobedo v. Illinois,* now the Court
fashions a constitutional rule that the police may

engage in no custodial interrogation without addition-ally advising the accused that he has a right under the Fifth Amendment to the presence of counsel during interrogation and that, if he is without funds, counsel will be furnished to him. When, at any point during an interrogation, the accused seeks affirmatively or impliedly to invoke his rights to silence or counsel, interrogation must be forgone or postponed. The Court further holds that failure to follow the new procedures requires inexorably the exclusion of any statement by the accused, as well as the fruits thereof. Such a strict constitutional specific inserted at the nerve center of crime detection may well kill the patient. Since there is at this time a paucity of information and an almost total lack of empirical knowledge on the practical operation of requirements truly comparable to those announced by the majority, I would be more restrained, lest we go too far too fast.[7]

Oral Arguments

Oral arguments were held on February 28th and March 1, 1966.

Those arguing included some of America's greatest attorneys. To help the reader better understand the decision, its

---

7. *Id.* at 500–01.

controversies, and complexities, I have decided to include three oral arguments: Mr. John Flynn on behalf of Miranda; Mr. Gary Nelson on behalf of the State of Arizona, and Mr. Duane Nedrud on behalf of the National District Attorneys Association.

Presenting the arguments in full enables the reader to better understand the issues and dilemmas before the Court; the questions the Justices posed to Flynn, Nelson, and Nedrud highlight their concerns and leanings. The answers reflect the diametrically opposed perspectives ultimately reflected in the majority and dissent.

The questions were direct and thoughtful; the responses were respectful and framed, naturally, in accordance with the particular position advocated. All three advocates clearly understood the significance of the moment and the ramifications of their positions.

Even when arguing on behalf of their clients, Flynn, Nelson, and Nedrud were respectful regarding the larger issues at stake. There is no doubt all three recognized the Court was considering extending protection to a suspect at the moment of custody. In subsequent years, there has been uncertainty and dispute regarding the practical application of the term *custody*. A careful reading of Warren's writings suggests that he understood the term to mean when the suspect is arrested and denied freedom of movement.

The essence of the *Miranda* holding is that it is *at that point* that the warnings established in the holding are to be extended to the suspect. That was the natural progression after *Escobedo*. Unclear was whether the mechanism for extension was to be the Fifth or Sixth Amendment. The oral arguments reflect that uncertainty: for Flynn, extending protection to the suspect was paramount; for Nelson and Nedrud, such an extension was highly problematic given the clear interests and concerns of their respective clients.

With that, we turn to the oral arguments.

MR. CHIEF JUSTICE WARREN: No. *759, Ernesto A. Miranda,* petitioner, versus *Arizona.* We'll wait just a few moments until you get seated.

Mr. Flynn, you may proceed.

ORAL ARGUMENT OF JOHN J. FLYNN, ESQ., ON BEHALF OF THE PETITIONER

MR. FLYNN: Mr. Chief Justice, may it please the Court:

This case concerns itself with the conviction of a defendant of two crimes of rape and kidnapping, the sentences on each count of 20 to 30 years to run concurrently.

I should point out to the Court, in an effort to avoid possible confusion, that the defendant was convicted in a companion case of the crime of robbery in a completely separate and independent act; however, the Supreme Court of the State of Arizona treated that conviction as a companion case in a companion decision, and portions of that record have been appended to the record in this case, as it bears on the issue before the Court.

Now the issue before the Court is the admission into evidence of the defendant's confession, under the facts and circumstances of this case, over the specific objections of his trial counsel that it had been given in the absence of counsel.

The Trial Court in June of 1963, prior to this Court's decision in *Escobedo,* allowed the confession into evidence. The Supreme Court of the State of Arizona in April of 1965, after this Court's decision in *Escobedo,* affirmed the conviction and the admission of the confession into evidence. This Court has granted us review.

The facts in the case indicate that the defendant was 23 years old, of Spanish-American extraction; that on the morning of March 13, 1963, he was arrested at his home, taken down to the police station by two officers named Young and Cooley; that at the police station he was immediately placed in a line-up. He was here identified by the prosecutrix in this case and later identified by the prosecutrix in the robbery case. Immediately after the interrogations, he was taken into the police confessional at approximately 11:30 a.m. and by 1:30 they had obtained from him an oral confession.

MR. JUSTICE BRENNAN: What is the "police confessional?"

MR. FLYNN: The interrogation room, described in the transcript as Interrogation Room No. 2, if Your Honor please.

He denied his guilt, according to the officers, at the commencement of the interrogation, and by 1:30 he had confessed. I believe the record indicates that at no time during the interrogation and prior to his oral confession was he advised either of his rights to remain silent, his right to counsel, or of his right to consult with counsel; nor, indeed, was such the practice in Arizona at that time, as admitted by the officers in their testimony.

The defendant was then asked to sign a confession, to which he agreed. The form handed him to write on contained a typed statement as follows, which precedes his hand-written confession:

"I, Ernesto A. Miranda, do hereby swear that I make this statement voluntarily and of my own free will, with no threats, coercion, or promises of immunity, and with full knowledge of my legal rights, understanding any statement I make may be used against me."

This statement was read to him by the officers, and he confessed in his own handwriting. Throughout the interrogation the defendant did not request counsel at any time. In due course the Trial Court appointed counsel to defend him in both cases, and defense counsel requested a psychiatric examination, which has been made—and the medical report—has been made a portion of the transcript of the record in this case, as it enlightens us to a portion or some of the factual information surrounding the defendant.

MR. JUSTICE FORTAS: Mr. Flynn, I am sorry to interrupt you, but you said that Miranda was not told that he might remain silent? Did you say that?

MR. FLYNN: That is correct, Your Honor.

MR. JUSTICE FORTAS: Is there a dispute as to that?

MR. FLYNN: Yes, there is, Your Honor, and I believe it arises as a result of the appendix to the robbery conviction. In this respect, I would answer Your Honor's question by referring to page 52 of the petitioner's brief, to the appendix at the top, at which the question was asked by Mr. Moore, the trial counsel:

Question: "Did you state to the defendant at any time before he made the statement you are about to answer to, that anything he said would be held against him?"

Answer: "No, sir."

Question: "You didn't warn him of that?"

Answer: "No, sir."

Question: "Did you warn him of his rights to an attorney?"

Answer: "No, sir."

"Mr. Moore: We object, not voluntarily given."

"Mr. Turoff: I don't believe that is necessary."

"The Court: Overruled."

On page 53, the succeeding page, a portion of the same record indicates further examination concerning this conversation, and starting approximately one-third down the page.

Question: "Had you offered the defendant any immunity?"

Answer: "No, sir."

Question: "In your presence, had Officer Cooley done any of these acts?"

Answer: "No, sir."

Question: "About what time did this conversation take place, Officer?"

Answer: "Approximately 1:30."

Question: "Shortly after Miss McDaniels made her first statement, is that correct?"

Answer: "Yes, sir."

Question: "Can you tell us now, Officer, regarding the charge of robbery, what was said to the defendant and what the defendant answered in your presence?"

Answer: "I asked Mr. Miranda if he recognized—" and there the questioning terminates.

MR. JUSTICE FORTAS: I was referring to page 4 of your brief in which you say that Officer Young believes that Miranda was told that he need not answer their questions.

MR. FLYNN: I was about to continue, if Your Honor please, to page 54, in which we find the question:

"You never warned him he was entitled to an attorney or anything he said would be held against him, did you?"

"Answer: We told him anything he said would be used against him; he wasn't required by law to tell us anything."

Consequently, this would answer Your Honor's question, except bearing in mind that the record clearly reveals that from the line-up and the identification to the interrogation room, the officers established the time as 11:30, and that the confession was completed and signed at 1:30.

Reading the testimony of the robbery conviction, it is apparent to me that the officers, when they recite or answered on page 54 of the transcript that he had been advised of his rights, were again relating to this formal typed heading, which would be at 1:30, at the time he signed a confession; that, hence, there really is no conflict in the record as to when he was advised of his rights.

The further history relating to this defendant found in the psychiatric examination would indicate that he had an eighth-grade education, and it was found by the Supreme Court that he had a prior criminal record and that he was mentally abnormal. He was found, however, to be competent to stand trial and legally sane at the time of the commission of the alleged acts.

Now, the critical aspect of the defendant's confession, I think, is eminently demonstrated when, during the trial, the prosecutrix was asked the question concerning penetration, in which she first responded that she thought it was by finger, under questioning by the prosecuting attorney. Immediately thereafter, she expressed uncertainty as to the manner or method of penetration and, after some prompting, responded to the prosecuting attorney that it had been, in fact, by the male organ. On cross-examination, she again expressed the uncertainty in relation to this penetration which, of course, is the essential element of the crime of first-degree rape in the State of Arizona, when she responded to his question that she simply was unsure whether it had been by finger or by penis.

Now of course the defendant's confession neatly corrects this "reasonable doubt" that otherwise would have been engendered, when in precise terminology he wrote, "Asked her to lie down, and she did. Could not get penis into vagina. Got about one-half(half) inch in."

The only thing missing, or the only thing that the officers failed to supply in words to this defendant at the time he wrote this confession, was in violation of Section 13–611, Arizona Revised Statutes. Then, of course, they would have had the classic confession of conviction, because they could have argued that the man even knew the statutory provisions relating to rape.

The State, as I read their response, takes no issue with the statement of facts as I have outlined them to this Court, except to say that we overstate his mental condition and minimize his educational background; and also the concern that is expressed by Mr. Justice Fortas concerning at what stage of the proceeding he may have been advised of his right to remain silent.

Now the Petitioner's position on the issue is simply this: The Arizona Supreme Court, we feel, has imprisoned this Court's decision in *Escobedo* on its facts, and by its decision is refusing to apply the principles of that case, and for all practical purposes has emasculated it. Certainly every court desiring to admit a confession can find distinguishing factors in *Escobedo* from the fact situation before it.

I would like to very briefly quote from the transcript of the record which contains the Arizona decision at page 87:

"It will be noted that the Court in the *Escobedo* case set forth the circumstances under which a statement would be held admissible, namely: One, the general inquiry into an unsolved crime must have begun to focus on a particular suspect; two, a suspect must have been taken into the police custody; three, the police in its interrogation must have elicited an incriminating statement; four, the suspect must have requested and been denied an opportunity to consult with his lawyer; five, the police must not have effectively warned the suspect of his constitutional rights to remain silent. When all of these five factors occur, then the *Escobedo* case is a controlling precedent."

The Arizona Supreme Court, having indicated its clear intention to imprison the *Escobedo* decision, set about to do precisely that. First, as to the focusing question, it indicated that this crime had occurred at night. Consequently, despite the positive identification of the defendant by two witnesses, which the State urged were entirely fair line-ups, the Supreme Court of Arizona indicated that even then perhaps under these facts, attention had not focused upon this defendant.

I think this is sheer sophistry and would indicate the obvious intent of the Arizona Supreme Court to confine *Escobedo* and to distinguish it whenever possible.

Next, the Court found that the defendant was advised of his rights in the reading of the typed portion immediately preceding its transcript. They permitted that document to lift itself by its own bootstraps, so to speak, and to indicate that here was a man who was knowledgeable concerning his legal rights, despite the facts and circumstances of his background and education. They further found that he was knowledgeable because he had a prior criminal record, though in the decision he indicated this would be knowledge of his rights in court and certainly not his rights at the time of the interrogation.

I think the numerous briefs filed in this case indicating the substantial split in the decisions throughout the various states, the circuits and the Federal district courts, indicate the interpretation that has been placed upon *Escobedo*. On the one hand, we have the California decision in *Dorado*. We have the Third Circuit decision in *Russo*, which would indicate that principle and logic are being applied to the decision, and in the words of Mr. Justice Goldberg, that when the process shifts from the investigation to one of accusation, and when the purpose is to elicit a confession from the defendant, then the adversary process comes into being.

On the other hand, the other cases that would distinguish this have found and give rise to what I submit is not really confusion by merely straining against the principles and logic in that decision.

MR. JUSTICE STEWART: What do you think is the result of the adversary process coming into being when this focusing takes place? What follows from that? Is there, then, a right to a lawyer?

MR. FLYNN: I think that the man at that time has the right to exercise, if he knows, and under the present state of the law in Arizona, if he is rich enough, and if he's educated enough to assert his Fifth Amendment right, and if he recognizes that he has a Fifth Amendment right to request counsel. But I simply say that at that stage of the proceeding, under the facts and circumstances in *Miranda* of a man of limited education, of a man who certainly is mentally abnormal who is certainly an indigent, that when that adversary process came into being that the police, at the very least, had an obligation to extend to this man not only his clear Fifth Amendment right, but to accord to him the right of counsel.

MR. JUSTICE STEWART: I suppose, if you really mean what you say or what you gather from what the *Escobedo* decision says, the adversary process starts at that point, and every single protection of the Constitution then comes into being, does it not? You have to bring a jury in there, I suppose?

MR. FLYNN: No, Your Honor, I wouldn't bring a jury in. I simply would extend to the man those constitutional rights which the police, at that time, took away from him.

MR. JUSTICE STEWART: That's begging the question. My question is, what are those rights when the focusing begins? Are these all the panoply of rights guaranteed to the defendant in a criminal trial?

MR. FLYNN: I think the first right is the Fifth Amendment right: the right not to incriminate oneself; the right to know you have that right; and the right to consult with counsel, at the very least, in order that you can exercise the right, Your Honor.

MR. JUSTICE STEWART: Well, I don't fully understand your answer, because if the adversary process then begins, then what you have is the equivalent of a trial, do you not? And then I suppose you have a right to a judge, and a jury, and everything else that goes with a trial right, then and there. If you have something less than that, then this is not an adversary proceeding and then you don't mean what you're saying.

MR. FLYNN: I think what I say—what I am interpreting "adversary proceeding" to mean is that at that time, a person who is poorly educated, who in essence is mentally abnormal, who is an indigent, that at an adversary proceeding, at the very least, he is entitled at that stage of the proceeding to be represented by counsel and to be advised by counsel of his rights under the Fifth Amendment of the Constitution; or, he has no such right.

MR. JUSTICE STEWART: Well, again I don't mean to quibble, and I apologize, but I think it's first important to define what those rights are—what his rights under the constitution are at that point. He can't be advised of his rights unless somebody knows what those rights are.

MR. FLYNN: Precisely my point. And the only person that can adequately advise a person like Ernesto Miranda is a lawyer.

MR. JUSTICE STEWART: And what would a lawyer advise him that his rights were?

MR. FLYNN: That he had a right not to incriminate himself; that he had the right not to make any statement; that he had a right to be free from further questioning by the police department; that he had the right, at the ultimate time, to be represented adequately by counsel in court; and that if he was too indigent or too poor to employ counsel, the state would furnish him counsel.

MR. JUSTICE STEWART: What is it that confers the right to a lawyer's advice at that point and not an earlier point? The Sixth Amendment?

MR. FLYNN: No. The attempt to erode, or to take away from him, the Fifth Amendment right that already existed—and that was the right not to convict himself, and be convicted out of his own mouth.

MR. JUSTICE STEWART: Didn't he have that right earlier?

MR. FLYNN: If he knew about it.

MR. JUSTICE STEWART: Before this became a so-called "adversary proceeding?"

MR. FLYNN: Yes, Your Honor, if he knew about it and if he was aware—if he was knowledgeable.

MR. JUSTICE STEWART: Then did he have the right to a lawyer's advice earlier?

MR. FLYNN: If he could afford it, yes; and if he was intelligent enough and strong enough to stand up against police interrogation and request it, yes.

MR. JUSTICE STEWART: What I'm getting at is, I don't understand the magic in this phrase of "focusing," and then all of a sudden it becomes an adversary proceeding. And then I suppose if you literally mean that it becomes an adversary proceeding, then you're entitled to all the rights that a defendant is given under the Constitution that would be given in a criminal trial. If you mean less than that, then you don't really mean it has now become the equivalent of a trial.

MR. FLYNN: Well, I simply mean that when it becomes an adversary proceeding, at the very least, a person in Ernest Miranda's position needs the benefit of counsel, and unless he is afforded that right of counsel he simply has, in essence, no Fifth or Sixth Amendment right, and there is no due process of law being afforded to a man in Ernest Miranda's position.

MR. JUSTICE FORTAS: Is it possible that prior to this so-called "focusing," or let's say prior to arrest—if those don't mean the same thing—that a citizen has an obligation to cooperate with the state, give the state information that he may have relevant to the crime; and that upon arrest, or upon this "focusing," that the state and the individual then assume the position of adversaries, and there is, at the very least, a change in that relationship between the individual and the state; and, therefore, in their mutual rights and responsibilities? I don't know whether that's what my Brother Stewart is getting at, and perhaps it is unfair to discuss this through you—

[Laughter.]

MR. JUSTICE FORTAS: —but if you have a comment on it, I'd like to hear it.

MR. FLYNN: I think the only comment that I could make is that, without getting ourselves into the area of precisely when focusing begins, that I must in this instance limit it to the fact situation and the circumstances of Ernest Miranda, because for every practical purpose, after the two-hour interrogation, the mere formality of supplying counsel to Ernest Miranda at the time of trial, is what I would submit would really be nothing more than a mockery of his Sixth Amendment right to be represented in court, to go through the formality, and a conviction takes place.

Well, this simply is not a matter of the record. It is in the robbery trial, and I think it so illustrates the position of what occurs in the case of persons who have confessed, as Ernest Miranda. The question was asked in the robbery trial—which preceded the rape trial by one day—of Mr. Moore:

"THE COURT: Are you ready to go to trial?"

"MR. MOORE: I have been ready. I haven't anything to do but—and sit down and listen."

MR. JUSTICE BLACK: May I ask you one question, Mr. Flynn, about the Fifth Amendment? Let's forget about the Sixth. The Amendment provides that no person shall be compelled to be a witness against himself. It's disassociated entirely from the right to counsel.

You have said several times it seems, during the case, that in determining whether or not a person shall be compelled to be a witness against himself, that it might depend to some extent on his literacy or his illiteracy, his wealth or his lack of wealth, his standing or his lack of standing—why does that have anything to do with it? Why does the Amendment not protect the rich, as well as the poor; the literate, as well as the illiterate?

MR. FLYNN: I would say that it certainly, and most assuredly, does protect; that in the state of the law today as pronounced by the Arizona Supreme Court, under those guiding principles, it certainly does protect the rich, the educated, and the strong—those rich enough to hire counsel, those who are educated enough to know what their rights are, and those who are strong enough to withstand police interrogation and assert those rights.

MR. JUSTICE BLACK: I am asking you only about the Fifth Amendment's provision that no person shall be compelled to be a witness against himself. Does that protect every person, or just some persons? I am not talking about in practical effect; I am talking about what the Amendment is supposed to do.

MR. FLYNN: It protects all persons.

MR. JUSTICE BLACK: Would literacy or illiteracy have anything to do with it if they compelled him to testify, whatever comes within the scope of that?

MR. FLYNN: At the interrogation stage, if he is too ignorant to know that he has the Fifth Amendment right, then certainly literacy has something to do with it, Your Honor. If the man at the time of the interrogation has never heard of the Fifth Amendment, knows nothing about its concept or its scope, knows nothing of his rights, then certainly his literacy—

MR. JUSTICE BLACK: —he'd have more rights, because of that? I don't understand. The Fifth Amendment right, alone, not to be compelled to be a witness against himself? What does that cover?

MR. FLYNN: Perhaps I have simply not expressed myself clearly.

MR. JUSTICE BLACK: Does that cover everybody?

MR. FLYNN: It covers everybody, Your Honor. Clearly in practical application, in view of the interrogation and the facts and circumstances of Miranda, it simply had no application because of the facts and circumstances in that particular case, and that's what I am attempting to express to the Court.

Now the Arizona Supreme Court went on, in essence we submit, to turn its decision primarily on the failure of the defendant in this case to request counsel, which is the only really distinguishing factor that they could find.

MR. JUSTICE STEWART: Is there any claim in this case that this confession was compelled was involuntary?

MR. FLYNN: No, Your Honor.

MR. JUSTICE STEWART: None at all?

MR. FLYNN: None at all.

MR. JUSTICE WHITE: Do you mean that there is no question that he was not compelled to give evidence against himself?

MR. FLYNN: We have raised no question that he was compelled to give this statement, in the sense that anyone forced him to do it by coercion, by threats, by promises, or compulsion of that kind.

MR. JUSTICE WHITE: "Of that kind?" Was it voluntary, or wasn't it?

MR. FLYNN: Voluntary in the sense that the man, at a time without knowledge of his rights—

MR. JUSTICE WHITE: Do you claim that his Fifth Amendment rights were violated?

MR. FLYNN: I would say his Fifth Amendment right was violated, to the extent—

MR. JUSTICE WHITE: Because he was compelled to do it?

MR. FLYNN: Because he was compelled to do it?

MR. JUSTICE WHITE: That's what the Amendment says.

MR. FLYNN: Yes, to the extent that he was, number one, too, poor to exercise it, and number two, mentally abnormal.

MR. JUSTICE WHITE: Whatever the Fifth is, you say he was compelled to do it?

MR. FLYNN: I say it was taken from him at a point in time when he absolutely should have been afforded the Sixth Amendment—

MR. JUSTICE WHITE: I'm talking about violating the Amendment, namely the provision that he was—to violate the Fifth Amendment right, he has to be compelled to do it, doesn't he?

MR. FLYNN: In the sense that Your Honor is presenting to me the word "compelled," you're correct.

MR. JUSTICE WHITE: I was talking about what the Constitution says.

MR. JUSTICE BLACK: He doesn't have to have a gun pointed at his head, does he?

MR. JUSTICE WHITE: Of course he doesn't. So he was compelled to do it, wasn't he, according to your theory?

MR. FLYNN: Not by gunpoint, as Mr. Justice Black has indicated. He was called upon to surrender a right that he didn't fully realize and appreciate that he had. It was taken from him.

MR. JUSTICE WHITE: But in all the circumstances— I'm just trying to find out if you claim that his Fifth Amendment rights were being violated. If they were, it must be because he was compelled to do it, under all circumstances.

MR. FLYNN: I would say that as a result of a lack of knowledge, or for lack of a better term "failure to advise," the denial of the right to counsel at the stage in the proceeding when he most certainly needed it, that this could, in and of itself—and certainly in most police interrogations—constitute compulsion.

MR. JUSTICE BLACK: Why wouldn't you add to that the fact that the State had him in its control and custody? Why would that not tend to show some kind of coercion or compulsion?

MR. FLYNN: The whole process of a person, I would assume, having been raised to tell the truth and respect authority.

MR. JUSTICE BLACK: Was he allowed to get away from there, at will?

MR. FLYNN: No, Your Honor. He was in confinement and under arrest.

MR. JUSTICE BLACK: The State had moved against him by taking him in to question him, did it not?

MR. FLYNN: That is correct.

Flynn, you would say that if the police had said to this young man, "Now you are a nice young man, and we don't want to hurt you, and so forth; we're your friends and if you'll just tell us how you committed this crime, we'll let you go home and we won't prosecute you," that that would be a violation of the Fifth Amendment, and that, technically speaking, would not be "compelling" him to do it. It would be an inducement, would it not?

MR. FLYNN: That is correct.

MR. CHIEF JUSTICE WARREN: I suppose you would argue that that is still within the Fifth Amendment, wouldn't you?

MR. FLYNN: It is an abdication of the Fifth Amendment right.

MR. CHIEF JUSTICE WARREN: That's what I mean.

MR. FLYNN: Because of the total circumstances existing at the time—the arrest, the custody, the lack of knowledge, the—

MR. CHIEF JUSTICE WARREN: In fact, we have had cases of that kind, that confessions were had, haven't we, where they said it would be better for you if you do; we'll let you go; and so forth?

MR. FLYNN: That, of course, is an implied promise of some help or immunity of some kind.

MR. CHIEF JUSTICE WARREN: Yes, but that isn't strictly compulsion that we have been talking about?

MR. FLYNN: That certainly is not compulsion in the sense of the word, as Mr. Justice White had implied it.

MR. JUSTICE BLACK: As I recall, in those cases—I agree with the Chief Justice—as I recall, in those cases that was put under the Fifth Amendment, and the words of the Fifth Amendment were referred to in the early case by Chief Justice White, I believe it was, and the fact that inducement is a compulsion and was brought in that category, and therefore it violated the Amendment against being compelled to give evidence against yourself.

MR. FLYNN: I am sure Mr. Justice Black has expressed it far better than —

MR. JUSTICE BLACK: So it's a question of what "compel" means, but it does not depend, I suppose—I haven't seen it in any of the cases—on the wealth, the standing, or the status of the person, so far as the right is concerned.

MR. FLYNN: Yes, I think perhaps that was a bad choice of words, in context, if Your Honor please, at the time I stated them.

I would like to state, in conclusion, that the Constitution of the State of Arizona, for example has, since statehood, provided to the citizens of our State language precisely the same as the Fourth Amendment to the Federal Constitution as it pertains to searches and seizures. Yet from 1914 until this Court's decision in *Mapp v. Ohio,* we simply did not enjoy the Fourth Amendment rights or the scope of the Fourth Amendment rights that were enjoyed by most of the other citizens of the other states of this Union, and those persons who were under Federal control.

In response to the *Amicus* for New York and the *Amicus* for the National Association of Defense Attorneys that would ask this Court to go slowly and to give the opportunity to the states, to the legislature, to the courts and to the bar association to undertake to solve this problem, I simply say that whatever the solutions may be, it would be another 46 years before the Sixth Amendment right in the scope that it was intended, I submit, by this Court in *Escobedo,* will reach the State of Arizona.

We're one of the most modern states in relation to the adoption of the American Law Institute rules. We have a comparable rule to Rule 5. To my knowledge, there has never been a criminal prosecution for failure to arraign a man. And there is no decision in Arizona that would even come close to the McNabb or Mallory Rule in Arizona. In fact, the same term that *Miranda* was decided, the Arizona Supreme Court indicated that despite the necessity and requirement of immediate arraignment before the nearest and most successful magistrate, that *Mallory v. McNabb* did not apply.

MR. CHIEF JUSTICE WARREN: Mr. Nelson?

ORAL ARGUMENT OF GARY K. NELSON, ESQ., ON BEHALF OF THE RESPONDENT

MR. NELSON: Mr. Chief Justice, may it please the Court, counsel:

I'm somewhat caught up in where to begin. I think perhaps the first and most important—one of the most important—things to say right now is concerning Mr. Flynn's last remarks. I, as a prosecutor, even of only short duration, take serious issue—as strenuous issue as I can take—before this Court, in the statement that it will take another 46 years in the State of Arizona for the right to counsel to become full-blown. I just simply think there is no reason for that statement to be made. If there is any reason for it to be made, or any possible justification for it to be made, then there is no point in going any further.

One issue that might be a good starting point is concerning the description of the Arizona court's supposed "off-the-cuff" referral to, or ignoring of, the *Escobedo* decision, or the attempt to void it clearly. There is no such thing in the Arizona Supreme Court opinion, and a reading of it shows that they agreed that they must follow this Court, not begrudgingly.

They simply stated that it's a fact, and then in exploring the case of *Escobedo* in the case of *Miranda* they try to find out what happened in *Miranda,* what the case of *Escobedo* says, and apply those principles. There's no attempt to avoid, and I don't think you can read it, implicitly or otherwise, in the Arizona Court's opinion. Clearly they did not base it on a request. They did not say we have A, B, C, D, and E, and F wasn't present, therefore it's not controlling. That is not what they said. They said other courts in that jurisdiction had gone off on that particular area. They mentioned that as a factor, but they discussed hundreds of—no, not hundreds—many other factors in *Miranda,* which differentiated it from *Escobedo.*

To get to the facts in *Miranda* I think it's very clear from the record that Mr. Miranda, as an individual defendant, does not particularly require any special rule. I certainly agree with Justice Black 100 percent that the Fifth Amendment, the Sixth Amendment, and every part of our Constitution applies to everyone—poor, rich, intellectual and so on. There is no possible difference for differentiation.

I don't argue that. I don't think any prosecutor of note argues it. But *Miranda* I think characteristically by the petitioner, is portrayed in this light in an attempt to make something that isn't there. Sure he only went through the 8th grade, and one of the psychiatrist said that he had an emotional illness.

I might say that there is another psychiatric report. It's not in the printed record, and I just discovered it in my file, but it is in the record before this Court—the record that was on appeal, and I would urge the Court to advert to that psychiatric report, also. And as to the fact that Mr. Miranda could not have made the statement that he made, I just don't think there is any basis for alleging that. The fact that he uses the medical words to describe the male and female sex organ rather than some four-letter vernacular words that he might have used, this doesn't condemn him just because he knew those words and maybe felt in this context in writing the statement that he could use them. There is no indication in the record that the police put these words in his mouth. The fact that this particular one-half inch penetration is something that the police conjured up in his mind is just simply not supportable by the record.

You read the psychiatric report that is in the record and he said he was upset when he found out that she had not had sexual relations before. Well, she told him that. The only way he found out was because, obviously from the record, as he said, he was only able to make penetration only a slight way simply because of the fact that the woman's hymen had not been ruptured. This is a clear fact that he knew why he made that statement and why it was accurate, not a fabrication of the police officers.

MR. JUSTICE FORTAS: Mr. Nelson, on page 19 of your brief you assert, "The petitioner was advised of his

Constitutional rights, specifically including his right to remain silent, the fact that his statement had to be voluntary, and that anything he did say could be used against him." Is the only basis for that the printed legend in the confession that he signed?

MR. NELSON: No, I don't believe I would have put in as strong a statement concerning his right to remain silent had not we agreed to stipulate to this other portion of the other record. But I believe that as long as that's in the record, I can make this statement because it's supported in the finding of the court, based on the interrogation of the officers, the testimony of the officers in the trial that is actually before this Court concerning their advise to him, and the findings of the Court based on his understanding, the reading of the statement, the testimony coupled with this. I believe, then, that the court below, which clearly found that to be true, that he had been fully advised, had a proper basis for finding all of these to exist, except that there is no quarrel that he was not specifically advised that he had a right to counsel.

MR. JUSTICE FORTAS: Is it your position that the record shows that he was advised of these rights somehow, some way, in addition to the legend on his confession? That's my question.

MR. NELSON: Yes.

MR. JUSTICE FORTAS: How? Where is that?

MR. NELSON: I believe the police officers testified to the fact that they told him of his rights and that they also, besides telling him—perhaps the record is a little unclear, in both cases, as to exactly when it took place—but I believe the record supports a statement that he was advised specifically by them of his rights and then he was adverted to the paragraph and perhaps even again the paragraph was read to him. But the record is not really all four-square. It is not that clear.

MR. JUSTICE FORTAS: Let us assume he was so advised—and I understand you to say that the record is not clear on that point—let us assume that he was advised of his rights. In your opinion does it make any difference when he was advised? That is, whether he was advised at the commencement of the interrogation, or whether he was advised only when he was ready to sign the confession—the written confession? Does that make any difference in the terms of the issues before us?

MR. NELSON: Assuming for a moment that some warning is going to be required, or should have been given, then I would think that to be of any effect it must be given before he had made any statements. Perhaps he might have refused to sign the written confession. Certainly still, the oral statement could have been introduced against him.

MR. JUSTICE FORTAS: So you think that the warning, if necessary, has to be given prior to the interrogation?

MR. NELSON: At some meaningful time, right. I would think it would have to be at some time prior to the fact that after—if they used it before, of course the warning would mean nothing. If they could introduce what they had obtained from the time before they gave the warning, and not afterwards.

MR. JUSTICE FORTAS: Is it your submission to us that a warning is necessary, before a confession, in the absence of counsel, can be taken and subsequently introduced in the trial?

MR. NELSON: No.

MR. JUSTICE FORTAS: What is your Position on that?

MR. NELSON: My Position basically is—concerning the warning—is that each case presents a factual situation in which the Court would have to determine, or a court or a judge or prosecutor at some level, would have to make a determination as to whether or not a defendant, because of the circumstances surrounding his confession, was denied a specific right—whether it be right to counsel, the right to not be compelled to testify against himself—and that the warning, or age or literacy, the circumstances, the length of the questioning, all these factors would be important. But I don't think you can put it to one simple thing such as a warning, because there are perhaps many more situations that we could think of where a warning would be completely inadequate.

MR. JUSTICE FORTAS: Well, tell me some of the factors that would be relevant in the absence of a warning.

MR. NELSON: His age, his experience, his background, the type of questioning, the atmosphere of questioning, the length of questioning, the time of day, perhaps—all of these factors.

MR. JUSTICE FORTAS: Do you think what we ought to do is to devise something like the *Betts* and *Brady* rule, special circumstances?

MR. NELSON: Well, I think that's what the *Escobedo* case indicates. In other words, I am—of course my Opinion is biased—if it's not something like that, then it is an absolute right to counsel. I don't think there can be any in-between unless some other theory. Under the way I read the decisions of this Court, if it is an absolute right to counsel, the same sort of right to counsel that attaches—

MR. JUSTICE FORTAS: We're not talking about right to counsel. We're talking about the warning. When is the warning necessary? As I understand you, you say that if the warning is necessary, if it should be held to be constitutionally necessary in the absence of counsel, then the warning has to be given at a meaningful time.

MR. NELSON: I would think so, certainly.

MR. JUSTICE FORTAS: And I then proceeded to ask you to give us the benefit of your views as to whether a warning was necessary. As I understand it, you say that you have to look at the circumstances of each case?

MR. NELSON: I would say, not absolutely.

MR. JUSTICE FORTAS: I ask you what are the relevant circumstances in each case—the relevant circumstances to look for in each particular case? And how about this particular case? Is the psychiatric report to which you refer, Psychiatric Report No. 2, at material variance with the one to which you are referring?

MR. NELSON: I don't think so. I'm not a psychiatrist, so I can't say. I think both reports say, in effect, the man has an emotional illness that should be treated, but that he knew what was going on. Both the reports say his mental faculties, whatever they were, were sharp, acute, and that he had no psychotic disorders. They both say basically the same thing. I think the diagnosis in the other report said a "sociopathic personality."

MR. JUSTICE FORTAS: So that if the *Betts* against *Brady* test were applied in the way that this Court did apply it prior to *Gideon,* I suppose it's quite arguable that Miranda, this petitioner here, was entitled to a warning. Would you agree to that?

MR. NELSON: It's arguable. I have extensively argued the fact that he wasn't of such a nature, as an individual who because of his mental condition or his educational background, as to require any more than he got.

In other words, I'm saying that he got every warning, except the right—the specific warning, of the right to counsel. He didn't have counsel. Counsel wasn't specifically denied to him, on the basis of a request to retain counsel. The only possible thing that happened to Mr. Miranda that, in my light, assuming that he had the capability of understanding at all, is the fact that he did not get the specific warning of his right to counsel.

MR. JUSTICE FORTAS: Well, even if we assume that he got all the other warnings, and putting aside the question of the right to counsel, assume that the record does show that he got these warnings, still is there any evidence—and I have to ask you again—does the record show that he got it at what you would call a meaningful time?

MR. NELSON: Yes. I think the police officers—they were never pinned down, in other words, as to whether at 11:30 when they went into Interrogation Room 2 they immediately warned him. This was not pinned down by either side. But they did say he was warned. And they went on to elaborate that he was warned I believe, if my recollection serves me correctly, in response to a specific question concerning the statement—they said that part of the statement was read to him again.

Now I believe that the Court could find from the record that he was warned at 11:30. If the warning is required in this particular case to protect his rights, and it is found,

as a matter of fact—which the court below did not find—
that it was not given until the written statement, then I
would suppose that it wasn't given at the proper time.

MR. JUSTICE FORTAS: Mr. Nelson, I certainly want
your views and only your views, and I don't want to
state anything unfairly, but am I correct in inferring
from what you have just said, in answer to my questions, that the State of Arizona does agree that there
are occasions when the United States Constitution
requires that a warning as to the right to remain silent
must be given to a person who is in custody, and must
be given at a meaningful time? Do I correctly state the
position that you are presenting to us here?

MR. NELSON: Not completely. I don't think that the
Arizona Supreme Court has worded its holdings, and
I cite to the Court the case that followed *Miranda*
and referred back to it concerning the point of waiver
and they go on to expand on their thinking. I don't
believe the Arizona Court has specifically said that
warnings, as such, are of a constitutional dimension.
The court has said that in some cases warnings may
be required in a given case.

In fact, in the *Goff* case, which I cite as the next case in
the Arizona Court's determination, they say it's important that all steps be taken at the earliest possible time,
when they are indicated by the fact situation, to ensure
that the State doesn't overreach, and that the man is
given every benefit of his rights under the Constitution;

but I don't believe that they have yet said, as a constitutional dimension, any specific warning at any specific situation need be given.

It is my argument concerning the factors surrounding *Escobedo* that if *Escobedo* is a completely distinct and separate determination of a Sixth Amendment right, as divorced from the Fifth Amendment right, which I think is pretty hard to do, then in order for it to be meaningful and effective—not just to the defendant but to the people of the State, of the country—it's got to announce a rule which forbids affirmative conduct on the basis of police officers or prosecutors calculated in a given situation to deny the man the implementation of his right, whether it be the right to counsel or the right against compulsory self-incrimination.

As I understand it, there is no right not to incriminate himself. The right is for him not to be compelled, whether it's subtle compulsion or direct, but it is still a right not to be compelled to incriminate yourself. At least this is my understanding, and he doesn't have a right not to incriminate himself. He has a right not to be compelled to incriminate himself by some means, either direct or devious. Now I think if the extreme position is adopted that says he has to either have counsel at this stage, or intellectually waive counsel, that a serious problem in the enforcement of our criminal law will occur.

First of all, let us make one thing certain. We need no empirical data as to one factor: what counsel will do if he is actually introduced. I am talking now about counsel for defendant. At least among lawyers there can be no doubt as to what counsel for the defendant is to do. He is to represent him 100 percent, win, lose, or draw—guilty or innocent. That's our system. When counsel is introduced at interrogation, interrogation ceases immediately.

MR. JUSTICE BLACK: Why?

MR. NELSON: Well, for one reason: first of all there are several different situations, but assume counsel is immediately introduced and he knows nothing about the case. He has not talked to the defendant. He has been appointed, say, to an indigent defendant who says "I want a lawyer. I need a lawyer right now. I don't want to talk to you without a lawyer."

He is given a lawyer. He talks to the defendant. First of all he stops the interrogation until he can talk with him. I would think, if he is going to represent him, he cannot allow him to say anything until he finds out what his story is, what he is going to say, and how it is going to affect him. So the interrogation would immediately stop, for that purpose. And after he has had an opportunity to confer with his client—let's assume another thing. Let's assume the client said, "Yes, I am guilty. I did it." He had all the requisite intents. He makes a statement to his lawyer in confidence that he did it, and asks his lawyer what he should do.

Well, the lawyer maybe doesn't know his past history. Maybe the lawyer would want to find out what the police have, if he can. So maybe more time, in order to properly represent him, would be taken up here—time when there would be no interrogation. Let's further assume that he advises his client, "Well, I think you ought to confess. I think there's a possibility for a light sentence. You did it. They have other evidence; or maybe they don't have any other evidence,"—let's say they don't have any other evidence—"and you can confess."

The fellow says, "Well, I don't want to confess. I don't want to go to the gas chamber if I don't have to. Is there anything else that you, as my lawyer, can do for me?" Well, what has he got to tell him? Under our system, he has got to tell him, "Yes, you don't have to say anything. And the fact that you don't say anything can't in any way hurt you, inferred or otherwise, and we can put the State to its burden of proof."

MR. JUSTICE BLACK: Why does our system compel his lawyer to do that?

MR. NELSON: He is compelled by the system to do this.

MR. JUSTICE BLACK: Well, why does it do it? For what purpose? What's the object on the part of the lawyer?

MR. NELSON: Because we believe that it's right, and proper, that the criminal defendant not be deprived of his life, liberty, or property, without due process of law.

MR. JUSTICE BLACK: And something about giving testimony against himself.

MR. NELSON: Right. I mean this is just one issue. The lawyer has to guard all these rights. But I'm saying that the practical effect of introducing counsel at the interrogation stage is going to stop the interrogation for any and all purposes, except what counsel decides will be in the best interest of his defendant. Otherwise, counsel will not be doing his job.

MR. JUSTICE BLACK: Isn't that about the same thing as the practical effect and object of the Amendment, which says he shall not be compelled to give testimony against himself? Is there any difference between the objects there, and purposes of the two—what the lawyer tells him, and what the Fifth Amendment tells him?

MR. NELSON: Well, certainly that's the object of what his lawyer tells him.

MR. JUSTICE BLACK: Isn't that the object of the Amendment?

MR. NELSON: Well, that is the question, of course. The Fifth Amendment, he has the right never to be compelled to incriminate himself at whatever stage, and this is, of course, involves a knowledgeable implementation of that right at this time, if he wants to.

What I am saying is that the State does not have to, at this stage, insist on that right being enforced or waived, because the pre-trial police interrogation does more than just develop confessions. It develops incriminating statements. It develops exculpatory statements which pin a story down to a defendant very closely after the crime is committed, or very closely after he has been taken into police custody, which prevents or effectively makes it unprofitable for him to perjure himself or change his testimony at trial should he take the stand.

MR. JUSTICE BLACK: Is there anything fantastic in the idea that the Fifth Amendment—that the protection against being compelled to testify against oneself—might be read reasonably as meaning there should be no pre-trial proceedings when he was there in the possession of the state?

MR. NELSON: Of course to me, I think there is. I think there is a valid interest—

MR. JUSTICE BLACK: There is a valid interest, of course, if they can convict him—and that's their business, to try to convict him.

MR. NELSON: Right. But I think this is another argument that I think must be made. Our adversary system, as such, is not completely adversary even at the trial stage in a criminal prosecution because Canon Five of the Canons of Ethics of the American Bar Association—which are law in Arizona by rule of court—says that the duty of the prosecution is not simply to go out and convict, but it is to see that justice is done.

In my short time, I have gotten as much satisfaction out of the cases in which I was compelled to confess error in a case where a man had been deprived of his rights of due process as I got satisfaction out of being upheld in a tight case in a court.

MR. JUSTICE FORTAS: Do you give defendants access to the State's evidence against him in your State?

MR. NELSON: Mr. Flynn would tell you more about that at the trial level. I don't believe that the rule has been interpreted very broadly. I think it has been interpreted narrowly. I think he can get his own statements and perhaps he can get the police officers' reports. There is a rule providing for motions, but the judges, as I understand it, have construed it fairly narrowly.

MR. JUSTICE FORTAS: So that it is possible to speculate, isn't it, that the State has limitations—places limitations upon its obligation to cooperate with the defendant, as witnessed by the denial of discovery to the defendant, discovery of the evidence that the State has against him?

MR. NELSON: Yes. Of course I'm sure the prosecutors would go along 100 percent with full discovery for both sides.

MR. JUSTICE FORTAS: Maybe the prosecutors that you know.

[Laughter.]

MR. NELSON: The defendant, of course, is compelled to no discovery, no ordinary discovery procedures in the scope we think of them in a civil case. I just say that I am not sure that the analogy is completely—

MR. JUSTICE FORTAS: What I was drawing your attention to is that there are, in our system, limitations upon the degree of cooperativeness on both sides. It's not just that the arrested person has, under the Constitution, a Privilege against self-incrimination; it is also that the state, when it assumes an adversary position even before that time, takes advantage of certain "reticence," shall I say, with respect to disclosure to the accused.

MR. NELSON: It surely does. But there is no compulsion. In fact, the compulsion is, to the contrary, on the defense side to cooperate, whereas there is complete compulsion—at least by my interpretation of the law— for the prosecutor to do as much, if it's available to him, to show that the defendant is innocent, as there is to prove he is guilty.

MR. JUSTICE FORTAS: "I think we have established, in this colloquy, that complete" is a little bit of an overstatement

MR. NELSON: It doesn't always work that way. I am sure that's the case.

Here again is another point. This is no reason, I don't think, for a constitutional rule which would, in effect, take care of what I consider to be exceptions to the rule rather than the general practice.

I might just say, since I notice that my time is about up, counsel made a statement to the effect, in answer to a question of one of the Justices—and I forgot which one—something about why Miranda talked; that "maybe he was raised to tell the truth; in our society you're raised to tell the truth and respect authority." This brings another thing into play, I believe, which is vitally important—and the prosecutors in my State consider it so—that if, in fact, you either have counsel or you don't, it thereby seriously circumscribes interrogation and confession. You eliminate an early part of one of the most important principles, hopefully, in our criminal law. And that is not just to convict, not just to deter or not just to put somebody away, but to rehabilitate them, and at the earliest possible moment. I don't have that many personal experiences, but we had a meeting of the prosecutors in our State. Many of the cases involving confession and the pre-trial interrogation were the cases where a man has at least admitted he has done something wrong. These were cases where the defendants were much more susceptible to rehabilitation, at this stage, and if you foreclose this, then you develop an attitude in the police officers—you take the personal attitude away.

Many a hardened police officer, when he has developed a case of tremendous circumstantial evidence against a man, and yet the man sits there and keeps telling him "I didn't do it," he is going to wonder. There is a personal factor there. He is going to wonder "Why doesn't this man confess? Why doesn't he say something about doing it?"

Even assuming, *arguendo*, it is not coercion—and I have no argument that whatever is considered coercion, whether it's subtle or otherwise, should not be used. Assuming the interrogation is good, except for that. He is going to wonder, and maybe he is going to go out and examine that eye witness who saw him at 2:00 o'clock in the morning under a dark street light, and examine that other evidence, because he wonders—that personal element—he ought to confess. Here is all of the evidence. It's a *prima facie* case. This is wiped out completely if you terribly circumscribe this particular pretrial investigation. This particular personal element is out, and he can say, "Well, I got the evidence. Maybe he's guilty or maybe not. I didn't talk to him. I don't know how he acts or how he turns up." And I think defendants could be hurt as much as the prosecution.

Mr. Duane Nedrud, argued as Amicus Curiae on behalf of the National District Attorneys Association.

MR. CHIEF JUSTCE WARREN: Mr. Nedrud?
MR. NEDRUD: Mr. Chief Justice, if it please the Court: My name is Duane Nedrud. I am counsel for the *amicus* National District Attorneys Association. My co-counsel is Miss Oberto. I thought that her presence might show that prosecuting attorneys aren't all bad or she wouldn't be working for us on a full time basis.

If I may use some words of one of the Justices of this Supreme Court, "The *Escobedo* decision and the *Dorado* interpretation makes it more necessary than ever that we stop and look where we are going. If we are talking about equality between rich and the poor, we are striving for a worthy objective. If we talking about equality between the policeman and the criminal, we are on dangerous ground."

I would remind this Court that we are not talking about the police versus the defendant. We are talking about the people versus the defendant. In the same way that we would not talk about the Army or the Marine Corps versus the Viet Cong, but we would talk about the United States versus the Viet Cong.

I have not mentioned in my brief anything about the Fifth or Sixth Amendment. I concede that this Court can interpret Amendments in the way that it sees fit. I am willing to agree with the ACLU in their brief, in one point where they quote me, although they do misquote me when they refer to *Malloy* and *Hayes* in substitution form, on pages 26 of their brief, instead of *Haley* and *Payne,* whom I consider entirely different; that an admonishment in the *Dorado* interpretation will not materially affect confessions.

If this is to be our objective—to limit the use of the confession in criminal cases—then you are taking from the police a most important piece of evidence in every case that they bring before a court of justice. Police officers are public servants. They are not attempting to put innocent people in jail. They want to follow the dictates of this Court, and they will follow them to the best of their ability, but they too are human beings. They do have, however, an experience and knowledge which many of us lack, because this is their job—the investigation of crime—and we have not, as lawyers, paid attention to their problems. We have seldom been down to the police station and asked, "What can we do to assist you in your problems?"

We are more inclined—and I talk about the prosecuting attorneys, and I am not referring to this Court any more than any other lawyer in the United States.

If I may use the present case of *Miranda* as an example, the defense admits that there is a voluntary confession. He says that we should not allow this confession because he did not have counsel present, because we would not have been able to convict him, because there was no other evidence except his own voluntary statement that his male organ had penetrated a half an inch. Otherwise, he would have been acquitted.

Is this what we are looking for, to acquit *Miranda* because he did not have counsel? The *amicus* here has presented data covering thousands of man-hours on the part of the members attempting to show the widespread use of confessions. I am not saying that the widespread use of confessions justifies their use. I am just attempting to present to you, through our members, the importance of the confession in our criminal administration of justice.

I believe that there is something beyond that which we are discussing here. I think that there is a need—and I have mentioned this, and I pray for it—that all public servants: law enforcement officers, prosecuting attorneys, trial courts, and Members of this Court, work together. We are not adversaries. There is a need, I think, on the part of the people, to be able to refer to "my policeman," "our police," "my court," and not "those cops."

MR. JUSTICE FORTAS: Do you think we ought to overrule *Escobedo*?

MR. NEDRUD: Sir?

MR. JUSTICE FORTAS: Is it your position that we should overrule *Escobedo*?

MR. NEDRUD: If I knew what *Escobedo* meant, I may say so, but I have said in my brief, Mr. Justice Fortas, that I think that *Escobedo* should never have been appealed in the facts of the case. I think that this Court rightly reversed the case on the facts.

MR. JUSTICE FORTAS: Well, you're not urging that we overrule *Escobedo*?

MR. NEDRUD: No, sir. It's our system of justice, in effect, which we need as a matter of change. I do not attempt to say that defense counsel is wrong when they attempt to do the best they can for counsel. This is our system of justice.

But I could tell you, for example, in the State of New York, that when the defense counsel is picked by those who are in the profession of crime—if I can use this—that they wonder who is "hot," for example, in winning cases now, and they are picked almost as if they were racehorses, because now they are winning. There is nothing so fickle as a criminal defendant. He wants only one thing. He wants to win. Now if a prosecuting attorney only wants to win, then we should not have that prosecuting attorney in office. We should make a change.

MR. CHIEF JUSTICE WARREN: May I ask you this, please, Mr. Nedrud? If you agree on the facts that *Escobedo* should have been reversed, what would you say as to the man who did not have a lawyer but who said he wanted a lawyer before he talked?

MR. NEDRUD: If he asked for a lawyer, and he does not waive his right to counsel, I think that he should have a lawyer. I think that even the state should—I would go so far as to say that I think the state should appoint him a lawyer, if he asks for a lawyer. I do not think, however, that we should in effect encourage him to have a lawyer.

MR. CHIEF JUSTICE WARREN: Why do you say we should not encourage him to have a lawyer? Are lawyers a menace?

MR. NEDRUD: Mr. Chief Justice, a lawyer must in our system of justice attempt to free the defendant. This is his job.

MR. CHIEF JUSTICE WARREN: Because it is his professional duty to raise any defenses the man has?

MR. NEDRUD: Yes, sir.

MR. CHIEF JUSTICE WARREN: Do you think, in doing that, is a menace to our administration of justice?

MR. NEDRUD: I think he is not a menace at the trial level. He is not a menace, per se, but he is, in doing his duty, going to prevent a confession from being obtained.

MR. CHIEF JUSTICE WARREN: When does he cease being a menace?

MR. NEDRUD: Mr. Chief Justice, I did not say he was a menace.

MR. CHIEF JUSTICE WARREN: You said he was if he interjected himself into it before the trial level.

MR. NEDRUD: I merely said he would prevent a confession from being obtained. And if this is what we are looking for, we should appoint a counsel even before the arrest stage, because the moment that a murder takes place the Government is out looking for the criminal.

MR. CHIEF JUSTICE WARREN: If a lawyer, as you say he is entitled to a lawyer under the facts of *Escobedo,* and the lawyer is entitled to tell him that he doesn't want him to talk to the police, why would it be a menace for another lawyer whom the defendant didn't want, to do the same thing?

MR. NEDRUD: Mr. Chief Justice, I am not disagreeing with you one iota. I am just saying that if, in effect, this is what should be done—if you want to equalize, for example, the defendant's right against the policeman—naturally he should have counsel if this is what we are striving for.

MR. CHIEF JUSTICE WARREN: Well, suppose we put it on the basis of not equalizing anything, or balancing anything, but on protecting the constitutional rights of the defendant not to be compelled to convict himself, on his own testimony.

MR. NEDRUD: Mr. Chief Justice, I of course do not interpret the Constitution. This is, of course, your prerogative, sir.

MR. CHIEF JUSTICE WARREN: How do you interpret it?

MR. NEDRUD: I do not interpret it that the defendant is entitled to a lawyer, until the trial stage.

MR. CHIEF JUSTICE WARREN: Until the trial starts?

MR. NEDRUD: Yes, sir.

MR. CHIEF JUSTICE WARREN: Where do you set that authority?

MR. NEDRUD: As I read the Constitution—you asked me my opinion, and I said I have no authority to interpret the Constitution—I am saying that this is the way I read the Constitution.

MR. CHIEF JUSTICE WARREN: Has that been the way the Court has read the Constitution in days gone by?

MR. NEDRUD: I believe so.

MR. JUSTICE DOUGLAS: Counsel, everybody knows that if he is appointed a lawyer at the beginning of trial, then the lawyer can't possibly represent him. He needs time to prepare for the trial, so the appointment must be at some point anterior to the trial. Our question here is at what point? How far anterior?

MR. NEDRUD: Mr. Justice Douglas, I am not concerned when the lawyer enters the stage, and maybe part of our problem is that the prosecuting attorney enters before he should.

MR. JUSTICE DOUGLAS: Under the procedures in some states, as you well know, very important rights can be lost many days, many weeks prior to the trial. We come down to the question, which begins with the Constitution, concededly—I think we'd say "concededly"—everyone is entitled to a lawyer at the trial, and also at some point anterior to the trial.

MR. NEDRUD: The question comes, I think, Mr. Justice Douglas, to whether or not we are going to allow the trial court to determine the guilt or the innocence, or the defense counsel. If the defense counsel comes in at the arrest stage, he will, as he should, prevent the defendant from confessing to his crime, and you will have fewer convictions. If this is what is wanted, this is what will occur.

MR. JUSTICE BLACK: I guess there is no doubt, is there, that the provision that provides for protection against compelling him to give testimony has a consequence of fewer convictions?

MR. NEDRUD: Mr. Justice Black, this is true. Moreover, again we are talking about the voluntary-involuntary rule, and I have not questioned this whatsoever. This is, I believe, a good rule. I have said that *Mapp* versus *Ohio* is a good rule. I believe, however, that there is a point of diminishing returns and at some stage the police must be in a position to protect us.

MR. JUSTICE BLACK: At some stage, according to our opinion, he is entitled to a lawyer—at some stage. And we have said, as I recall, that it's at the stage when he needs it. At least after he has been detailed. What about the point where a man is seized by Government agents and, as you say, they are "our agents," they are "our officers." There is no antagonism. But what about the fact that when they're seized by someone who has the power to detain him, keep him away from his friends and his relatives and in seclusion if it's desired? Can you think of any time when he needs a lawyer more than at that point—at the point of detention?

MR. NEDRUD: Mr. Justice Black, again the question is, are we interested in convicting the defendant? Or are we interested in protecting, or acquitting him? This is the only point that I can, in effect, make if you say that this defendant needs counsel at this time.

For example, if I may use this illustration: I worked when I was a professor of law—which I was, prior to taking this position—I worked on the defense project for the American Bar Association. In the questionnaire, there was a statement: "When is the ideal time for counsel to be appointed for the defendant?" The question is, when is the ideal time "for whom?" The people? Or the Defendant? Now if it is for the defendant, then it is the earliest possible opportunity. If it is for the people, it should not be until a critical stage. If it is *White v. Maryland,* I agree it should be at the preliminary hearing stage. If it is the question of arraignment, as in *Alabama,* I agree. If it is at the trial stage, and he has lost none of his rights which can be interpreted in one way or another, then I say that it should be at the trial stage.

MR. JUSTICE BLACK: Well, as a prosecutor, I have found out over many years that it's a very critical stage when a person is taken to the police headquarters. There is nothing wrong with it. That is part of our government. A person is taken to police headquarters under arrest, under detention. He can't leave if he wants to, unless they let him. Would you call that "voluntary" for him then—for them to have him there, in that situation, and probe him about his probable conviction of crime? Would you think of that as voluntary?

MR. NEDRUD: Being voluntarily in the police station? No.

MR. JUSTICE HARLAN: I suppose you would say, wouldn't you, it's a question of fact for somebody to decide, in the context of different circumstances that have arisen?

MR. NEDRUD: I would hope, Mr. Justice Harlan, that Court has "protected," as I referred to it in my brief, by an involuntary rule of the totality of circumstances, and I hope that the Court would also continue to invoke this rule, but not go so far as to prevent the police from protecting us.

Thank you, sir.[8]

What do we learn from the opinion, dissent, and oral arguments? The question is posed through the lens of the question that we have set out to answer. That is our primary interest and focus. Earl Warren undoubtedly carried the day. His position "won," albeit a narrow 5-4 majority. The dissents were sharp and biting, raising legitimate and important points. Harlan and White were very critical of their "Chief" as Warren was called.[9] Clark's position is, frankly, unclear. That is in sharp contrast to the majority and dissents. Both are clear, leaving no doubt regarding their perspectives on this most important of issues. Because of the their clarity, the majority and dissents establish two diametrically opposing perspectives regarding the relationship between the state and the individual, now in custody, about to be interrogated. At that very moment, the individual is at his most vulnerable; the state is at its most powerful.

---

8. Docket No. 759, Ernest A. Miranda vs. The State of Arizona Oral Arguments, Feb. 28,1996, http://users.soc.umn.edu/~samaha/cases/miranda_v_arizona _oral_arguments.htm.

9. Brennan referred to Warren as "Super Chief."

The core of the conflicting views must not be minimized: Warren powerfully waved yellow flags of caution regarding law enforcement; the dissents suggested that Warren was exaggerating. Warren's deep skepticism of how police interrogated suspects was dismissed by the dissent; to say the least, they did not share his concern. In addition, there was deep conflict between the two sides regarding the protection of constitutional rights: Warren's framing the issues as a Fifth Amendment issue was a powerful stake he drove into the ground; the dissent did not agree that Warren was protecting constitutionally guaranteed rights.

The disagreement was raw, simultaneously legal and practical, and visceral in tone and content. The lengthy excerpts above are illuminating in that regard. The majority–dissent split was undeniable; in direct contrast to the unanimous decision in *Brown*, that would not be recreated in *Miranda*. Warren, the master politician and tactician who cajoled a very different Court in 1954, was unable to do so in 1966.

However, as much as a unanimous decision was a laudable goal, Warren's primary focus was protecting the suspect from law enforcement. From Warren's perspective, this was essential for the time had come for the privilege against self-incrimination to be extended to the interrogation setting.

Warren did not rank the *Miranda* decision as his most important; nevertheless, it is hard to exaggerate its extraordinary importance on a number of different levels.

The hostile public reaction in many quarters, including "Impeach Earl Warren" signs and billboards on the nation's highways, illuminates the intense feelings rising from the decision.

The oral arguments presented sharply contrasting positions: in arguing on behalf of Miranda, Mr. Flynn emphasized the requirement to protect the vulnerable suspect; in arguing on behalf of the State of Arizona and the National Association of District Attorneys, Mr. Nelson and Mr. Nedrud focused on larger societal interests and the harm to law enforcement. The majority opinion reflects, in large part, Flynn's argument; the dissent reflects, in large part, the Nelson and Nedrud argument.

However, as important as the oral arguments were, the critical work was done by Chief Justice Earl Warren. This was his decision: this was his articulation of how America should treat suspects and how the vulnerable should be protected. There is no gray in the decision, there is no "on the one hand, on the other hand" and there is no shying away from boldly and clearly addressing a critical issue.

Warren was unapologetic in his criticism of law enforcement; it was based on his personal knowledge. We must never lose sight, not only of Warren's extensive professional experience, but also of his direct involvement in the interrogation in a California murder case that he, as Chief Justice, would have blanched at. *Miranda* was the crowning achievement of the Warren Court criminal procedure revolution.

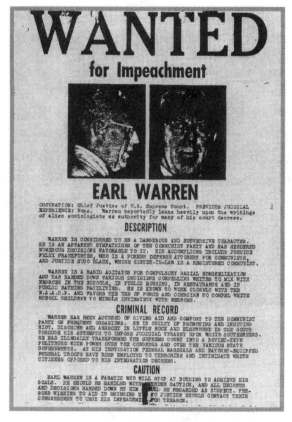

https://readtiger.com/wkp/en/Earl_Warren

With that, we turn our attention to asking what is a terrorist and how shall we define terrorism? This is necessary in order to answer whether Warren would extend *Miranda* to terrorists as compared to criminal suspects.

The task is complicated by the plethora of preferred definitions and the lack of unanimity, domestically and internationally, in this effort.

Chapter Seven

Post-*Miranda*, Terrorism, and Interrogations

Post-Miranda

According to Professor Geoffrey Stone, in the years after the *Miranda* decision, the Supreme Court had eleven opportunities to strengthen the holding; in all these eleven opportunities, the Court chose otherwise.[1]

So, where are we in 2017?

The *Miranda* of 1966 has been weakened; the title of Kamisar's law review article "The Rise, Decline and Fall (?) of Miranda" compellingly captures the moment.[2]

---

1. Geoffrey R. Stone, *The Miranda Doctrine in the Burger Court*, Sup. Ct. Rev. 99 (1977).
2. Yale Kamisar, *The Rise, Decline, and Fall (?) of Miranda*, 87 WASH. L. REV. 965 (2012).

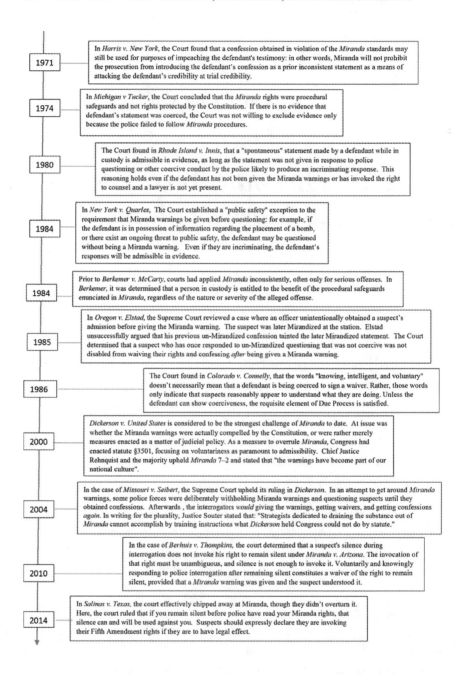

1971

In *Harris v. New York*, the Court found that a confession obtained in violation of the *Miranda* standards may still be used for purposes of impeaching the defendant's testimony: in other words, Miranda will not prohibit the prosecution from introducing the defendant's confession as a prior inconsistent statement as a means of attacking the defendant's credibility at trial credibility.

1974

In *Michigan v Tucker*, the Court concluded that the *Miranda* rights were procedural safeguards and not rights protected by the Constitution. If there is no evidence that defendant's statement was coerced, the Court was not willing to exclude evidence only because the police failed to follow *Miranda* procedures.

1980

The Court found in *Rhode Island v. Innis*, that a "spontaneous" statement made by a defendant while in custody is admissible in evidence, as long as the statement was not given in response to police questioning or other coercive conduct by the police likely to produce an incriminating response. This reasoning holds even if the defendant has not been given the Miranda warnings or has invoked the right to counsel and a lawyer is not yet present.

1984

In *New York v. Quarles*, The Court established a "public safety" exception to the requirement that Miranda warnings be given before questioning: for example, if the defendant is in possession of information regarding the placement of a bomb, or there exist an ongoing threat to public safety, the defendant may be questioned without being a Miranda warning. Even if they are incriminating, the defendant's responses will be admissible in evidence.

1984

Prior to *Berkemer v. McCarty*, courts had applied *Miranda* inconsistently, often only for serious offenses. In *Berkemer*, it was determined that a person in custody is entitled to the benefit of the procedural safeguards enunciated in *Miranda*, regardless of the nature or severity of the alleged offense.

1985

In *Oregon v. Elstad*, the Supreme Court reviewed a case where an officer unintentionally obtained a suspect's admission before giving the Miranda warning. The suspect was later Mirandized at the station. Elstad unsuccessfully argued that his previous un-Mirandized confession tainted the later Mirandized statement. The Court determined that a suspect who has once responded to un-Mirandized questioning that was not coercive was not disabled from waiving their rights and confessing *after* being given a Miranda warning.

1986

The Court found in *Colorado v. Connelly*, that the words "knowing, intelligent, and voluntary" doesn't necessarily mean that a defendant is being coerced to sign a waiver. Rather, those words only indicate that suspects reasonably appear to understand what they are doing. Unless the defendant can show coerciveness, the requisite element of Due Process is satisfied.

2000

Dickerson v. United States is considered to be the strongest challenge of *Miranda* to date. At issue was whether the Miranda warnings were actually compelled by the Constitution, or were rather merely measures enacted as a matter of judicial policy. As a measure to overrule *Miranda*, Congress had enacted statute §3501, focusing on voluntariness as paramount to admissibility. Chief Justice Rehnquist and the majority upheld *Miranda* 7–2 and stated that "the warnings have become part of our national culture".

2004

In the case of *Missouri v. Seibert*, the Supreme Court upheld its ruling in *Dickerson*. In an attempt to get around *Miranda* warnings, some police forces were deliberately withholding Miranda warnings and questioning suspects until they obtained confessions. Afterwards , the interrogators *would* giving the warnings, getting waivers, and getting confessions *again*. In writing for the plurality, Justice Souter stated that: "Strategists dedicated to draining the substance out of *Miranda* cannot accomplish by training instructions what *Dickerson* held Congress could not do by statute."

2010

In the case of *Berhuis v. Thompkins*, the court determined that a suspect's silence during interrogation does not invoke his right to remain silent under *Miranda v. Arizona*. The invocation of that right must be unambiguous, and silence is not enough to invoke it. Voluntarily and knowingly responding to police interrogation after remaining silent constitutes a waiver of the right to remain silent, provided that a *Miranda* warning was given and the suspect understood it.

2014

In *Salinas v. Texas*, the court effectively chipped away at Miranda, though they didn't overturn it. Here, the court ruled that if you remain silent before police have read your Miranda rights, that silence can and will be used against you. Suspects should expressly declare they are invoking their Fifth Amendment rights if they are to have legal effect.

In referencing Stone's 1977 article, Kamisar writes:

> A decade after Miranda had been decided, Professor Geoffrey Stone took a close look at the eleven decisions the U.S. Supreme Court had handed down 'concerning the scope and application of Miranda.' In ten of these cases, the Court had interpreted Miranda so as not to exclude the challenged evidence. In the remaining case, the eleventh case, the Court had excluded the evidence on other grounds. In effect, then, noted Professor Stone, ten years after Miranda had been handed down, 'the Court has not held a single item of evidence inadmissible on the authority of Miranda.' To use baseball terminology, in Miranda's first eleven 'at bats' it went zero for eleven.[3]

How does that bode for terrorists? What protections do we extend to those among us who seek to kill us? Is it a fair assumption that if Miranda protections have been weakened with respect to criminals that suspected terrorists should receive even less protection?

The questions, sufficiently complicated under ordinary circumstances, take on greater urgency in a combustible political environment, marked by strong passions and fear of terrorism. That fear, regardless of whether or not it is justified, has become a feature of the American landscape.

---

3. Yale Kamisar, *The Miranda Case Fifty Years Later* (Boston University, 2017).

Are they *criminals* as Earl Warren understood criminals? Are they Americans subject to being *killed without trial* as articulated by the Obama Administration's White Paper?[4] According to the White Paper:

> Lethal operations taken under the guise of national self-defense falls within a "well-established variant of the public authority justification and therefore would not be murder."[5]

Are they such a threat to American safety and security that we need to create a new category to define them? The answer impacts how we view the Warren–*Miranda*–terrorism question

In the courtroom, the defendant is represented by counsel. That is distinct from the interrogation room. There, unless the suspect responds affirmatively to the right to have an attorney, the only people in the room are who those designated by the state and the suspect. That setting and its inherent asymmetrical alignment dramatically demonstrates

---

4. The White Paper is a "A confidential Justice Department memo concludes that the U.S. government can order the killing of American citizens if they are believed to be 'senior operational leaders' of al-Qaida or 'an associated force'—even if there is no intelligence indicating they are engaged in an active plot to attack the U.S." http://investigations.nbcnews.com/_news/2013/02/04/16843014-justice-department-memo-reveals-legal-case-for-drone-strikes-on-americans?lite.

5. Memorandum from US Department of Justice, Lawfulness of Lethal Operation Directed Against a US Citizen who is a senior leader of Al-Qaeda or an Associated Force (2013), http://msnbcmedia.msn.com/i/msnbc/sections/news/020413_DOJ_White_Paper.pdf.

individual vulnerability and the limits of rights and protections.

Do we turn a blind eye to what happens to a suspected terrorist in the interrogation setting? Do we say, "just desserts" if a suspected terrorist is denied Miranda protections? Turning a collective blind eye is enticing. It is far easier not to see. There is something secure, perhaps comforting, in not asking. We hear on the news that a terrorist attack occurred; we inquire as to the welfare of the injured and express concern and sympathy for those killed and their families.

Politicians trot out tired clichés about defeating terrorism, finding those responsible for the reprehensible attacks and bringing them to justice. It is a pattern that repeats itself. I have heard this too many times to count. I have been involved more often than I can remember. While both reactions, the public and politicians, are understandable, it misses a larger point: the rights of those suspected of the act.

My emphasis on this issue does not reflect sympathy or empathy for those responsible. It is directly related to my concern that excess is but a minute away; violations of individual rights are just outside the door. While the public and many politicians are only too willing to break that door, there is extraordinary risk in fostering that environment. Tolerance of extremism in reaction to terrorism does not bode well for democracy.

The rush to judgment and the calls for retribution are reflective of set-piece responses. It is a play with the parts and lines well known. The omnipresent social media enhances the chatter; it legitimizes the calls for action. It is low-hanging fruit for those seeking to score points. While perhaps this is understandable from a public relations perspective, it is very dangerous.

The danger is to society and the suspect alike. The consequences of a false confession extend beyond the individual suspect. False confessions ultimately impact society's relationship with the individual—in particular, the vulnerable individual regardless of the act of which he or she is accused.

Some might argue that wrongful convictions are more troubling than wrongful confessions. There is no competition between the two. Both are deeply troubling. Concern regarding wrongful convictions is particularly acute when the death penalty is imposed. The extraordinary work of the Innocence Project highlights that.[6]

However, there is a crucial difference between the two: in the interrogation setting, the individual is alone with interrogators; in the courtroom, the individual is represented by an attorney. History is replete with examples of wrongful convictions and coerced confessions. Warren's opinion

---

6. My colleague Professor Jensie Anderson has played a significant role in these efforts: The Rocky Mountain Innocence Center examines serious felony cases, regardless of whether capital or noncapital. There have been a total of 1,913 exonerations in this country—156 were death penalty exonerations. Please see http://www.law.umich.edu/special/exoneration/Pages/about.aspx; http://www.deathpenaltyinfo.org/innocence-and-death-penalty.

reflects deep concern regarding the latter because they clearly lead to the former.

Warren did not write *Miranda* in a time of terrorism; his America is a very different America from today. That is not to suggest his America was tranquil. It was not. However, in spite of the crimes committed by radical groups in the years following the decision, there was no discussion about not extending its protections to members of radical groups. That is, they were treated like "regular criminals."

There were no exceptions predicated on the nature of crime or the identity of the criminal. Warren's opinion was very clear that protections must be extended uniformly and consistently. The majority's language did not suggest tolerance for exceptions predicated on the nature of crime or the identity of the criminal. However, it is safe to assume that Earl Warren did not predict, much less consider, the terrorism that is today's reality. There is no suggestion of that. It would be, frankly, unreasonable to expect him to have terrorism on his radar. That was, simply put, not the world as he knew it in 1966.

Terrorism and Terrorists: How to Define?

Terminology and definitions are important; so is understanding the times and their particular historical context.

Countless words have been written and spoken about terrorism and terrorists.

They have become integral parts of the contemporary landscape; in the hands of politicians, both are "political footballs." That is understandable. It is also unfortunate because the threat confronting modern society demands seriousness and somber analysis. More often than not, that is lacking.

However, it is an exaggeration to suggest that terrorism threatens western society. To do so is to engage in hyperbolic rhetoric for political gain. That is not to suggest that terrorists do not actively seek to kill, injure, and intimidate on a consistent basis. They do. Similarly, that is not to suggest that western society has a compelling and consistent response to terrorism. It does not.

Both facts, unpleasant as they maybe, were my professional reality for twenty years. They are, without doubt, the personal reality for all engaged members of society.

Nevertheless, it is of the utmost importance that the threat not be exaggerated; the consequences of overstating a threat are minimization of individual rights in the name of national security. That is particularly important regarding limits of interrogation and determining what rights and protections are to be extended to the suspected terrorist when interrogated.

The illegal interrogation measures authorized by the Bush Administration in the aftermath of 9/11 graphically highlight an "over-the-top" response to terrorism. The consequences and ramifications are significant and, in some cases, irreversible when torture results in the death of the interrogated suspect.

In 2017, the word *terrorism* is used liberally, widely, and instinctually. Politicians are quick to call an act of violence an "act of terrorism." The label is compelling and effective. Political opportunism dictates declaring attacks as terrorism. Whether that is ultimately correct or not is, unfortunately, irrelevant. The twenty-second sound-bite culture encourages a rush to judgment; the twenty-four-hour news cycle guarantees endless repetition of comments, regardless of their veracity.

The fact that there is no agreed definition of the word is, seemingly, irrelevant. What is important is the immediate proclamation by politicians and others regarding the scourge of "terrorism." The rush to label an attack as "terrorism" has political implications; doing so can have clear electoral benefit. From law enforcement's perspective, defining an act as terrorist is a double-edged sword; on the one hand, it reflects a failure to protect the public; on the other hand, it justifies allocation of additional resources. The same holds true for the national intelligence and security communities who readily characterize an attack as "terrorism." There is a sense of a self-fulfilling prophecy: if sufficiently discussed, it must be true.

Terrorism is perceived as something different, distinct from traditional warfare that pits nation-states equipped with tanks, planes, and ships; the essence of terrorism is asymmetrical conflict between the nation-state and a non-state actor. Nation-states struggle with what jurisprudential paradigm to apply to terrorism. The oft-asked question whether terrorists are criminals or "something else" vexes decision makers. The dilemma is difficult to resolve for it has significant legal, political, cultural, and practical implications.

My interactions over the course of two decades with individuals suspected of involvement in terrorism—whether Palestinian or Jewish—led me to the conclusion that religious extremism is the primary motivator for contemporary terrorism. That is not intended to castigate religion or people of faith. Were this book written in the 1970s, political ideology would have been the principal driver of European terrorism and the American movements previously referenced. Religion played no role in either.

The nation-state's arsenal is significantly greater than that of the non-state actor; nevertheless, the nation-state rooted in the rule of law is beholden to principles of international law and of self-imposed restraint. This is in direct contrast to the non-state actor that is neither signatory to international conventions or treaties nor subject to externally imposed restrictions of law or morality.

The definitional discussion regarding terrorism has vexed decision makers, military officers, the intelligence community, academics, and the broader public for decades. There are over a hundred offered definitions of the word *terrorism*; different agencies within the US executive branch have distinct definitions. The international community cannot agree on a commonly accepted definition. The lack of a uniform definition is not accidental. Much as Supreme Court Justice Potter Stewart famously said of pornography, "I know it when I see it,"[7] of terrorism it has been said "one man's terrorist is another man's freedom fighter."[8]

Definitions are a complex and tricky undertaking. Decision makers resist defining the term because it restricts their operational wiggle room; politicians try to avoid the discussion because there are endless "buts" and "exceptions"; the public, depending on political perspective, prefers a very broad or conversely narrow definition. The former gives wide latitude to targeting terrorists; the latter limits who is defined as a legitimate target.[9]

The definition below is one I offer in my other works and to my students. It reflects both my professional experience in the IDF and my academic research and scholarship. Not all readers will agree with the definition and may suggest their own. That is reasonable and to be expected.

---

7. *Jacobellis v. State of Ohio*, 378 U.S. 184, 197 (1964).

8. Ronald Regan, Radio Address to the Nation on Terrorism (May 31, 1986) (transcript available at http://www.presidency.ucsb.edu/ws/?pid=37376).

9. When testifying before the US House of Representatives Committee on Homeland Security, I suggested defining "homeland security" and "terrorism" were essential to the rule of law. The body language of Republicans and Democrats was beyond telling, signaling significant discomfort and profound hesitation in doing so. While their political calculations were understandable, the reluctance was, ultimately, disappointing and short-sighted.

Terrorism is an act committed by an individual or group of individuals predidcated on one of four motivations: religious, political, social or economic. The act can be violent though need not be; killing, injuring or intimidating innocent civilians are equally valid results as the intent is to influence government policy in accordance with one of the four motivations. Targeting innocent civilians is the essence of a terrorist attack.

According to this definition, attacking soldiers or policemen is not an act of terrorism for they are not innocent civilians.[10] What distinguishes terrorism is the deliberate targeting of innocent civilians, regardless of gender, age, race, and ethnicity. Distinct from efforts by the nation-state—*not always successful*—to target only those posing a threat to national security and public order, terrorists indiscriminately attack innocent civilians whose deaths are defined as legitimate.

---

10. In 1996, a soldier who served under my command was injured in a suicide bombing; that evening—in accordance with Israel Defense Forces standing orders—I met with the parents. The soldier's mother, who was very emotional and distraught, insisted her daughter was the victim of a terrorist attack. While I agreed with her that the attack was, indeed, a terrorist attack, her daughter, as a soldier, was not the victim of a terrorist attack. When I relayed this conversation to my commander, his immediate response was twofold: I was correct from a legal perspective but showed an utter lack of judgment. He was right; of that there is no doubt. While my soldier recovered and returned to service, a number of innocent civilians were killed.

The distinction is at the crux between the nation-state and non-state actors. That is not to suggest that innocent civilians are not killed by the nation-state. Such a claim would be preposterous. Collateral damage—the inadvertent deaths of innocent civilians—is inherent to engagement. However, the nation-state, in contrast to terrorists, does not intend to kill innocent civilians.

From the terrorist's perspective, an attack that kills a limited number of people is no less successful than an act that killed hundreds. Terrorist organizations embrace the actor, regardless of the attack's result; the act itself is to be celebrated.[11] The act itself is of primary importance because of the psychological impact on society. Given that one of the goals of an attack is to intimidate the civilian population, the attack is sufficient in and of itself.

Terrorist organizations take a long-term view regarding attainment of their goals in contrast with contemporary society predicated on immediate gratification. That is an important difference: nation-states have, unfortunately, created a "defeat terrorism" motif that focuses on eradicating terrorism, whereas terrorist organizations do not have a particular timeline or deadline regarding attainment of their goals and aims. The "defeat terrorism" slogan creates

---

11. As an example, see Jack Fenwick, *Sick ISIS supporters celebrate online after horror Nice terror attack leaves scores dead*, Express (July 15, 2016), http://www .express.co.uk/news/world/689701/nice-attack-dead-france-terror-isis -supporters-islamic-state-social-media-french.

false expectations among the public and justifies imposing harsh measures in order to attain "victory."

The limit of interrogation is one of the most important challenges facing democracies. The chart below highlights how different US government agencies define terrorism.

FBI	The Federal Bureau of Investigation builds on the Code of Federal Regulations "the unlawful use of force or violence against persons or property to intimidate or coerce a government, the civilian population, or any segment thereof, in furtherance of political or social objectives."[12]
CIA	The CIA uses the definition contained in Title 22 of US Code: "premeditated, politically motivated violence perpetrated against noncombatant targets by subnational groups or clandestine agents."
DHS	In its founding document, the Department of Homeland Security defines terrorism as any activity involving an act that is "dangerous to human life or potentially destructive of critical infrastructure or key resources," violates the criminal laws of the United States, and appears intended to "intimidate or coerce a civilian population, influence the policy of a government by intimidation or coercion, or affect the conduct of a government by mass destruction, assassination, or kidnapping."
DOJ	The USA PATRIOT Act of 2001 defines domestic terrorism as "activities that (A) involve acts dangerous to human life that are a violation of the criminal laws of the U.S. or of any state; (B) appear to be intended (i) to intimidate or coerce a civilian population; (ii) to influence the policy of a government by intimidation or coercion; or (iii) to affect the conduct of a government by mass destruction, assassination, or kidnapping; and (C) occur primarily within the territorial jurisdiction of the U.S."[13]

12. US Department of State, *Terrorism*, Country Reports on Terrorism (April 20, 2007), www.nij.gov/topics/crime/terrorism/Pages/welcome.aspx.
13. USA Patriot Act of 2001, Pub. L. No. 107–56, 115 Stat 272.

DOD	The Department of Justice defines terrorism as "the unlawful use of violence or threat of violence to instill fear and coerce governments or societies. Terrorism is often motivated by religious, political, or other ideological beliefs and committed in the pursuit of goals that are usually political." This definition represents a distinction between the motivations of terrorism and the goals of terrorism.
DOS	Title 22 of the US Code, Section 2656f(d) defines terrorism as "premeditated, politically motivated violence perpetrated against noncombatant targets by subnational groups or clandestine agents, usually intended to influence an audience."[14]

Food for Thought

The excerpt below, a most disturbing account of an interrogation clearly "gone wrong," is included for one reason: to highlight the danger of an interrogation without protections and limits. It did not occur in Detroit, San Francisco, Pittsburgh, or any other US city. The interrogators were not police detectives, FBI agents, or sheriff deputies. The suspect had not been brought into custody for the crime of burglary, armed robbery, rape, or murder.

In that sense, there is little correlation between the tragic incident and the interrogations Earl Warren wrote about. There is a seeming incongruity between the fate of the Afghan detainee tortured by US military personnel and the fate of suspects interrogated in US jails. Nevertheless, it is important to pause and contemplate the consequences

---

14. US Department of State, *supra* note 172.

of subjecting individuals suspected of involvement in terrorism to a protection-free interrogation. Perhaps, the discussion below can serve as a warning as to the consequences of not protecting suspects, regardless of the crimes they are suspected of committing. It is my belief Earl Warren would chafe at the situation presented below and agree that such an interrogation **must not be tolerated, under any circumstance**.

> Even as the young Afghan man was dying before them, his American jailers continued to torment him.
>
> The prisoner, a slight, 22-year-old taxi driver known only as Dilawar, was hauled from his cell at the detention center in Bagram, Afghanistan, at around 2 a.m. to answer questions about a rocket attack on an American base. When he arrived in the interrogation room, an interpreter who was present said, his legs were bouncing uncontrollably in the plastic chair and his hands were numb. He had been chained by the wrists to the top of his cell for much of the previous four days.
>
> Mr. Dilawar asked for a drink of water, and one of the two interrogators, Specialist Joshua R. Claus, 21, picked up a large plastic bottle. But first he punched a hole in the bottom, the interpreter said, so as the prisoner fumbled weakly with the cap, the water poured out over his orange prison scrubs. The soldier then grabbed the bottle back and began squirting the water forcefully into Mr. Dilawar's face.

"Come on, drink!" the interpreter said Specialist Claus had shouted, as the prisoner gagged on the spray. "Drink!"

At the interrogators' behest, a guard tried to force the young man to his knees. But his legs, which had been pummeled by guards for several days, could no longer bend. An interrogator told Mr. Dilawar that he could see a doctor after they finished with him. When he was finally sent back to his cell, though, the guards were instructed only to chain the prisoner back to the ceiling.

"Leave him up," one of the guards quoted Specialist Claus as saying.

Several hours passed before an emergency room doctor finally saw Mr. Dilawar. By then he was dead, his body beginning to stiffen. It would be many months before Army investigators learned a final horrific detail: most of the interrogators had believed Mr. Dilawar was an innocent man who simply drove his taxi past the American base at the wrong time. Whether Mr. Dilawar was in the "wrong place at the wrong time" or a "wanted" terrorist, there is no justification for what happened to him. It is beyond unacceptable. It serves as "word to the wise" highlighting what can—and does—go wrong when pressure on the interrogator is great and the suspect is subjected to the unrestrained whims of the interrogator. It is a dangerous combination. Earl Warren knew this only too well. That is the essence of

Miranda. That is, frankly, why he—and he alone—could write the opinion in the manner he did.

To have another Justice write the decision would not have had the same impact. For the decision to have been written in a less direct, forceful manner would have diminished the reactions among law enforcement. There was an obvious audience that drew Warren's greatest focus: those entrusted with interrogating suspects. Reading the above—though it did not take place on US soil as a "regular" criminal interrogation—reinforces the power and importance of Warren's decision.

The story of Mr. Dilawar's brutal death at the Bagram Collection Point—and that of another detainee, Habibullah, who died there six days earlier in December 2002— emerges from a nearly 2,000-page confidential file of the Army's criminal investigation into the case.[15]

Like a narrative counterpart to the digital images from Abu Ghraib, the Bagram file depicts young, poorly trained soldiers involved in repeated incidents of abuse. The harsh treatment, which has resulted in criminal charges against seven soldiers, extended beyond the two deaths.

In some instances, testimony shows, it was directed or carried out by interrogators to extract information. In others, it was punishment meted out by military police guards.

---

15. A copy was obtained by The New York Times.

Sometimes, the torment seems to have been driven by little more than boredom or cruelty, or both.[16]

A democracy that allows, in the name of national security, torture of suspected terrorists casts significant doubt on claims to respecting and honoring individual rights. The Constitution Project's Task Force on Detainee Treatment examined "the federal government's policies and actions related to the capture, detention and prosecution of suspected terrorists in US custody during the Clinton, Bush and Obama Administrations."[17]

The task force findings were stark and disturbing:

Finding 1

US forces, in many instances, used interrogation techniques on detainees that constitute torture. American personnel conducted an even larger number of interrogations that involved "cruel, inhuman, or degrading" treatment. Both categories of actions violate US laws and international treaties. Such conduct was directly counter to values of the Constitution and our nation.

Finding 2

The nation's most senior of officials, through some of their actions and failures to act in the months and

---

16. http://www.nytimes.com/2005/05/20/world/asia/in-us-report-brutal-details-of-2-afghan-inmates-deaths.html.

17. https://constitutionproject.org/task-force-of-detainee-treatment/.

years immediately following the September 11 attacks, bear ultimate responsibility for allowing and contributing to the spread of illegal and improper interrogation techniques used by some US personnel on detainees in several theaters. Responsibility also falls on other government officials and certain military leaders.

Finding 3

There is no firm or persuasive evidence that the widespread use of harsh interrogation techniques by US forces produced significant information of value. There is substantial evidence that much of the information adduced from the use of such techniques was not useful or reliable.

Finding 6

Lawyers in the Justice Department's Office of Legal Counsel (OLC) repeatedly gave erroneous legal sanction to certain activities that amounted to torture and cruel, inhuman, or degrading treatment in violation of US and international law, and in doing so, did not properly serve their clients: the president and the American people.[18]

Referencing the conduct of the CIA and US military personnel in Iraq and Afghanistan is not intended to draw a direct parallel to how the FBI and police departments

---

18. https://detaineetaskforce.org/pdf/Findings-and-Recommendations.pdf.

interrogate suspected terrorists on US soil. Nevertheless, it is instructive for our purposes. Dismissal without stopping to pause is not risk free.

Applying Miranda rights and protections in Iraq, Afghanistan, Yemen, Somalia, Pakistan, and other "hot spots" where US military personnel and intelligence officials interrogate combatants is a nonstarter. There is no intention to extend the *Miranda* holding to such an environment. That will not happen. However, there are important—and disturbing—lessons we can learn from the material cited above.

Terrorists are determined to cause as much harm as possible. Nation-states are engaged in a constant effort to understand their motivations, and gather intelligence in a never-ending effort to prevent future attacks and to punish those responsible for an attack. It is, in many ways, a never-ending game of "cat and mouse."

I write these lines while in Israel, forty-eight hours after the latest terror attack in Jerusalem. The attack, claimed by IS—a claim immediately rejected by HAMAS and Israeli security authorities—resulted in the killing of Hadas Malka, a twenty-three–year-old woman who served in the Border Police. Three terrorists were killed in the attack.[19]

Important for our purposes is the political rhetoric that came in the attack's aftermath. It is a well-rehearsed play with politicians uttering empty words of warning to terrorist

---

19. http://www.haaretz.com/israel-news/1.796248.

organizations; the public weighing in, commensurate with their particular political viewpoint; the media rushing to get comments from family and friends; terrorist organizations claiming credit for the attack (and competing with each other); and the security forces stating there was no intelligence suggestive of a planned attack and reassuring the public that no measures will be spared either to find those responsible for the attack or to prevent future attacks.

I have been around this block more times than I can count; it is a rerun for the umpteenth time. All players know their roles and lines.

What is never fully resolved, however, are the actual definitions of the terms casually bandied about. By example: Israel's leading daily, Ha'aretz's headline was that Malka was "killed," whereas the Army radio station said she was "murdered." Regarding the terrorists, the initial media report was that they were "neutralized"; shortly afterward it was announced that they were "eliminated." The discussion is neither amorphous nor merely academic. How we define an actor and his or her actions determines how they are categorized, which significantly impacts what rights they are to be accorded, or not.

The question whether separate categories should be created for distinct threats and different crimes is of great importance. How it is resolved impacts not only the actor—and what rights are to be extended—but it also impacts society and how it balances individual rights with national security considerations.

There are different models and proposals that can be adopted and adapted; at its most basic, the question in the context of terrorism is whether the nation-state extends the same protections to a suspected terrorist that it does to a suspected criminal. To answer that requires resolving whether or not terrorism is nothing more than a criminal act and whether or not a terrorist is but a criminal.

We undertake this dialogue with the understanding we will not resolve these questions in this book. That is beyond our scope. What is within our scope is seeking to understand how Warren would have understood—and defined—terrorism and those responsible for what society, in 2017, calls "acts of terrorism." Terrorism as a concept is not new; quite the opposite. History is replete with examples. What is seemingly different is the extent to which society is increasingly focused on the act and the actor responsible for what is called terrorism.

While different theories abound for the uptick in engaged focus on terrorism, it is reasonable to suggest the events of Tuesday, September 11, 2001 are a crucial "landmark." The events of that day are forever embedded in the memories of Americans; Al-Qaeda culturally, politically, socially, and practically changed the American landscape. Whether one lived in New York City, Washington, DC, Salt Lake City, or San Francisco, Americans woke up on Wednesday September 12, 2001 to a very different nation.

Public opinion polls reveal Americans' fears of terrorism over the years.

How worried are you that you or someone in your family will become a victim of terrorism -- very worried, somewhat worried, not too worried, or not worried at all?

% Very/Somewhat worried

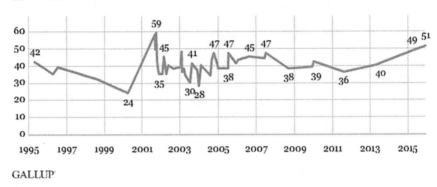

GALLUP

Perhaps because of the difference in number of casualties, the scale of the attacks including number of participants and targets, or the impact on the country, 9/11 is considered the critical turning point in the history of terrorism in the United States. The significance of 9/11 cannot be minimized; the phrase "post-9/11 world" is not an exaggeration. It reflects an important reality: recognition, both in the United States and internationally, that something profoundly changed in the contemporary world. While the shock of that day has worn off, its impact is felt, for example, every time we fly or go to a sporting event. TSA security lines are "exhibit A." Undoubtedly, others can suggest ways in which 9/11 has changed their lives. While the shock has long worn off and the overwhelming sense of patriotism has been restored to more natural levels, there is no doubt that America changed on that day.

How worried are you that you or someone in your family will become a victim of terrorism -- very worried, somewhat worried, not too worried, or not worried at all?

	Very worried	Somewhat worried	Not too worried	Not worried at all	Know a victim (vol.)	No opinion
	%	%	%	%	%	%
2015 Dec 8-9	19	32	28	20	--	1
2015 Jun 2-7	15	34	25	24	--	2
2013 Apr 24-25	11	29	33	27	--	*
2011 Aug 11-14	9	27	32	31	*	*
2010 Jan 8-10	9	33	35	22	*	1
2009 Dec 11-13	12	27	34	28	*	*
2008 Sep 5-7 ^	9	29	38	24	--	*
2007 Jul 6-8	13	34	31	21	*	*
2007 Jun 11-14	12	32	33	22	*	*
2006 Aug 18-20	11	34	34	21	*	*
2006 Jan 20-22 ^	14	29	34	23	--	1
2005 Dec 16-18	11	30	37	22	--	*
2005 Jul 22-24	14	33	30	23	*	*
2005 Jun 16-19	8	30	36	26	*	*
2005 Jan 7-9	10	28	37	24	*	1
2004 Dec 17-19	13	28	34	25	*	*
2004 Oct 14-16	13	34	33	20	*	*
2004 Sep 3-5 ^	11	32	36	21	--	*
2004 Aug 9-11 ^	8	26	36	30	--	*
2004 Feb 9-12	10	30	36	24	*	*
2004 Jan 2-5	5	23	42	30	*	*
2003 Dec 5-7	9	28	38	25	*	--
2003 Aug 25-26	11	30	33	26	*	*
2003 Jul 18-20 ^	6	24	38	32	*	*
2003 Apr 22-23 ^	8	26	39	26	*	1
2003 Mar 22-23	8	30	38	24	--	*
2003 Feb 17-19	8	28	33	31	*	--
2003 Feb 7-9 ^	13	35	34	18	*	*
2003 Jan 23-25	8	31	36	25	--	*
2002 Sep 2-4	8	30	37	25	*	*
2002 May 28-29	9	31	37	22	1	*
2002 Apr 22-24	8	27	39	25	1	*
2002 Mar 4-7	12	33	32	23	*	*
2002 Feb 4-6 ^	8	27	39	25	--	1
2001 Nov 26-27	8	27	34	30	1	*
2001 Nov 2-4	11	28	34	26	*	1
2001 Oct 19-21 #	13	30	33	23	*	1
2001 Oct 11-14 #	18	33	35	14	*	1
2001 Oct 5-6 #	24	35	27	14	*	*
2001 Sep 21-22 #	14	35	32	18	*	1
2001 Sep 14-15 #	18	33	35	13	*	1
2001 Sep 11 # &	23	35	24	16	1	1
2000 Apr 7-9 ^	4	20	41	34	--	1
1998 Aug 20 @ &	10	22	38	29	--	1
1996 Jul 20-21 **	13	26	34	27	--	*
1996 Apr 9-10 **	13	22	33	32	--	*
1995 Apr 21-23 **	14	28	33	24	--	1

* Less than 0.5%
(vol.) = Volunteered response
^ Asked of a half sample
# WORDING: How worried are you that you or someone in your family will become a victim of a terrorist attack -- very worried, somewhat worried, not too worried, or not worried at all?
& Based on one night poll of national adults
@ WORDING: How worried are you that someone in your family will become a victim of a terrorist attack similar to the bombing in Oklahoma City?
** WORDING: How worried are you that you or someone in your family will become a victim of a terrorist attack similar to the bombing in Oklahoma City?

Prior to that Tuesday, the American public had largely been protected from the terrorism that is a part of life in many other countries. The international community had, for years, looked with envy at the United States. That envy was mixed with a sense that Americans were naïve regarding threats that other people faced. While the world expressed sympathy and horror in the aftermath of 9/11, there was also a sense that *now* American decision makers and the public at large would "understand." That was particularly true regarding Islamic extremism.

In the wake of 9/11, the international community adopted a number of conventions including the Declaration on Measures to Eliminate International Terrorism, the 1997 International Convention for the Suppression of Terrorist Bombings, the 1999 International Convention for the Suppression of the Financing of Terrorism, and the International Convention for the Suppression of Acts of Nuclear Terrorism.[20]

With that we turn our attention to five specific attacks. That is necessary for us to answer our question.

---

20. Security Council, *International Laws*, Counter-Terrorism Committee (June 21, 2011), http://www.un.org/en/sc/ctc/laws.html.

Chapter Eight

Five Attacks: Applying *Miranda* to Terrorism?

"When you see thugs being thrown into the back of a paddy wagon, you just see them thrown in; rough. I said, 'please don't be too nice. . . . They kidnap, they extort, they rape, and they rob. They prey on children. They shouldn't be here. . . . They are animals."

"We cannot accept this violence one day more. . . . You're not going to allow it and we're backing you up one hundred precent [sic]."

Five Attacks

In narrowing the focus to acts committed on US soil or by Americans, we are excluding acts of terrorism committed against Americans and American assets outside the United States.

I have chosen to focus on the five attacks below; those responsible were interrogated in the United States, brought to trial in the United States, and the question of extending Miranda rights was a matter of some controversy.[1]

Others may suggest additional examples of terrorist attacks on American soil. That is legitimate and to be expected.

Attacks in which the perpetrator was killed, including 9/11, San Bernadino,[2] and Orlando,[3] are not included as the interrogation dilemma was not relevant. The Ft. Hood attack is not included as Major Hassan was subject to the Uniform Code of Military Justice.[4] Attacks such as Columbine,[5] Charleston,[6] and Sandy Hook,[7] are not included, either because the perpetrator was killed or because law enforcement did not reference the act as "terrorism." That is not to suggest that some commentators, members of the public and elected officials did not use terminology

---

1. Emily Mann's play, Hoodwinked, compellingly shed light on this controversy: Emily Mann, *Hoodwinked*, http://arts.princeton.edu/events/hood winked/.

2. http://www.latimes.com/local/california/la-me-san-bernardino-shooting -terror-investigation-htmlstory.html.

3. http://www.cnn.com/2016/06/12/us/orlando-nightclub-shooting/.

4. http://www.history.com/this-day-in-history/army-major-kills-13-people -in-fort-hood-shooting-spree.

5. History.com Staff, *Columbine High School shootings*, History.com (2009), http://www.history.com/topics/columbine-high-school-shootings.

6. NPR, *Charleston Shooting*, Stories about Charleston Shooting (2017), http:// www.npr.org/tags/415878235/charleston-shooting.

7. History.com Staff, *Gunman kills students and adults at Newtown, Connecticut, elementary school*, History.com (2013), http://www.history.com/this-day-in -history/gunman-kills-students-and-adults-at-newtown-connecticut-elementary -school.

associated with terrorism. As previously discussed, that is a pattern—and problem—that repeats itself in the aftermath of an attack. That is relevant to note for the issue of terminology, sensationalizing and politicizing pose a constant—and unfortunate—challenge to national security and law enforcement.

In the aftermath of 9/11, the instinctual response to an event involving significant loss of life is "terrorism." That is not necessarily correct. It can also be wrong. The consequences, however, are significant for it suggests tolerance of minimizing otherwise protected rights. It is for that reason that applying the words of Earl Warren to suspected terrorists is essential.

The invariable "over-response," the inevitable beating of the drums, and the shrill verbiage are the very reasons that Miranda protections must be extended to suspected terrorists. To suggest otherwise is to recommend an interrogation culture fraught with danger for the interrogator, suspect, and society.

The five attacks below—which have been widely documented, discussed, and analyzed—are relevant for our purposes as they highlight the crux of the matter. The attacks are the essence of terrorism, regardless of how terrorism is defined. That is, whichever of the available-commonly accepted definitions we adopt, the attacks are terrorist attacks, in contrast to criminal attacks, as commonly understood.

The five attacks, as the graphic below illustrates, were violent, destructive, and effective from the actors' perspective. This was terrorism.

The question: should Miranda be extended to the actors? More precisely: would Earl Warren extend the actors Miranda protections?

The five attacks have been chosen deliberately: they represent significant, powerful acts of terrorism. Meaning, these attacks "push the envelope" of whether or not terrorists are to be extended rights. Extend *Miranda* to those responsible for these actions and *Miranda* will, by force of logic, be extended to other acts of terrorism.

e from the World Trade Centre after the exp'

The 1993 World Trade Center Bombing

Date: February 26, 1993

A previous attack to the one carried out by Al-Qaeda in 2001 on the World Trade Center. A truck bomb was detonated below the North Tower of the World Trade Center in New York City. The attack was planned by a group of terrorists including Ramzi Yousef, Mahmud Abouhalima, Mohammad Salameh, Nidal A. Ayyad, Abdul Rahman Yasin, and Ahmed Ajaj. They received financing from Khalid Sheikh Mohammed, Yousef's uncle. Yousef claimed the attacks were carried out in response to US involvement in Israel and the Middle East. The attacks killed six people and injured more than a thousand.

The 1995 Oklahoma City Bombing

Date: April 19, 1995

The Oklahoma City bombing was a domestic terrorist car bombing of the Alfred P. Murrah Federal Building in downtown Oklahoma City, Oklahoma. The attack killed 168 people, and injured more than 168 others. The actors responsible were Timothy McVeigh, Terry Nichols, and Michael Fortier, who met in 1988 at Fort Benning during basic training for the US Army. Michael Fortier, McVeigh's accomplice, was his Army roommate. The bombing was motivated as an angered response to federal government's handling of the 1992 Federal Bureau of Investigation (FBI) standoff with Randy Weaver at Ruby Ridge as well as the Waco siege. As a result of the bombing, the US Congress passed the Antiterrorism and Effective Death Penalty Act of 1996, which tightened the standards for habeas corpus in the United States, as well as legislation designed to increase the protection around federal buildings to deter future terrorist attacks

The 2009 "Underwear Bomber"

Date: December 25, 2009

On Christmas Day, 2009, a young Nigerian man, Umar Farouk Abdulmutallab, also known as Umar Abdul Mutallab and Omar Farooq al-Nigeri attempted to detonate plastic explosives hidden in his underwear while on board Northwest Airlines Flight 253 en route from Amsterdam to Detroit, Michigan. Born to wealthy family in Nigeria, Abdulmutallab was motivated to bomb the plane following conversations with Al-Qaeda in the Arabian Peninsula (AQAP). Contacts between Abdulmutallab and Anwar al-Awlaki, an American Yemeni Muslim lecturer and senior Al-Qaeda talent recruiter and motivator were also found to have motivated the attack. There were no casualties. In response to the attack, President Barack Obama vowed that the federal government would track down all of those responsible for the attack, and any attack being planned against the United States. He also ordered a review of detection and watchlist procedures.

The 2010 Times Square Bombing

Date: May 1, 2010

This bombing was an attempted terrorist attack in Times Square in New York in which two street vendors alerted New York City security personnel after they spotted smoke coming from a vehicle, and a car bomb was discovered. The bomb was disarmed before it could fully detonate. The bomber, Faisal Shahzad, a thirty-year-old Pakistan-born resident of Bridgeport, Connecticut, stated he was motivated by his anger over the repeated CIA drone attacks in Pakistan. As a result of this attack,

Senator Joe Lieberman, a Connecticut independent and chairman of the Senate Homeland Security Committee, introduced bipartisan legislation under which Americans joining or working with foreign terrorist groups would be stripped of their US citizenship.

The 2013 Boston Marathon Bombing
Date: April 15, 2013

At the annual Boston Marathon in 2013, two homemade bombs were detonated twelve seconds and 210 yards (190 m) apart at 2:49 p.m., near the finish line, leaving three dead and several hundred injured. Chechen American brothers Dzhokhar Tsarnaev and Tamerlan Tsarnaev were accused for the attack. During questioning Dzhokhar alleged that he and his brother were motivated by extremist Islamist beliefs and the wars in Iraq and Afghanistan, that they were self-radicalized and unconnected to any outside terrorist groups, and that he was following his brother's lead.

To Whom Does Society Owe a Duty?

That question has been discussed by philosophers, politicians, scholars, faith leaders, and the general public for hundreds of years. The easy answer is that the vulnerable members of society deserve its greatest protection; on their behalf, we must be vigilant and steadfast.

This is not burden free. It imposes on us the requirement to be sensitive to the frailties of others while recognizing that society is rugged and discourse can be rigorous, vigorous, and robust. That is legitimate and understandable. As Voltaire famously said: "I disapprove of what you say, but I will defend to the death your right to say it."

However, there is a sharp distinction between the right to free speech as guaranteed in the First Amendment and the right to act on that speech, thereby causing harm to another. One of the most important questions facing contemporary society is the extent to which intolerance must be tolerated.

Restated: what is the price of extremism and is the cost justifiable?

That cost moves from the intangible and amorphous when harm is its result. Harm is harm, whether physical or emotional. It is something society must not tolerate. That is particularly important in a politically charged era, marked by stridency and discord facilitated, if not exacerbated by social media.

It is impossible to ignore the profoundly disturbing tone and tenor of conversation in the United States in recent years. We ignore it at our peril. Hate is a reality in present-day America. There are a number of reasons for this. While we may disagree as to their cause, we must come together to punish those who attack others because of who and what they are. That must not be tolerated.

Swastikas in New York City's subways, bomb threats to Jewish Community Centers, destruction of Jewish cemeteries, physical attacks against homosexuals, reported harassment of people not speaking English on cell phones, and alleged urinating on a Muslim prayer rug at the University of Michigan are but a representative example of hatred in America today.

This is, tragically, not the first time the vileness of hate has permeated into our national culture and debate. The pages of history are filled with examples. One only has to look at pictures of lynched African Americans to understand the harm posed by hate.

The hyperbolic rhetoric of contemporary politics is a powerful reminder of the tenuous balance between national security and individual rights and liberties. That rhetoric makes asking the question this book poses highly relevant for there are powerful contrasting visions and philosophies of how to protect those rights. The question of whether or not the middle ground can be reestablished is a source of increasing discussion and concern.

This is particularly relevant with respect to preservation of individual rights in the immediate aftermath of an actual terrorist attack or a perceived threat, regardless of its concreteness. American history is pockmarked with such examples, ranging from President Lincoln's decision to suspend the writ of *habeas corpus* during the Civil War to President Wilson's efforts to limit the free speech of those who opposed the draft in the First World War. President Roosevelt's decision to internment decision in the aftermath of Pearl Harbor can be viewed as yet another example of executive power significantly minimizing individual rights.

The question of rights, and to whom are they extended, weighed heavily on my mind while writing this book. Democracy is a tenuous and fragile balance between individual rights and the public good; how society responds to the question "to whom is a duty owed" is critical, especially when individual rights are threatened.

The reasons why rights may be at stake vary; there is no one dominant or pervasive theme that satisfactorily explains this troubling and persistent reality. Nevertheless, American history, unfortunately, reflects vacillations regarding the extent individual rights are respected and upheld.

As to the America of today, these lines are written in the aftermath of the US Court of Appeals upholding the stay ordered by the US District Court regarding President Trump's Executive Order "immigration ban." Whether or not the immigration ban is a Muslim ban is a matter, for some, of interpretation. Like many others, that is exactly how I understood it for that reflects candidate Trump's promise to the electorate. As President, Trump has done nothing to persuade me otherwise.

When President Trump, both as candidate and in office, used the phrase "extreme vetting," I wondered what Earl

Warren would say. While writing this book, I found myself oftentimes reflecting on how Warren would react to President Trump.

Answering that question depends, frankly, on which Warren we speak of: Attorney General Warren or Chief Justice Warren. I have come to the conclusion that they are not one and the same; to what extent the former impacted the latter is an open and legitimate question. Warren as Attorney General was aggressive, unapologetic, and narrow-minded regarding Japanese Americans. He viewed them negatively and was convinced, devoid of concrete evidence, that they posed a threat to American national security. He was unable, or at least unwilling, to distinguish between individuals; for him, the class of Japanese Americans were one entity who needed to be dealt with "en masse." That was wrong and misbegotten.

There is great risk in finger-pointing, name-calling, and broad denunciations. This is particularly the case when hyperbolic rhetoric replaces discussion and debate. The risk is great when individual rights are at stake. The need for vigilance is paramount, even if protection of individual rights is not politically expedient or beneficial. The German theologian, Martin Niemöller, penned words relevant to our times and to the question we are asking:

> *First they came for the Socialists, and I did not speak out—*
> *Because I was not a Socialist.*

*Then they came for the Trade Unionists, and I did not
      speak out—*
Because I was not a Trade Unionist.
Then they came for the Jews, and I did not speak out—
Because I was not a Jew.
*Then they came for me—and there was no one left to
      speak for me.*[8]

Social media significantly enhances the power and danger of words. The negative ramifications of misinformation, disinformation, and lies have never been greater. The ease with which information, whether correct or not, is disseminated accentuates the need to aggressively protect individual rights, particularly because of the increasing difficulty in subjecting information to rigorous and robust fact-checking. There are endless examples of inaccurate claims and once they are "out there" in cyberspace, the potential for damage becomes palpable.

Regardless of one's politics, the 2016 US presidential campaign was unlike many of its predecessors. It was different in tone and tenor. There was a virulence, hatred, and violent undertone that was profoundly unsettling for many. The traditional means of political conduct and rhetoric were not relevant; new rules were applied. For some, those new rules were unsettling; for others, they were welcome

---

8. US Holocaust Memorial Museum. Martin Niemöller: "First They Came for the Socialists . . ." Holocaust Encyclopedia, https://www.ushmm.org/wlc/en/arti cle.php?ModuleId=10007392.

for they enabled articulating decades-long resentments, frustrations, and anger. Whether this new tone is here to stay or is a transient moment remains to be seen. Time will tell. Stridency and anger must not be underestimated; its dangers must be recognized.

While Earl Warren lived in a different era, there are certain similarities. The 1950s, after all, were deeply tainted by the stain Senator Joseph McCarthy (R-Wisconsin) imposed on America. McCarthyism reflects the very worst of American instincts: careers ruined and lives destroyed in the name of the "Communist threat" highlighted by McCarthy's witch-hunts. The tragic combination of xenophobia, nationalism, fearmongering, and a lack of national leadership had terrible consequences for many.

This was a dark period in American history; few politicians, including President Eisenhower, were willing to stare McCarthy down. It was not until the iconic CBS News reporter, Edward R. Murrow, and Secretary of the Army, Joseph Welsh, forcefully called McCarthy out did the tide turn. This failure to confront a bombastic fearmongerer must serve as a warning to Americans today.

The question is particularly relevant, given the threats America faces today. The threat is, it must be noted, twofold: threats from terrorists—domestic and international alike—and the threat to our liberties emanating from overreaction to terrorism. The fear of communism posed two threats to society and individuals alike: the possible threat the USSR posed to America and the consequences to individuals marked, unfairly, as communists or "fellow travelers." Woody Allen's movie "The Front"[9] brilliantly captured the price paid by writers, directors, and others accused of supporting communism or of being communists.

The question is whether an articulated threat of terrorism limits individual rights. This is a particularly relevant question in 2017 as the Supreme Court arguably turns "right" in the name of protecting American national security. Denying Miranda rights would be a natural result of this shift.

While different countries have different judicial regimes, a comparative analysis is instructive. That is not to suggest one regime is preferable over another; rather, it is intended to shed light on how different democracies respond to similar challenges and crisis. There is, I am convinced, significant value in such an undertaking. There is one important caveat that: the intention in such an undertaking is not to suggest superiority/inferiority but rather to learn from how different regimes resolve similar struggles and tensions.

My career in the Israel Defense Forces (IDF) consistently highlighted the importance of a powerful Supreme Court committed to judicial activism. The Israel Supreme Court, particularly under retired President (Chief Justice) Aharon Barak, opened its doors to Palestinian residents of the West Bank and Gaza Strip who felt aggrieved by measures implemented by the IDF.

---

9. THE FRONT (Columbia Pictures Corporation, 1976).

In the late 1990s, IDF Commanders came to understand that their actions were subject to judicial scrutiny and, if need be, robust intervention by the Court. Their recognition was sometimes reluctant; for some, this was interference with their discretion if not "stepping on their turf." Be that as it may, Barak's opinions emphasized that "national security is not a magical phrase" and that "logistical burdens of the State need not be borne by the individual."

The question of Israeli interrogation methods regarding Palestinian suspects has been a matter of much discussion both in Israel and in the international community. Claims of torture by Palestinian suspects have been heard for decades; those claims were rejected by the Israeli Security forces. Human rights organizations pressed the issue on innumerable occasions; Israeli officials met with visiting delegations to discuss the interrogation and judicial process regarding Palestinian residents of the West Bank and Gaza Strip.[10] The Supreme Court consistently chose not to intervene in how interrogations were conducted.

However, in a cutting-edge decision of enormous importance, the Israeli Supreme Court, sitting as the High Court of Justice, in 1998, imposed limits on interrogators. Loud—very loud—criticism swiftly came from many quarters suggesting the Court does not understand the reality of terrorism.

---

10. Over the course of my IDF service, I met with different Human Rights organizations who visited Israel on fact-finding missions prior to writing reports.

Chief Justice Earl Warren and President (Chief Justice) Aahron Barak

While all Justices have one vote, the Chief Justice is truly "first among equals." In previous writings, I have compared Barak with the late Chief Justice William Rehnquist.[11] Barak was the epitome of judicial activism; Rehnquist was the manifestation of judicial reticence. As the Warren Court's Criminal Procedure "revolution" holdings dramatically demonstrated, Earl Warren resembled Barak, not Rehnquist. Barak was widely criticized in many quarters; he was considered by those on the Israeli political and religious right wing to be soft on terrorism, too liberal and disengaged from the reality of life in the "tough" neighborhood called the Middle East.

Warren's language in *Miranda* establishes a similar regime: individual rights must not take a back seat to state power regardless of the threat posed to public order and national security. There is, I suggest, a clear similarity between C.J. Warren and President Barak: their opinions reflect profound suspicion of executive power—Warren focused on police departments, whereas Barak focused on the IDF—and the need to protect the individual. Both were heavily criticized; both were seen as weakening state power, thereby endangering the innocent civilian population.

---

11. Amos N. Guiora, *Going Toe to Toe: President Barak's and Chief Justice Rehnquist's Theories of Judicial Activism*, 29 Hastings Int'l & Comp. L. Rev. 51 (2005).

Warren was accused of putting criminals on the street, Barak of unnecessarily limiting operational counterterrorism.

Their emphasis on, and respect for, individual liberties became a political "football." The political right wing in both countries championed the cause of undue judicial interference. In Israel, a political slogan was created, "let the IDF win."[12] Battle lines were clearly drawn. The same held true for Warren. Nevertheless, both Warren and Barak were committed to the rule of law regardless of the loud and persistent voices in the public arena that harm resulted judicial interference.

Warren was vilified for being soft on crime, thereby hamstringing law enforcement in their efforts to protect the public from violent elements. Barak was viewed as limiting the IDF's ability to control Palestinian terrorism and Warren was perceived as limiting law enforcement's ability to forcefully respond to black violence.

Both, I believe, understood that they were addressing a pressing need: for Barak, it was articulating the parameters of the rule of law regarding operational counterterrorism; for Warren, it was the need to impose limits on law enforcement regardless of the reality of urban riots and street crime. There are, without a doubt, great risks in this undertaking: voices claiming that the Israeli and US Supreme Courts were endangering the public were loud—in some cases,

---

12. T'nu l'tzahal l'natzeach.

loud and threatening. It was made known to the public that Barak had a full-time security detail, at home and at work.

However, neither were deterred from what they considered their core mission. That is not to "sanctify" them; rather, it is to highlight that the judicial articulation of individual rights and the commensurate limiting of state power requires a Chief Justice committed to these two principles.

Barak's holding in *Public Committee against Torture in Israel v. The State of Israel* brings this life, vividly[13]:

> We conclude, therefore, that, according to the existing state of the law, neither the government nor the heads of the security services have the authority to establish directives regarding the use of physical means during the interrogation of suspects suspected of hostile terrorist activities, beyond the general rules which can be inferred from the very concept of an interrogation itself. Similarly, the individual GSS investigator—like any police officer—does not possess the authority to employ physical means that infringe a suspect's liberty during the interrogation, unless these means are inherent to the very essence of an interrogation and are both fair and reasonable.

> An investigator who employs these methods exceeds his authority. His responsibility shall be fixed

---

13. H.C. 5100/94 (Israel 1999). *Public Committee against Torture in Israel v. The State of Israel.*

according to law. His potential criminal liability shall be examined in the context of the "necessity defense." Provided the conditions of the defense are met by the circumstances of the case, the investigator may find refuge under its wings. Just as the existence of the "necessity defense" does not bestow authority, the lack of authority does not negate the applicability of the necessity defense or of other defenses from criminal liability. The Attorney-General can establish guidelines regarding circumstances in which investigators shall not stand trial, if they claim to have acted from "necessity." A statutory provision is necessary to authorize the use of physical means during the course of an interrogation, beyond what is permitted by the ordinary "law of investigation," and in order to provide the individual GSS investigator with the authority to employ these methods. The "necessity defense" cannot serve as a basis for such authority.[14]

Barak added:

Deciding these petitions weighed heavily on this Court. True, from the legal perspective, the road before us is smooth. We are, however, part of Israeli society. Its problems are known to us and we live its history. We are not isolated in an ivory tower. We live the life of this country. We are aware of the harsh

---

14. *Public Committee against Torture, supra* note 105, at 36.

reality of terrorism in which we are, at times, immersed. The possibility that this decision will hamper the ability to properly deal with terrorists and terrorism disturbs us. We are, however, judges. We must decide according to the law. This is the standard that we set for ourselves. When we sit to judge, we ourselves are judged. Therefore, in deciding the law, we must act according to our purest conscience.[15]

What is similarly remarkable about the *Miranda* opinion is its timing. It is unsurprising that an "Impeach Earl Warren" campaign commenced following the Miranda decision. There was a disconnect between the general population and law enforcement with Supreme Court decision making. In graphic terms, while the streets were burning, the Court was protecting those responsible. That is, in many ways, Warren's finest hour.

Undoubtedly, and understandably, some will point to Warren's holding in *Brown v. Board of Education*—particularly his remarkable ability to forge a unanimous decision—as the pinnacle of his extraordinary stewardship. Highlighting *Miranda* is not intended to minimize *Brown*. Both changed America. Both reflect the very best of American values, principles, and good.

Nixon said of the Supreme Court, "It is the court's duty to protect legitimate rights but not to raise unreasonable

---

15. *Id.* at 37.

obstacles to enforcement of the law."[16] According to Professor Michael Flamm, Nixon became "more critical and less judicious as the race (against Humphrey, ANG) tightened in late October."[17]

According to Nixon:

> "Some of our courts have gone too far in their decisions weakening the peace forces as against the criminal forces in the United States of America"; Nixon pledged to appoint justices "who will respect the Constitution."[18]

After his election, President Nixon nominated to the Supreme Court Chief Justice Warren Burger, Justice Harry Blackmun, Justice Lewis Powell, and Justice William Rehnquist. Burger reflected Nixon's negativity regarding the Warren Court. To what extent the historical enmity between Nixon and Warren influenced Nixon's criticism of the Court is a matter of historical conjecture.

The Warren Revolution largely ended with these appointments. The Burger Court was the antithesis of the liberal, progressive protection of individual rights orientation of the Warren Court.

---

16. Michael W. Flamm, *Law and Order: Street Crime, Civil Unrest, and the Crisis of Liberalism in the 1960s* 175 (2007).

17. *Id.*

18. *Id.* at 176.

Chapter Nine

Final Word

This book has been a journey in examining the life of an extraordinary Chief Justice through multiple lenses. To answer the question posed at the outset required examining both the times he lived and contemporary society. His career spanned decades; his contribution to American society is remarkable. However, as we came to see, his career was permanently stained by a terrible event. While he came to "own" it, his brief reference to it in his memoirs is just that, brief. It is also, frankly, unsatisfying.

However, it is important for our purposes for two reasons: what recommendations did Warren make at a time of crisis and what did he subsequently learn from that action. As to Warren's conduct in the aftermath of Pearl Harbor, Warren, I believe, had a clear agenda intended to position himself politically in California. Important to recall that in the early 1940s, Earl Warren was first and foremost a politician. There is no evidence I have found indicating that Warren entertained any thoughts of ascending to the judiciary, whether on a state or national level. As an ambitious politician, with his eye on higher office, the attack on Pearl Harbor presented an opportunity.

That is not to suggest that Attorney General Warren was a cynic. That is not the impression I gained from meeting with those who knew Warren or reading about him. Rather, Warren was a product of his times and his ambition. That is understandable and not particularly unusual.

What is unusual, and hence what makes Warren an extraordinary figure is the *Miranda* decision. For me, extraordinarily positive; for others, extraordinarily negative. In that sense, Warren was a divisive person. Or more accurately, his opinions were divisive. One in particular: *Miranda v. Arizona*.

I have read its critics; I have met with those who are convinced the decision was profoundly wrong. I strongly disagree with them. My disagreement is, in large part, based on my professional career. While I well understand the terrible consequences and costs of terrorism, I am convinced that protecting the suspect in the interrogation setting—regardless of the suspected act—is the crux of a democracy wedded to protecting individuals from state power.

That is not to minimize victim rights. However, this is not a zero-sum game; this is not a "black–white" paradigm where one right is at the expense of the other. Similarly, confessions that "clean the slate" are, ultimately, a stain on law enforcement if they are "false" confessions. Warren's conviction that interrogations are inherently coercive reflects his understanding of the reality of false confessions, and of their significance.

It is, then, for that reason that I am convinced that were Earl Warren alive, he would answer my question in the following manner: "Miranda rights for all suspects. No ands, ifs or buts."

That clarity is reflected in the directness of the opinion. Warren's conviction in the absolute necessity to impose limits on law enforcement seeps through every word in the opinion. Warren was clear in his criticisms of law enforcement. Warren did not believe law enforcement was "hamstrung" as a result of the holding. That was not his intention. He was unsparing in his criticisms of law enforcement. He considered them "lazy."

The decision to limit state power and to protect the suspect was based on his experience and understanding of the nature of the interrogator–suspect relationship.

That profound—for that is the best word—concern would, in my opinion, unequivocally extend to today's terrorism. That is the most correct and faithful reading of Earl Warren's opinion, which represents the apex of the Warren Court's criminal procedure revolution.

Index